ON CAMERA

On Camera

Essential know-how for programme-makers

Harris Watts

Revised edition published in 1997 by Aavo,
8 Edis Street, London NW1 8LG

First published in 1982 as *The Programme-Maker's Handbook,
or Goodbye Totter TV* by Starstream Books

Revised and expanded edition published by BBC Books
as *On Camera – How to produce film and video* in 1984 and
re-printed nine times 1984 – 1994

ISBN 0 9507582 3 X

Illustrated by Bryan Reading
Typography by Nicola Barnacle and Daniel Edwards
Printed and bound by Lontec, Borehamwood, Herts.
Set in Monotype Bembo

My thanks to Mike Crisp, Mike Derby, Gareth Watkins and Andy Benjamin, my colleagues at BBC Television Training, for checking various parts of the book. Also to Tony Mayne, Malcolm Campbell, Rosie Turner, Lino Ferrari and Peter Bridgman, who looked through the parts of the book concerned with their specialities. And especially to Bill Bell, also my colleague at Television Training, who helped me with the technology when I was out of my depth.

Harris Watts is an experienced producer of current affairs and science documentaries and was a senior instructor in the BBC's Television Training department for many years. His book, *Directing On Camera*, about single-camera direction, was published by Aavo in 1992 and his *On Camera* training tapes have won awards in six international competitions.

The contents of the tapes are as follows:

Programme 1 **The camera**
The camera – lenses and apertures – shot sizes and camera movements – crossing the line
Duration 34 min 9 sec

Programme 2 **Planning a programme**
(directed by Mike Crisp)
How – and how not to – cover an event
Duration 17 min 11 sec

Programme 3 **Interviews**
Sixty minute profile – one-camera interview – two-camera interview – walking interviews – car interviews
Duration 20 min 15 sec

Programme 4 **Editing**
Working out the structure – editing interviews
Duration 19 min 35 sec

Programme 6 **Sound**
The need for sound – microphones – interviews – background noise
Duration 27 min

Programme 7 **Lighting**
Opening sequence – people – light and colour – places – people and places
Duration 29 min 5 sec

The full set is available on three 60-minute VHS tapes from Aavo, 8 Edis Street, London NW1 8LG.
Telephone and Fax: 0171 722 9243.

For Christina, Jonathan, Matthew, Lucy and Amy

Contents

Foreword

When Harris Watts first wrote the predecessor to this current volume – *The Programme Maker's Handbook* – in 1982, UK television was a relatively cosy setup. The BBC had two channels. There was also ITV and a young upstart called Channel Four. In those far-off days the BBC nurtured and trained its staff, ITV sometimes did likewise and Channel Four took calculated risks.

Today, nearly a decade and a half on, it's like looking back at another world. The growth of satellite and cable has opened up the airwaves (and cable-ducts) to thousands of people who might otherwise have never had the chance to get their hands dirty making a show. And the BBC and ITV have both undergone the most radical of changes.

The downside – and there's always a downside – is that when too much inexperience gathers together in one place, disaster is certain to enter camera left. Of course it's not life or death. But television is ultimately about money. And broadcasters or backers can get pretty sore when they see their money going the wrong way down the tube.

Television needs trouble-shooters. Which is where Harris comes in camera right. Previous editions of *On Camera* have enjoyed a dog-eared existence as the Bible for aspiring researchers, producers and directors. But just as broadcasting has changed, so too has the technology that enables the production team to get their masterpiece on to our screen. Lightweight cameras and non-linear editing have revolutionized shooting and editing techniques; studio galleries can resemble Mission Control, Houston; graphics continue to astonish even the most jaundiced eye.

This edition of *On Camera* has been thoroughly revised and in some places totally rewritten to take account of all these changes and more.

To those new to television, to those who want to be in television and to those who just want to know what on earth is going on, I commend this book. Television remains the most powerful medium of communication yet devised. It's usually great to watch and usually great to make. And if I may paraphrase Orson Welles on seeing a film set for the first time, it's the best train set a boy (or girl) could have. Enjoy playing with it. But above all, make sure your audience enjoys it just as much as you.

Michael Grade *Chief Executive, Channel Four*

Introduction to the third edition

What's new about the new *On Camera*?

The structure is the same: *Basics* (programme-making step-by-step) followed by *Briefings* (specific topics discussed in detail). Every section ends with a summary. The first edition of *On Camera*, which was called *The Programme-Maker's Handbook (Goodbye Totter TV)*, introduced this structure in 1982 and it continues to make the book accessible both as a programme-maker's guide and as a work of reference.

The second edition of *On Camera*, published in 1984, was subtitled *How to produce film and video*. The new subtitle, *Essential know-how for programme-makers*, emphasizes the producers and directors. The debate about film and video is over: film hasn't died but hardly anyone uses it for their first programmes. The new *On Camera* assumes you are using video and, when appropriate, adds a comment about film – it was the other way round in the first two editions. This repositioning has led to numerous changes throughout the book.

There are other changes in response to new technology. The chapter about editing has been rewritten to cover non-linear editing and to guide the reader through the variety of editing routes now available. The briefings entitled *Chromakey* and *Technology for the non-technical* have also been completely revised, with the technology briefing taking you through encoding, fields and frames, component and composite recording, digital technology, compression and a lot more.

On Camera has no intention of losing its reputation as the industry's most helpful and friendly guide.

Ideas

Most how-to-do-it television guides start with a short lecture on the importance of ideas in programme-making. I will do so as well. But the truth is that San Totta TV manages quite well without ideas – instead its producers use formulas for their programmes.

formulas Caesar Andante's *Sports Round-Up* takes a camera to a few convenient games each week. He then adds an introduction from the studio to each videotape and that's his slot filled for the week. Virginia Donna's *Women At Large* programme has a slightly more ambitious formula: every week there is a cooking demonstration, a song from a children's choir in the studio and the rest of the programme is filled with an interview or report about some meeting organized by the Women's Institute of San Totta. Light entertainment, religious, children's and chat programmes all have their own formulas.

Tottam™ TV

'WOMEN AT LARGE'

Producer: Virginia Donna

~~WEEK 1~~ *WEEK 2*
  WEEK 3
Contents: *WEEK 4*
     WEEK 5
1. Titles
2. Children's choir
3. Recipe
4. Women's Circle Report
5. Credits

Unchanged formulas become boring

Nothing wrong with that: all formulas started off as ideas once – good ideas, or they wouldn't have developed into formulas. And formulas offer some useful advantages. Producers aren't exposed to the risk of failure – they know their programmes will work. Viewers know exactly what to expect from each programme and a few acquire the habit of

viewing regularly. San TTV's General Manager, Magnus
Vision, is happy too: his programmes have a safe following
and nothing radical or unexpected is broadcast which might
ruffle the conservative tastes of the government VIP s he has
to get his funds from.

But in the long run formulas have a built-in element of
failure, a sort of biodegradable element which guarantees
that they will eventually rot away. Because in the long run
formulas become tired and predictable and boring. You
know that has happened when you can predict more than
50 per cent of a programme's contents before you've seen it.

The way to avoid this sorry end is to keep your formula
fresh by always looking for ways to improve it. In countries
with a long tradition of television you will be surprised how
even programmes with a highly successful formula (like the
news) have changed over the years – the result of new ideas
introduced to keep an old and indispensable formula
popular and alive.

But if you don't have a formula, you need an idea.

ideas So what in television is an idea?

To answer that, we first have to think about another
question: what is television for? The usual answer to this
question lists two objectives for programmes:

1. To entertain.
2. To inform.

For our purposes these are perfectly good objectives.
They also provide a simple test for a programme idea.
All you need do is ask yourself:

1. Does my idea entertain?
2. Does my idea inform?

A 'yes' to question one is necessary for each and every
programme idea without exception. All programmes
must entertain the viewer in some way or quite simply
there won't be any viewers, just people who have left
their television on by mistake, or are waiting for the
next programme. In fact the most useful definition for
entertainment is 'something which people want to watch'.
It needn't entertain only in the song-and-dance sense.

It can interest, surprise, amuse, shock, stimulate or provoke
the audience, but it must make them want to watch. That's
entertainment.

A 'yes' to question two ('informing') is necessary for all
programmes except those intended purely as entertainment
(song-and-dance programmes, comedy, music programmes
and so on). Informing means leaving the viewer at the end
of the programme knowing a little more about something
than he or she knew at the beginning.

If you have an idea which deserves a 'yes' to question
two, you have a programme idea. But beware – your idea
must also deserve a 'yes' to question one ('entertaining') if
it's worth pursuing. What's the point of being informative
if you're so unentertaining (so boring and predictable) that
no one wants to watch? Reading the telephone directory
on air, for example, could be called informative, but it's
unlikely to be entertaining. Remember: people aren't paid
to watch.

Another point about being informative: television
TV and is surprisingly bad at conveying detailed information to an
information audience. Newspapers, for example, can deliver far more
information far faster. It would take about an hour to read
out four pages of a broadsheet paper on television. Showing
pictures other than that of the newsreader would slow
things down even more. To make things worse, television
viewers all have to receive their information at the same
speed (this can delay the quick-witted and confuse the
slow) and no one can go back to look again at the bits he
or she didn't catch the first time round.

On the other hand the great advantage of television is
that it can bring facts to life and present them in an
entertaining way. But only a very limited number of facts
in a given time. So you the producer have to be ruthless
about deciding which are the most important facts and
present only those in your programme. Doing this and
being fair and balanced at the same time is one of the most
difficult things a producer has to do. But it has to be done:
programmes clogged with facts leave the viewers so bored
and bewildered that in the end they leave you.

So where are these entertaining and informative
thinking programme ideas going to come from? Thinking up ideas
up ideas and ways of presenting them effectively is of course the
most important and creative part of the producer's job – it's
even more important than the procedures and techniques
which this book contains. The idea behind the programme
must be the master; technique must be the servant. That's
the right order of priorities and you should always stick
to it: never let production techniques dictate the content
of your programme.

Because thinking up ideas is the creative heart of the
producer's job it's not something that I – or anyone else –
can do for you. But I can offer you some hints on
identifying ideas.

1. Is there something you want to say to the world?
strong Do you have strong feelings about some subjects?
feelings If you do, then you are one of those people who will
have little trouble thinking of programme ideas. Obviously

the things which make your blood boil are things which other people will also have strong opinions about and so you have the makings of a programme setting out the facts for everyone to consider. But don't let your strong feelings unbalance your sense of fairness; television is not a personal soapbox.

interests

2. Think about what you are really interested in and the chances are that you will have a programme idea that will interest other human beings.

It's sometimes difficult to identify your own interests. (I know, if anyone asks me what my hobbies are, my mind immediately goes blank.) The way to do it is to analyze your own behaviour. Which bit of the newspaper do you read first? (Fashion? Sport? News?) What sort of music do you listen to and who are your favourite performers? What were the subjects of the last few interesting conversations you had? (Knitting? Jet planes? Pets?) Which books do you browse through in the bookshop? Which films and TV programmes on which subjects do you prefer? The answers to these questions will probably suggest some topics which you could do something with. These are the areas you should be combing for your programme ideas.

See Briefing 18 for more about viewers

I recommend your own interests as the place to start looking because this is where you are most likely to find the subjects which interest other people. Most people are just like you (and me): they enjoy seeing programmes about all sorts of people (successful or unsuccessful, courageous or cowardly, amusing or gifted or bungling or any adjective you care to name except boring); they enjoy programmes about animals and children and curiosities like eggs without yolks and extrasensory perception. They aren't immediately attracted by programmes about export statistics, energy gaps and computer languages because on the whole they don't understand these subjects. I am not saying that you should always go for the sensational or trivial and avoid important subjects like the last three. But making informative and entertaining programmes about subjects like the last three is infinitely more difficult than making informative and entertaining programmes about the other subjects I have mentioned. So give yourself a chance of making successful programmes by picking subjects which people will want to watch, particularly for your first few programmes.

keep an
ideas file

3. It's unfortunate that the time when you most desperately need an idea is always the time when you can't think of anything. Avoid this embarrassing state of mind by keeping an ideas file. In this file you should jot down possible subjects for programmes, the names of interesting books or people who might provide a topic, cuttings from newspapers and magazines and anything else which might come in useful. You'll soon find that the problem with the ideas file is keeping it to reasonable proportions. But never mind – with a bulging ideas file behind you, you'll get through even your least inspired days without too much anguish.

Of course, you aren't always given the luxury of choosing your own subjects for programmes. Often you'll be asked to do a programme about something which may not interest you and you won't be able to say no. But once you have accepted the assignment it's your job as producer to come up with an idea that will make the programme work. This happened once to Totta's current affairs producer, Eustace Sugar. He was asked to do a programme about the San Totta Army (San TA for short) to celebrate Constitution Day. Eustace thought for a bit and made the following proposal: he would visit all three of the country's military bases with a camera crew and ...

Unfortunately, there was no 'and'. That was as far as his idea went. Not a thought about what he was going to shoot when he got there. Was Eustace's programme idea a good one? Let's apply our two questions.

1. Does it entertain?

Answer – no. Undoubtedly there are interesting things
going on at the military bases, but Eustace is unlikely to find
them since he has no idea what he's looking for.

2. Does it inform?

Again no. Eustace has no idea what he wants to tell his
viewers about the army. So by setting out to tell them about
everything he sees at the bases he ends up by swamping
them with information and telling them nothing.

What Eustace needs is a bit of research to come up
with a programme idea which is both entertaining and
informative. Perhaps a look at how the army has developed
in the last 10 years and will develop in the next 10. Or a
report on how the military system can turn unsophisticated
villagers into skilled handlers of complex modern weapons
in a comparatively short time.

Now those are real programme ideas, Eustace.
But to think of them – and certainly to turn them into
programmes – you need to do some research. And that's
the next chapter.

SUMMARY
IDEAS

Keep formulas fresh by looking for new ways of improving them.

Test all new programme ideas by asking
1. *Does it entertain?*
   YES *required for all ideas.*
2. *Does it inform?*
   YES *also required for all ideas*
   (except purely entertainment programmes).

Television is not good at conveying large amounts of detailed information. So you have to select only the most important facts to put in your programme and leave the others out.

Hints for thinking up good ideas
1. *Do programmes about things you feel strongly about.*
2. *Give yourself a chance of making successful programmes by picking subjects that interest people (the extraordinary interests people more than export statistics).*
3. *Keep an ideas file.*

Research

Totta producers are not very keen on research.

In one way it seems rather inferior work, something for secretaries and very junior production assistants (there are no San TTV researchers). In another way it seems to be rather superior work, in fact something beyond the competence of programme-makers, something which government information officers or the clever chaps at the national museum can provide.

As a result, Totta programmes aren't researched at all. Eustace Sugar, as we know, makes a habit of turning up with his crew at a location and shooting whatever happens to be going on. Romeo Landmark, the sports commentator, rarely knows the name of more than three players in each team when he's commentating on a football match. He certainly has no facts and figures about the recent records of the two teams.

For more ambitious programmes, such as hour-long documentaries, Oscar Boney, the former school inspector turned producer, gets a local expert to write a summary of the topic he's chosen. The resulting document is called a 'script'. And, as Oscar says, who needs research if you have a script?

The answer is: everyone needs research. Even if there's a handy summary written by some expert.

There are two points to be remembered about research:

1. Every programme needs it.
2. Producers should do their own.

Fairly obvious points, but they are often ignored. As a producer you must obviously have some knowledge of the

topic you are making a programme about. This doesn't
mean that you need to know as much as or more than the
expert. But you do need to know enough to be able to
decide what to put into the programme and what to leave
out. The choice of facts which you think worth including
may not always be the same as the choice the expert would
make, but provided you can justify it intelligently, your
choice will probably be the most effective one for
television.

do your own research

It follows therefore that you should do your own
research, because as you find out more and more about the
programme subject you are the only person who is looking
out for the points which will come over most effectively
on television. No one will be able to recognize these points
better than you. Your outside experts certainly won't be
able to: that's not their job. Government information
officers know more about publicity than programme-
making. The clever chaps at the national museum are more
interested in collecting than selecting facts. And academics
are always aiming at the definitive written (not televisual)
account. When it comes to finding and selecting facts for
television, you are the expert.

Think in visual sequences

think in pictures

You are also the only person who will be – or should be –
thinking in pictures and sequences of pictures. An author
working on a book finds his thoughts grouping themselves
into paragraphs; a television producer should find his
thoughts forming themselves into picture sequences. You
have to look for the good individual shot which sums up
a situation, but you can't construct a good programme out

of a succession of isolated shots, any more than you can write a good book by jotting down isolated facts. So always look for situations which will yield not only pictures but sequences of pictures. These are the building blocks of your programme.

So how do you research? The answer is – in any way possible. Read anything you can find on the subject. Telephone likely informants and go and talk to them personally if they sound interesting. Ask around to see if your friends and colleagues have useful contacts. Visit places and exhibitions. Look up references in the library. View previous programmes on the subject. Think, use your imagination and discuss your subject with anyone who will listen. Be open to new ideas – research should be an enjoyable, enlightening experience, not a desperate search for material to prop up your prejudices.

Now is also the time to start thinking about music, if you intend using it in your programme. It could affect the way you handle your pictures. If you have a researcher, do the most important pieces of research together and split up for the rest, comparing notes afterwards.

using a tape-recorder If you can lay hands on a tape-recorder, record any important conversations with people who might contribute to your programme. Make the recordings good enough to be edited and used over the relevant sequences in the finished programme; often you find that people are never again as fresh and interesting as the first time you meet them. But check that using a recording made like this does not violate any agreement with the sound recordists' union. If it does, think about taking a sound recordist along for first meetings with key contributors to the programme, particularly if they are old or likely to be nervous (it's probably too expensive to have a sound recordist with you on all your research meetings).

Of course, how you research depends on how much time you have. If you have any choice in the matter (and often you won't), give yourself enough time to become clear in your own mind what the programme will say and how it will say it. When you know that, you've done most of your research.

keep a notebook

A final point – keep a notebook for each production. Put in it the facts and figures you have found out from your research, lists of the names and addresses of everyone involved in the programme, lists of possible sequences, notes of your expenses and so on. Read through it at intervals while you are doing your production: ideas which you rejected at an earlier stage may be worth reviving now that your programme has more shape to it. Re-reading a well-kept notebook can help bring order to that jumble of half-thought-out ideas swirling round inside your head. And when the production is finished, don't throw away the notebook. The contacts and ideas in it may be useful for another programme some day.

SUMMARY
RESEARCH

Every programme needs research.

As a producer you should do your own so that
1. *You know enough about the subject to select the important points for television yourself.*
2. *You recognize the material that will come across best on television – no one else can do this for you or as well as you.*

Think in pictures and sequences of pictures.

Follow up all likely leads.

Be open to new ideas.

Start thinking about your choice of music.

Record first conversations with likely contributors.

Keep a notebook.

Recce

Recce is short for reconnaissance, a word most often found
on the lips of soldiers, who use it to describe going ahead
of the main body of troops to spy out the land. Though,
of course, like television people, soldiers more often say
'recce' than reconnaissance.

In television as in war, a recce, though often impossible,
is always advisable. Why?

There is no one major reason, just a host of minor ones.

Obviously if you have visited the location and have had
a good look at what you intend to do, you are more likely to
make economic and effective use of your time on location
with the crew. Being well prepared always pays dividends
– both for programmes and budget.

recce people

Other benefits flow from meeting the people you intend
to interview (yes – you recce people as well). Talking with
them about your plans gives everyone a chance to sort out
their ideas in advance. On the day itself you will often find
that a camera – like a gun – doesn't promote clear thinking.

The discussion on the recce also makes non-television
people realize how much work goes into making a
programme. Finished programmes flow so effortlessly
from TV sets that most people assume that making the
programme is also effortless. They envisage cameramen
stepping from fast cars shooting from the hip, a quick chat
followed by a short interview and that's it – the whole
process as brief and bloodless as a well-organized bank raid.
As a result, they tend to allocate far too little time for their
part of the programme.

Don't disillusion them too much – or they might
withdraw their co-operation. But as you do your recce, the

truth will slowly dawn on them that programme-making
is more like working than robbing a bank.

So what do you do on a recce? The following checklist
will be helpful.

1. Look around

Have a good look around the location and see what it has
to offer.

2. Talk to people

Talk to people there at length. Be curious about anything
and everything which promises something relevant for your
programme. Something they say or you notice may suggest
a new idea for – or way of – doing your story.

Check the sun

3. Check the sun

Check where the sun will be when you come back for
the shoot. This is important. A late afternoon sun low on
the horizon can make some scenes impossible to shoot.
A bright sun behind a building can cast so black a shadow
on its front that no videotape or film stock will produce an
acceptable picture.

4. List sequences

Make a list of the sequences you intend to film and discuss
it with the people there. Ask them to help with any
arrangements.

5. List shots

Work out a rough list of the shots you want for each
sequence. Try and think of some which are a bit unusual but
still fit into your story: perhaps a high shot from the top of
the camera car or a street–level shot with the cameraman
standing in a ditch (preferably without water in it). An
unusual angle can often turn a commonplace scene into an
interesting shot. So ask to shoot from low roofs, high cranes,
conveyor belts and so on. Remember that as a television
producer you can frequently get permission to put your
camera in positions which would be forbidden to members
of the public (on the front of railway engines, half–way up
ships' masts, underground in mines and so on). Use this
advantage to the full; you're there on behalf of your viewers.
Look out in particular for the shot which 'says it all' – the
shot which, in one unforgettable instant, sums up the
nurse's devotion to the patient; the shot which captures
the fan's enthusiasm for the footballer.

The most interesting shots are often to be found at the
point where things are changing: the first time the new
machine is switched on in the factory, the moment the air
hostess tries on her new uniform, the day the ship is towed
off for scrapping. Buildings are more interesting while they
are going up or coming down, schools when their pupils
are beginning or ending their break in the playground. On
the whole television is wasted presenting things which are

Show things changing   static; it's at its best when showing things which are
happening or changing before the viewer's eyes. You know
you've found that sort of shot or sequence when what the
cameraman is doing is not the most interesting thing
happening on the location.

6. Electricity

Check that there is electricity for your lights and what
sort of plugs are in use. Check also on any high-powered
electrical, radar, magnetic or x-ray devices in the vicinity.
They can create havoc, particularly for video recorders and
radio mikes. Industry and the military seem to be using
more and more of such devices. If you find any, warn your
crew and ask for their advice.

7. TV and computer screens

Make a note of any TV or computer screens that will be in
shot (the make, model and screen refresh rate will all be
helpful) so that you can warn the crew. They may need to
bring along special equipment to get rid of the roll bar and
stabilize the screens on screen.

8. Safety

Think about safety. As producer/director you are required
by law to take reasonable care not only for your own safety

but also for the safety of the crew and everyone taking part
in the programme. Ask the people on the spot for advice
and help with any special equipment that they are familiar
with: for example, helmets on building sites, life jackets
on boats (not just for non-swimmers), safety harnesses for
working at heights. Explosives and weapons are obviously
dangerous and require expert handling; but special
precautions may also be needed if you are working with
animals, any type of fire, underground, among ruins, in
heavy traffic, on motorways or at night. If you are planning
any kind of stunt, get expert help. Special effects designers
and stunt men can make it possible to shoot in safety things
that will look satisfyingly dangerous on screen. They cost
a lot less than an accident.

9. Sound

Listen to the noises on the location. They will be more
noticeable on the recording than they are in real life, so
consider ways of controlling them, such as using another
mike, moving to a different position or shooting at a
different time. Continuous noise from places like the
building site next door, a busy road or an airport can be
made more tolerable by setting up a shot which incidentally
shows the source of the noise. Quiet sounds like air-
conditioners or aquarium pumps are best dealt with by
asking if they can be switched off while you shoot. Ask
about this on the recce to allow time for any special
arrangements to be made. Don't forget also to ask about
flying times at the helicopter training school just over the
horizon, or about the factory full of circular saws which
happens to be working half-time on the recce day. Its return
to full-time working on the shooting day may halve your
working time.

10. Shooting permission

Double-check that you have permission to shoot from all
the people you need to ask. Does this include the police?
Minor officials like public relations officers are often reluc-
tant to admit that they aren't actually entitled to give permission. You have to be tactful about finding out who is.

11. Fix the shooting day

Make sure your contacts know the day and time you intend
to come back for shooting, and what is expected of them
on the day. Check that market days, early closing or late
shopping days, school terms or holidays, high or low tides,
unexpected fairs, carnivals, festivals or sports events won't
interfere with your shooting.

12. Refreshments and parking

Check that there is a place nearby where your crew can
get food and drink (and go to the toilet) if shooting will
take more than a short time. If in town, find or arrange
somewhere to park. If out of town, select an area where
parked cars will be out of shot.

13. Special equipment

Make a note of any non-standard equipment you might
need: special mounts or lenses for the camera, light filters
for 'star' or diffusion effects, extra sound equipment, a
clockwork camera for filming in coalmines or on oil or gas
tankers where there is a danger that electrical sparks may
set off an explosion. Walkie-talkies are indispensable for
any scene where the camera is some distance from the
action: for example, shots of cars or boats travelling. Will
the crew need wellington boots, bathing costumes or other
special clothing?

14. Take a stills camera

It's often useful to take a stills camera with you on the recce.
A photograph can help the cameraman choose the right
lights for the interior you have in mind, or give the graphic
artist an idea for a style which will fit the programme.
Photographs are indispensable if you are doing a drama
partly on location and partly in the studio: the set designer,
costume designer, props buyer and studio lighting and
sound supervisors will all need a good set of photographs
if they can't visit the location themselves.

15. Publicity stills

Your stills camera will also remind you to look for publicity
shots for the programme. If you see anything promising,
make a note to arrange for a stills photographer to be
present on the shooting day.

16. How to get there

Lastly, make sure that you can give clear and accurate instructions on how to reach the location. A sketch map is often useful. If the location is in the middle of nowhere it may be a good idea to arrange to meet somewhere easy to find and then travel in convoy. Or, alternatively, if there will be a large number of crew and participants, put up cards with distinctive arrows and a code word at key road junctions. Don't mention TV or you may attract an unwanted crowd. And remember to take down the signs after the shoot.

You can become one of the organizers at programmed events

recceing programmed events

Occasionally you will be asked to tape or film an event which hasn't been arranged purely for your benefit and which you therefore won't be able to stop and start as you wish (presentation and opening ceremonies, graduation days and so on). When you recce these events you have to decide which part of the proceedings you are interested in and then go on to find out as much detail as possible about what is actually going to happen in these sections. Often the organizers of the event won't have thought through all the details, in which case you can tactfully become one of the organizers and help them arrange the proceedings as much as possible to your mutual benefit.

All this preparation can involve you in a great deal of work, particularly if you intend to include a large part of – or even all – the events in the programme (rarely necessary unless you are doing an outside broadcast). But the preparation is vital if your camera crew (or crews) are to avoid getting themselves into a terrible tangle because they don't know who does what next.

The classic case was Vincent Toolgate's coverage of a mixed old people's choir (Vincent is San TTV's news producer). The ladies were lined up on one side of the stage and the men on the other, with the solo singer in the middle. The cameraman started on a wide shot and then when the men started singing he slowly zoomed in to cover them. Just before he finished the zoom they stopped singing and the ladies started. He wobbled for a moment, wondering whether to pan to the ladies, and decided against it. The ladies went on singing for a time so he then decided to pan to them. Just as he finished his pan, the ladies stopped singing and the men started …

You can see that the possibilities for confusion are endless. A proper recce (preferably during a rehearsal for an event such as this) and Vincent could have avoided all the problems. If the cameraman could have accompanied him on the recce, so much the better. But that's a refinement which Totta hasn't thought of yet.

SUMMARY
RECCE

Always advisable, not always possible.

Recce is part of the research. Use it to
 1. *Look around the location.*
 2. *Talk to people there.*
 3. *Check the position of the sun.*
 4. *Work out possible sequences.*
 5. *Look for interesting shots, particularly those which show things changing or 'say it all'.*
 6. *Check the electricity supply. Check on high-power hazards for video recorders and mikes.*
 7. *Note details of TV and computer screens.*
 8. *Think about safety and assess the need for special equipment, advice or help.*
 9. *Check for noise problems, both obvious and hidden.*
 10. *Double-check shooting permissions.*
 11. *Check contacts are clear about shooting times and dates. Check local calendar of events for possible shooting snags.*
 12. *Check feeding and toilet arrangements. Arrange car parking.*
 13. *Are walkie-talkies or special equipment needed for camera, sound or crew?*
 14. *Take photographs to help studio-based technicians.*
 15. *Look for publicity shots. If you think of any, make a note to arrange for a stills photographer to come on shooting day.*
 16. *Can you give clear 'how to get there' instructions?*

Recce programmed events in great detail.

Take a cameraman on recces, if possible.

Options

San Totta TV is safe TV. Its producers stick to the techniques they know and avoid experiments. That way there's no chance of having a big failure with a programme. Unfortunately there's also no chance of having a big success.

So San TTV's viewers are restricted to a diet of talking heads and filmlets with muzak for sound tracks (synchronized sound is so rare that most viewers think it's locally unavailable). All programmes are fronted by presenters sitting in the same San TTV Presenter's Chair; viewers know it's the same one because they can recognize its squeak. The presentation announcements each day are also the same; the announcers read from a standard script in which only the programme titles change: 'And now, for your entertainment and enjoyment, San TTV proudly presents ...' In fact Totta's producers have been sticking to the same techniques so faithfully since the station opened that they've forgotten that there are other possibilities.

Non-Totta producers should always try and broaden their personal range of production techniques. So here is a list of techniques, an inventory of options which any television producer might use. The list is not complete. What list of this type could be? New techniques are always being developed and some talented producers can successfully use techniques which other equally talented producers can't.

Of course not all the techniques which follow can be used in the same programme. But experiment a little if you think a particular technique would help what you are trying to say. You will be pleasantly surprised how much difference a bit of extra effort and imagination can make.

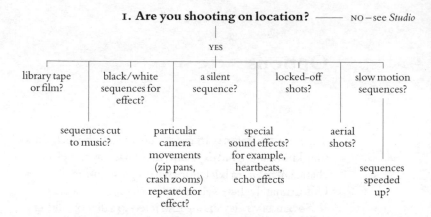

1. Are you shooting on location? —— NO – see *Studio*

YES

| library tape or film? | black/white sequences for effect? | a silent sequence? | locked-off shots? | slow motion sequences? |

| sequences cut to music? | particular camera movements (zip pans, crash zooms) repeated for effect? | special sound effects? for example, heartbeats, echo effects | aerial shots? |

sequences speeded up?

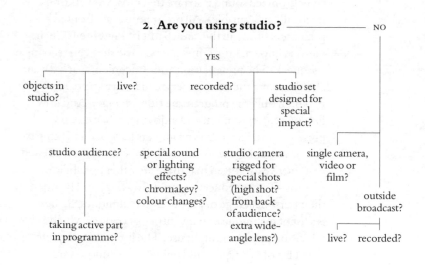

2. Are you using studio? ——————— NO

YES

| objects in studio? | live? | recorded? | studio set designed for special impact? |

| studio audience? | special sound or lighting effects? chromakey? colour changes? | studio camera rigged for special shots (high shot? from back of audience? extra wide-angle lens?) | single camera, video or film? |

outside broadcast?

| taking active part in programme? | | live? recorded? |

3. Are you using a reporter / presenter? —— NO
see *Dramatized*

YES

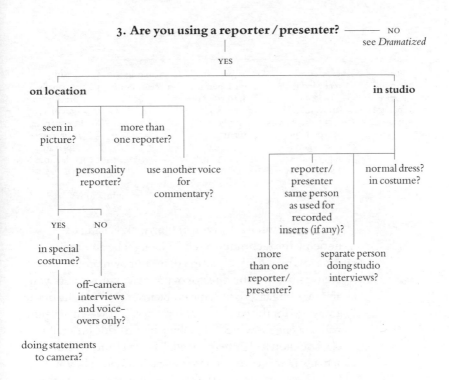

on location   **in studio**

seen in picture?

more than one reporter?

personality reporter?

use another voice for commentary?

reporter/ presenter same person as used for recorded inserts (if any)?

normal dress? in costume?

YES   NO

in special costume?

more than one reporter/ presenter?

separate person doing studio interviews?

off-camera interviews and voice-overs only?

doing statements to camera?

4. Is your programme dramatized?

on film or video?

in studio?

one person doing all parts solo? several actors? children playing some or all parts?

script specially written? partly improvised? historical words re-enacted?

music? song? dance?

location improved with constructed sets, props, lights? or non-naturalistic abstract set – in a cave, against the sky or on a mountain?

other possibilities: puppets? cartoons? models? shadows?

costume historical? formal? casual?

archive or undramatized sequences mixed with dramatized?

5. Are you using graphics?

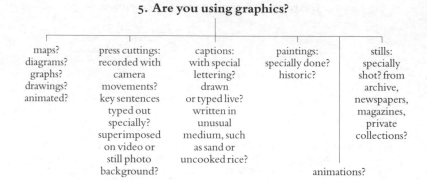

| maps?
diagrams?
graphs?
drawings?
animated? | press cuttings:
recorded with
camera
movements?
key sentences
typed out
specially?
superimposed
on video or
still photo
background? | captions:
with special
lettering?
drawn
or typed live?
written in
unusual
medium, such
as sand or
uncooked rice? | paintings:
specially done?
historic? | stills:
specially
shot? from
archive,
newspapers,
magazines,
private
collections? |

animations?

When you watch television or films make a habit of noticing the techniques used. You might be able to use some of them (suitably adapted) in your own programmes. Remember that the director or producer whose work you are watching faced the same problems as you – did he or she always go for the easiest solution? I have just watched a film with a scene showing a boy taking his first ride on a wild black stallion he has befriended. The first time the boy actually manages to get onto the stallion's back, boy and horse are swimming in the sea. The director chose to film the whole scene from under water so that all we see are the boy's legs carefully getting astride the horse. An imaginative, original idea which works beautifully.

Simpler ideas used with imagination and originality can work just as well – try very hard to get some into your programmes. But make sure the techniques you choose help to communicate the point you want to make. Techniques that aren't quite right can get in the way of your message.

SUMMARY
OPTIONS

Television offers a vast range of techniques for getting the message across to the audience, many of them simple to use. Don't always go for the obvious – see if there is a better, more imaginative technique for communicating what you want to say.

Enlarge your own armoury of techniques by watching how other directors handle their material. You could adapt some of their ideas for your own programmes.

Techniques should promote, not confuse the message you are trying to get across.

Treatment

The preliminary research is now finished. It may have lasted a month, a week or the time it takes to make a telephone call. At the very least you will have thought things over, asked a few questions, got some answers and worked out a way of doing your programme.

Now you are ready to do the treatment. This consists of putting down on paper all the things you intend to put into the programme in note form, with the visuals on the left and an indication of what the sound will be on the right. Something like this:

Opening of new bridge over Rigwe River

picture	sound
1. crowd arrives for opening ceremony	commentary: new bridge opening today – bridge replacing ferry
2. ferry on last trip	ferry working since 1936 – last trip at noon on Sunday
3. interview ferry captain cutaway of rowing skiffs	sync: 'end of an era – ferry replaced rowing skiffs – early hostility to ferry – sad to be going'
4. library film: new bridge being built	commentary: new bridge started two years ago – then use original commentary
5. interview consultant engineer	sync: 'difficulties building bridge'
6. crowd assembled for opening	vox pop: what difference will new bridge make to everyday life?
7. arrival of VIPs and opening ceremony	sync, and comm on events as needed
8. celebrations	ditto

This is probably as much detail as you need in your treatment. But why bother doing a treatment at all?

The advantages will emerge as you do it. Putting down on paper what you intend to do concentrates the mind – that's the first advantage. It also gives you a way of addressing important questions like:

– do you have a story?
– have you planned enough sequences to tell it well?
– have you left anything out?
– how long will your planned sequences take to shoot?
– how long will they run on screen?

All this, and more, will emerge as you do your treatment. With experience you will be able to recognize the strong and weak points in your story, and this knowledge will serve you well when you come to shooting it. You don't have to stick slavishly to every sequence you've planned. While you are shooting, new facts may emerge (you never stop learning); or some events you had high hopes for may turn out to be disappointing. If either of these happens, there is nothing to stop you changing your planned sequence. Treatments are preparation, not prescription.

Some events may be
disappointing

Totta producers of course avoid doing a treatment at all costs. Virginia Donna once did a treatment for her weekly women's programme but decided it looked a bit bare – a true reflection of her programme, since it never departs from its very basic formula.

Eustace Sugar doesn't like putting his ideas on paper; he finds he can't think of anything to put down. He once did a programme about San Video traffic jams which consisted of 25 minutes of – you guessed it – traffic jams. And nothing else. The treatment for this programme (if there had been one) would have read 'shots of traffic jams'. Even Eustace would have realized that there was something wrong with this as a programme idea!

How long will the programme be if you do all the sequences you have in your treatment? Have you planned enough, or too much?

The trick here is to estimate the likely length of each **estimating** sequence and then add up the estimates. You will find **duration** it helps if the list of points in the sound column of your treatment is as complete as possible. If you allow 15 seconds for each point plus something for pictures without commentary, your total won't be far out. Let's see how this works with the Rigwe River treatment.

Sequence 1

crowd arrives for opening ceremony	commentary: new bridge opening today – bridge replacing ferry

Duration estimate:
Two points, 15 secs each = 30 secs. Allow extra 5 secs for opening of programme (commentary can't begin immediately programme does). But don't bother with odd seconds too much. So total for sequence = ½ min.

Sequence 2

ferry on last trip	ferry working since 1936
	– last trip at noon on Sunday

Duration estimate:
Two points, about 15 secs each = 30 secs. Allow extra for
shots of ferry's last trip: arriving, tying up at quay, blowing
whistle and so on: 30 secs. Total = 1 min.

Sequence 3

interview ferry captain	sync: 'end of an era – ferry
cutaway of rowing skiffs	replaced rowing skiffs
	– early hostility to ferry –
	sad to be going'

Duration estimate:
Four points, 15 secs each = 1 min. Allow extra time for
captain talking round subject, say 30 secs. Total = 1½ mins
(note cutaway photo of rowing skiff is to be used over sound
of captain talking. So no extra time is needed).

Sequence 4

library film: new bridge	commentary: new bridge
being built	started two years ago – then
	use original commentary

Duration estimate:
The library film is particularly interesting as it says the
bridge will take only six months to build! Allow time to
introduce the library film (15 secs), plus 15 secs to make
your commentary point (new bridge started two years ago),
plus 1½ mins for the original commentary on the library
film. Total = 2 mins.

Sequence 5

interview consultant	sync: 'difficulties building
engineer	bridge'

Duration estimate:
One point = 15 secs. but obviously the engineer will want
to give details of his difficulties and his talk is bound to
ramble a little. So allow 1½ mins.

Sequence 6

crowd assembled for opening	vox pop: what difference will new bridge make to everyday life?

Duration estimate:

Allow 15 secs to set up the question for the vox pop (a technique in which you ask lots of people the same question and then use short extracts from their answers without repeating the question); then about 15 secs for each of six answers. Total = 1¾ min. Call it 2 mins for ease of calculation.

See Briefing 9 for more about vox pops

And so on.

The advantage of making a separate estimate for each sequence is that your overestimates and underestimates will tend to cancel out, leaving you with a fairly accurate idea of how long your sequences will run. But to be on the safe side, make sure your sequences add up to about 25 per cent more than you need. It's much easier to cut things out of programmes than to put them in. Indeed programmes usually benefit from being planned a little overlong and then shortened.

How long will the programme take to shoot? It depends on the story, your preparation and how fast you and the crew can work. The only rule is that everything takes longer than you expect.

estimating shooting time

For a rough guide, however, calculate as follows. Allow 20 minutes after you arrive on location to unpack the gear and set up for the first shot. Each setup or camera position after the first will take about 10 minutes – though you will be lucky to do six in an hour. Allow 10 minutes if you have to move more than a few yards for a new setup. Each interview will take 30-45 minutes and you should allow another 15-20 minutes to get the gear back into the car. On this basis the Rigwe bridge story will take just over three hours to shoot:

unpacking/packing (2 x 20 mins)	40 mins
5 setups	50 mins
moves	10 mins
2 interviews (45 mins each)	1hr 30 mins
total	**3hr 10 mins**

This estimate is, of course, very rough. Ten minutes for the vox pops is almost certainly an underestimate; the arrival of the VIPs and the opening ceremony will also take longer. And will the interviewees (the captain of the ferry and the consultant engineer) be ready for their interviews when you want them or will you have to wait?

Ignore the rough edges: the value of the calculation is that it tells you that the Rigwe bridge story is going to take at least half a day to shoot, not including travel time, if you shoot it as a magazine story. As a documentary it will take the best part of a day, as your more elaborate treatment – including shots of the captain skippering his ferry, the men in the engine room and so on – will tell you. If you add travel time and meal breaks to the calculations based on the treatment, you can work out how many shooting days you need – or start trimming the treatment to fit the number of days you can afford.

taking stock   Besides help with planning and timing a story, treatments yield a further bonus: they give you a chance to stand back and take stock of the way the programme is going. Has the research uncovered a good story and interesting contributors? Are there enough sequences and pictures to make the story come alive on screen? Is the programme idea still entertaining and informative now you know more about it? This is the time to test your project by using the questions in the first chapter.

identifying   You may sometimes have difficulty doing a treatment
your story   along the lines I have suggested. Often this difficulty is itself a sign that you have not thought things through. Your mind is such a jumble of facts and ideas that you can't decide what the story is or how you should tell it. If this is your problem, try turning to a friend and telling him or her in about 20 simple, everyday words what your programme is about (just as if your friend had asked). For example, 'I'm showing the opening of the new bridge and looking at how people used to cross the Rigwe River before'. The very effort of putting your story in a few simple words tells you (a) if you have a story, (b) what the story is, and (c) if it's entertaining and informative. Your brain will find the words for the story if

you let it, as long as you stick to simple, spoken language. Often it's the pompous phrases (like 'Rigwe River Overbridge Construction Project – Final Phase') which obstruct your understanding of what the story is about. Then once you have identified your story you can organize your material to put it in the most effective way.

Beware if the summary of your story is something vague like 'this film shows the work of the police' or 'this film shows the things that go on in our military bases' (this was Eustace Sugar's story). Such stories suggest no reason why any viewer should watch; they promise nothing informative or interesting. If instead you say: 'I want to show the new techniques the police are using to cope with the rising crime rate', you have identified a specific story which is likely to yield something worth watching.

Another useful tip for finding your story is to ask yourself 'Why am I doing this story now? Could it be done next year, or could it have been done last year?' Thinking about these questions forces you to pinpoint the relevance of your story to the viewer now.

shot lists   For short films with perhaps only one or two sequences, doing a treatment can be excessive. A list of shots may be all you need.

storyboards   The other way of planning a short film is to do a storyboard, where each frame represents a shot. The storyboard doesn't have to be a work of art – pin men or sausage men are fine. I find sausage men convey movement

Sausage men are easy to draw

better than pin men and are easier to draw: all you have to do is produce a string of sausages – one for each section of the body – so that an arm or leg has three sausages, the head and neck are a sausage each, and so on. Make a note of the shot size and any camera movement under each frame.

Storyboard

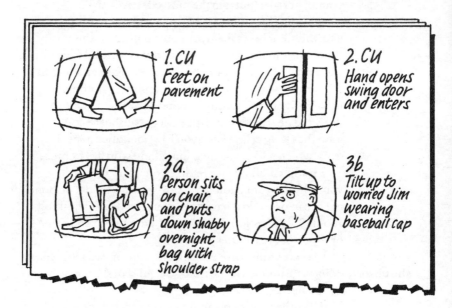

Storyboards are a lot of work and so are impractical for longer films (though many full-length Hollywood features are storyboarded before shooting). Even if you storyboard only the tricky sequences, the effort is worthwhile. Storyboards give you a feel for the film, make you 'think pictures', give you advance warning of problems like crossing the line and help you sort them out.

Finally, how do you break down action into shots? What **breaking** size should the shots be? The answer is to work out what **action into** you want the viewers to see – and then set up the shots to **shots** show them. Each shot should be dictated by its content and the needs of the viewer. It has to be close enough to emphasize the action you want viewers to see – the most common mistake made by beginners is to shoot everything too wide. It should run as long as it shows the action satisfactorily and holds the viewers' interest on the screen. When it stops doing those jobs, it's time to look for another.

your mental TV

If you find it difficult at first to break down action into shots (it never becomes easy!), close your eyes and imagine a television set showing the sequence you want to shoot.

See Briefing 1 for more on shot sizes and camera moves

Watch the sequence, remember each picture (whether it's in close-up, medium shot or long shot, how the camera moves and so on) and there you have your breakdown of individual shots. If you forget one of the shots you can always rerun the sequence on your mental TV.

SUMMARY
TREATMENT

When preliminary research is over, do a treatment.
Put pictures on the left, sound on the right.

Check your treatment to see if you have
  − *a workable programme idea*
  − *enough material to cover the story at the length you want*
  − *left anything out.*

Estimate the total duration by estimating the duration of each sequence and adding them up.

Estimate shooting time by allowing 10 minutes per setup and adding 20 minutes unpacking and 20 minutes packing time.

Sit back and take stock of your programme.

Identify your story. If having difficulty
  − *try telling the story to someone in a few words*
  − *why are you doing this story now?*
  − *'see' the story on your mental TV.*

For shorter films, a shot list may be enough.

For shorter films or tricky sequences in longer films, do a storyboard.

Location shooting

Totta's documentary producer, Oscar Boney, never goes on location with the crew when the time comes to shoot his programme. Quite unofficially, of course. 'Well,' he reasons to himself, 'I don't really know what I want to shoot anyway and perhaps the cameraman can sort out something good. After all, he's had more experience on location than I have. Anyway I'm much too busy to go out now. I've got to fill out my car allowance claim and ...'

At least Oscar scores two out of three for his reasons. He isn't sure what he wants to shoot (very little research, no recce, no treatment) and the cameraman is more experienced in location shooting than he is. Though you would have to stop Oscar's allowances before he admitted it in public.

The drawbacks of this stay-at-home policy are obvious. Oscar's absence may indeed have no noticeable effect on any individual shot. But the overall coverage will certainly suffer because the cameraman has spent even less time than Oscar working out what the programme is about. Besides, cameramen who can operate the camera and successfully direct at the same time are very rare indeed – there's simply too much for one person to do. And Oscar himself will suffer: if he doesn't go on location with his crew he misses the shooting experience he could be acquiring and has no chance of improving his personal expertise. So he manages at one stroke to deprive himself of two chances: the chance of making a good programme now (if it is good, it won't be because of him), and the chance of making better ones in the future. Because, believe me, there's no teacher like experience.

**brief the
cameraman**

So what do you, as a fairly new producer, do with an experienced cameraman (or camerawoman) on location?

First of all explain to him (or her) briefly what the programme is about and show him the relevant part of the treatment. Don't be discouraged if he doesn't want to know about the programme and doesn't want to read the treatment; some cameramen like to work on a shot-by-shot basis and ignore everything else. If you meet this sort of cameraman, very briefly tell him what the story is anyway; there's always a chance he might become interested.

Then, start shooting the most important bits of the story first. That way if the equipment fails or the weather worsens, you have at least recorded something. In fact, as technology becomes more and more reliable, the weather is likely to be the greater hazard. So it's a good idea to do your exteriors first if the weather is right rather than run the risk of it changing for the worse.

*Do exteriors before
the weather changes*

shooting order

You don't have to do the shots in the order in which they are planned to appear in the finished story. But don't change the natural order unless there's a good reason; jumping about unnecessarily can complicate matters and lead to continuity problems. The thing to avoid is taking the camera back to a position once you have left it – that's an obvious waste of time. The way to avoid this is to sort out in advance all the shots you need with the camera in one position and then shoot them one after another. Then you move to your next position and shoot there. This is not only a logical way to proceed but also has other benefits.

poison-in-the-pop-bottle story

Suppose, for example, that you are doing a story about shops that are breaking the law by selling poisonous weedkiller in old soft-drink bottles and are not even bothering to put warning labels on the bottles. You show your reporter going into the shop to buy some of the offending bottles; then he comes out holding the bottles to make a statement to camera. It's obviously quicker and easier to do both exterior shots first, even though in the finished film they will be separated by the shots of the reporter buying the bottles and interviewing the shopkeeper inside.

You will notice that even with a short story like this there are at least two ways of putting the shots together for the finished programme.

either	**or**
ext. shop	ext. shop
reporter enters shop	reporter enters shop
buys poison	buys poison
comes out of shop	interviews shopkeeper
statement to camera	comes out of shop
interviews shopkeeper	statement to camera

The crucial point is the position of the interview, which will make a big difference to the emphasis of the story. The thought will occur to you at the treatment stage that the position depends on what the shopkeeper says (which in turn depends to some extent on what you ask him). Will he get angry when you ask him why he is selling a poisonous substance in bottles in which it could be mistaken for a soft drink? Or will he simply shrug his shoulders and say that all the shopkeepers do it?

If he gets very angry, he may prevent your reporter doing his statement in front of the shop after the interview – that's a good reason for filming the statement before the interview. That way, you know you are safe; you have already recorded the statement. And of course, if the shopkeeper stays cool during the interview, there's nothing to stop you doing another version of the statement after the interview, one that takes into account what the shopkeeper said. If you do that, you have given yourself a choice of ways in which to cut the story. And that means you have a chance of producing a better story – one choice must be better than the others.

You should now be able to see how helpful it is to think about your shooting order. The main advantage is that it makes you think through the story. This helps you to foresee problems and plan how to cover the various possibilities. In this story the logic of doing exterior shots before interior suggests that you should shoot the reporter's statement with the bottles before you shoot the reporter buying the bottles. This happens to fit in with your plan to shoot the statement before the buying and the interview (in case the shopkeeper becomes angry). It might even be worthwhile doing two versions of the statement in advance, one to set up the interview and one to sum up the story. This will again increase your options in the cutting room.

How much should you shoot?

The limiting factor is not the cost of videotape or how **shooting** long you have to shoot, but editing time. There is no point **ratios** shooting hours of material if you don't have the time to cut it. The fastest sort of editing is 'painting', the news technique of covering a pre-recorded commentary with generalized 'wallpaper' shots: this can be thrown together

very quickly. Other editing takes longer: two-minute
magazine items will take at least twice as long to edit as they
did to shoot. Longer films need about three times their
shooting time for editing, special effects, graphics and
dubbing.

How much you shoot depends also on how good you
want your story to be. For the poison-in-the-pop-bottles
film you need at least a two to one ratio (two minutes shot
for each one used). Three to one would be better; you must
provide the editor with enough to give him or her – and
yourself – a chance to put together something good. Longer
documentaries need at least five to one; up to 10 to one is
acceptable.

But don't run away with the idea that shooting
everything that moves will in itself give you a better story.
Oscar Boney once turned in a ratio of 45 to one. No one
at Totta could be bothered with this pile of cassettes (all
unlabelled, of course); it would have taken over a week just
to view and log the material. Editing was a random affair,
relying on Oscar's memory and pot luck ('try the tape that's
fallen out of the box'). What you shoot is as important as
how much

To shoot a programme well you have to pull off a
difficult trick: you have to pay an enormous amount of
attention to every detail in every shot and yet at the same
time you must never lose sight of the overall shape of the
programme. Here are some points to bear in mind.

Homework
Do your homework thoroughly (research, recce, treatment,
etc.). For longer films, when it may be some time since
you did the treatment, go back to it each evening during
the shoot and look again at your ideas for tomorrow's
sequences. Do a storyboard or shot list for next day's
sequences. If you already have one, look through it
carefully – you may need to rethink your approach to
take into account the shooting you have done so far.

Every shot is important

Shoot every shot as if it were the most important in the programme. After all, while it is on screen, it will be the most important shot in the programme.

Master shots

Some directors start shooting each sequence by covering the main action all the way through with a wide shot, a 'master' shot. They then get the contributors to repeat the action for close-ups, cutaways and reaction shots to cut into the master. This approach works better in some situations than others. The master shot often looks less and less satisfactory as the action develops – and then looks more and more tired each time it is used in the finished sequence. A better approach is to decide what you want the viewers to see at each stage of the action and then move the camera to get the size and angle you want. This should give you the best shots for each part of the action instead of a compromise shot all the way through.

The GV or geography shot

For each location or building in which you are shooting, take a wide shot – a GV (General View) or 'establisher' – to show where the action is taking place. Also do a wide shot of people in scenes or exchanges that will be on screen for some time (a long interview, a courtroom scene, or a meal or picnic). This shot, often known as the 'geography' shot, shows people's positions relative to each other and to the location. It relieves the feeling of disorientation viewers get if you cover a long scene only with mid-shots and close-ups. Take GVs and geography shots even if you don't think you will need them. You will be surprised how often they get you out of trouble when you are editing.

The introductory shot for interviewees

For each person interviewed you should do at least one shot showing the person doing something other than being interviewed. You don't have to use the shot in the finished programme but it's sensible to have one available. If you can shoot your interviewee doing something which gives the

viewer an insight into the sort of person he or she is
(gardening or running up the stairs or exercising the dog),
so much the better. The important things to remember are
that the background for this introductory shot should be
different from the background for the interview and that
your interviewee should go out of the picture at the end
of the shot. If he or she doesn't exit, you will have to do
a 'jump' cut to get from the introductory to the interview
shot and that may not be acceptable.

Avoid jump cuts
You are in the editing room, you have a shot of a man
running down the street and as he comes near the camera
you cut straight to a shot of him sitting in his armchair
reading the newspaper. You have just put a jump cut into
your programme: the man has 'jumped' instantly between
two locations and the effect is not pleasant.

The time to avoid jump cuts is when you are shooting.
Let travelling subjects, such as people, cars and aeroplanes
leave the picture before you stop shooting; in the example
above you should carry on shooting till the man has run past
the camera. Or shoot a close-up of the man's drink next to
the armchair before showing him sitting there. To avoid a
jump cut, the editor needs some pictures without the man
to put between the shots of the man in the two locations.

You should always plan your shooting to avoid jump
cuts; shortening shots in the cutting room will give you
more than enough jumps to worry about anyway. Ways of
getting round these are discussed in what follows and in the
chapter on editing.

Cutaways
There are two sorts of jump cuts: one is a by-product
from editing sound, and the other is the price we pay for
television's marvellous ability to telescope time. You need
cutaways to get over both sorts of jump cut, if you can't
avoid them any other way.

Let's deal first with the jump that comes from the sound
shortening edit. You want to shorten an answer in an interview. It's
sound fairly easy to shorten the sound without the viewer noticing

that anything is missing. It isn't so easy with the picture –
there is an obvious jump when the pictures at the beginning
and end of the cut are put next to each other. To cover this
jump you have to cut away to something else (hence the
term 'cutaway').

Interview cutaways are dealt with in detail in the next
chapter. Here I just want to make the point that no one has
yet come up with a totally satisfactory way of dealing with
this sort of jump cut: virtually all the solutions are make-
shift because there is usually no visual, dramatic, or logical
reason to take the viewer's attention away from the
interviewee.

In fact many directors and programmes take the view
that jump cuts are preferable to cutaways because they are
more honest and less distracting.

**short–cutting
time**

The other sort of cutaway is much easier to use because
it springs naturally from television's marvellous ability to
short-cut the passing of time. Suppose you are shooting
a funeral procession moving slowly down the road to the
cemetery. You can hold the shot of the approaching
procession for a fairly long time (even longer if you have
some suitable music on the sound track). But long before
the procession turns into the cemetery gates the viewer's
interest in the shot will have dwindled. What could be more
natural than to cut away from the approaching procession to
one or more shots of weeping mourners and then cut back
to the procession turning into the cemetery gates? Notice
that the cutaway(s) of the mourners need be on the screen
only a fraction of the time that it really takes the procession
to reach the cemetery gates and the sequence will still look
right to the viewer – that's what I mean by television's
'ability to short-cut the passing of time'.

When shooting you'll frequently find yourself wanting
to short-cut the time it really takes to do things like getting
into a car and driving away, cooking a meal, painting a
picture or going through a supermarket checkout. You can
often get over the jump in time by covering the beginning
and the end of the action from different angles or with

You'll frequently find yourself wanting to short-cut time

different shot sizes. The person leaving in his car, for example: start on a wide shot of the person getting in and then cut to a low-angle shot of the car moving off. This short-cuts the time spent fumbling for the right key, fastening the seat belt, checking the mirrors, starting the motor, releasing the handbrake and so on.

But more often than not you need cutaways (don't forget to do them – you're going to need them). People's faces, close-up details of the main action, perhaps shots from the point of view of the main object in the sequence (in the funeral example perhaps a view of the spectators along the route as seen by someone in the procession): these move the story on and aren't there just to avoid jump cuts. The best cutaways contribute to the content of your programme.

Wallpaper shots

Your exterior GVs and your introductory shots for
interviewees are both examples of wallpaper shots.
You need wallpaper shots like these to give the viewer
something to look at while the commentary is talking
about things which can't be illustrated directly. Traffic,
pedestrians, people eating or shopping, children playing,
landscapes, aircraft taking off and landing all make
acceptable wallpaper (and are much used).

Your treatment will tell you roughly how much
wallpaper you need; make sure you shoot enough. But
beware if half or more of your shots are wallpaper: viewers
want to see specific shots that tell the story on their screens,
not generalized fillers. The more relevant the wallpaper is,
the more acceptable it is.

Insert shots

The finger on the switch, the dial on the machine, the
time on the wristwatch: these are some of the things which
you may want viewers to see but which don't stand out
well enough in the wide shots. So do close-ups of them,
repeating the complete action (the finger comes into
shot, flicks the switch, goes out of shot) to give the editor
maximum freedom to choose the best possible cutting
points for the insert. Remember any action you shoot in
close-up should be performed slightly slower than normal.
Fast, jerky actions go in and out of the close-up frame so
quickly that they look snatched.

Overlaps

Don't forget your overlaps – for both sound and vision.
For insert shots, always repeat the complete action in close-
up, not just the part you think you are going to use. In the
poison-in-the-pop-bottle story, when you were shooting
the reporter entering the shop, you should have continued
the shot until well after he had gone through the door and
was no longer visible from outside. Then when you were
shooting his coming through the door with your camera
inside the shop, you should have started with a shot of the
empty door with no reporter there. You then cue him to

walk into shot and through the door. So in effect you
have two shots and two sound recordings of him walking
through the door – one from outside and one from inside.
Overlaps give the editor and you a chance to choose the
best point to cut between both shots of the action. Or you
may decide that one shot will do.

Three for the price of one

Here's a way of getting three shots for the price of one.
Whenever you do a zoom, ask the cameraman to hold the
beginning of the zoom and also the shot at the end of the
zoom for about 10 seconds each. This gives you a choice of
three shots to use in the editing room and it's only taken an
extra 30 seconds of shooting time (10 seconds to ask the
cameraman and 10 seconds for each hold). It also gives you
the chance of dropping the zooming part of the shot during
editing and just using the two holds. Too many zooms can
spoil a film, especially if there's no good reason for them.
You should in particular avoid the ugly 'yo-yo' effect you
get when you zoom in and then out again on the same shot.

Don't rely on library film

Cameramen who are in a hurry on location will sometimes
say to you: 'You don't need to wait around for the shots
you want (of a police car or ambulance or the National
Assembly Building) because there are hundreds of shots in
the library – 'I know, because I shot some myself only last
week'.

Don't be misled. First of all, the cameraman won't know
if the shot he has in mind wasn't recycled with the rest of the
surplus material after editing. Then, if the shot has survived,
it will probably take you ages to find it. If you do manage
to find it, it will probably be minus its sync sound track
(which was mixed with another track) and it may also have
a dissolve at one or both ends so that it isn't long enough.
Finally, if it is useable, it's extremely unlikely to say exactly
what you want it to say. There are a hundred ways of
shooting a police car or ambulance or the National
Assembly Building. There is only a one-in-a-hundred
chance that the size and angle of the library shots are exactly

what you want. If you are on the right location and can see what you want, shoot it there and then.

Sorry, Mr Cameraman.

Crossing the line

The best way to avoid crossing the line is to use your mental TV. When people talk, they normally look at each other. So if one person faces right on screen, the other should face left. If you see a car travelling towards the right of the screen, it must continue to travel to the right in the next shot or it will appear to have turned round. If a golfer hits the ball right to left in one shot, you have to arrange matters so that the ball travels right to left in the next shot or it will appear to have done a U-turn between the two shots.

The line in the phrase 'crossing the line' is the border where left and right swap over when put on screen. With the camera on one side of the line the train in the illustration below will appear to be moving right; with the camera on the other side of the line the train will be moving left. The

Crossing the line

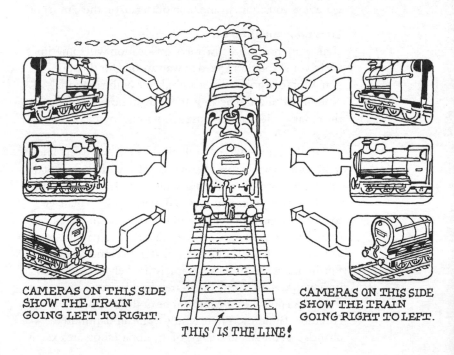

CAMERAS ON THIS SIDE
SHOW THE TRAIN
GOING LEFT TO RIGHT.

THIS IS THE LINE!

CAMERAS ON THIS SIDE
SHOW THE TRAIN
GOING RIGHT TO LEFT.

line runs along the track; more precisely, it is the course
the train is following. With two people talking (my example
above) the line runs through their heads; in golf the line
runs along the path the ball is travelling.

In theory, to avoid crossing the line, you have to keep
your camera on the same side of the action in successive
shots. But the problem rapidly becomes more complicated.
If you shoot a man and a woman walking right to left and
talking to each other and the man is furthest away from the
camera, a shot of the woman from the man's point of view
will reverse the direction in which they appear to be
walking. In this situation the need to have one speaker
facing right on screen and the other one left conflicts
with the need to keep them walking in the same direction.
The way round the problem (if it bothers you) is to avoid
individual points of view. Stick to shots from one side of the
path they are treading and vary the angle, if you need to, by
taking shots from directly in front or behind.

tricky situations If you are shooting four people sitting round a dinner
table or playing cards, the crossing-the-line problem
becomes tricky, as there is a different line for any two
people. The answer here is to do a wide shot (a geography
shot) to show where everyone is sitting and every time you
move the camera decide which is the most important line
to respect. As a safety measure do cutaways of each person
looking at each of the others in turn. You then know
you are covered for any eventuality. In fact, if you are
shooting and you aren't sure where the line is (or you and
the cameraman disagree – it happens quite often), don't
waste time arguing or working out which side to do the
shot. Do it from both sides; it's quicker than talking about
it and you know you're covered.

Finally, don't get too obsessed with not crossing the
line. The convention is broken in nearly every pop video
you see on screen with singers facing right and left in
successive shots. It's a good idea to avoid the mistake when
you can. But keep things in proportion: crossing the line
may confuse or irritate your viewers, nothing worse. It's
not the end of the world.

Sound

The person who is forgotten most often on location is

always
record
sound

the sound recordist. He or she needs to know the shot
you have in mind just as much as the cameraman. So make
a point of briefing him about each shot when you are
setting it up. You may have to change the shot slightly to
help the recordist get his microphone in the right place.
It's obviously useful to find this out as early as possible.
Record sound with every shot – it doesn't cost extra. Some
directors don't bother with sound if there isn't any speech in
the shot. This saves time on location (very little) but creates
a lot of work later for the person who has to piece together
an effects track from library disks. Often, because there
isn't time to create an effects track, the shots without sound
have to be covered with music, a precious asset that should
be used for emotional and creative reasons and not as a
technical filler. Pictures without effects have half the power
they should have. If you want good effects, record them
when you are shooting; then use the dubbing theatre and
effects library to make your location sound even better.

intrusive
sounds

One of the most per-
sistent sound problems on
location is the noise from
sources not seen in the shot.
Your brain automatically turns down
the volume when you are shooting
(you are concentrating on the shot)
but the microphone picks them all
up and they will sound louder
on the recording than they
did in real life. Even the hum
from something relatively quiet like
a refrigerator can ruin a recording; if
viewers are wondering where the noise
is coming from, they won't be listening
to the sound you want them to hear.
Many of these noises can be stopped
temporarily. Switch off the
refrigerator just before

you start shooting; you can often deal with radios and other devices in the same way. Workmen using pneumatic drills (they always seem to turn up near locations) can usually be persuaded to down tools for a few moments with a little money. Switch off phones (don't forget the mobiles) before starting to shoot; they have a habit of ringing at awkward moments. You'll have to stop shooting while aircraft pass overhead or, if you can't stop, carry on recording after the action has ended so that the aircraft sound can be gently faded out during the dub. If you can't get rid of off-camera sound, you may have to find a quieter location to shoot something like a long interview. Or make sure that the source of the sound is seen in at least one shot in the

See Briefing 6 for sequence; after all, people would expect an interview
more about sound in a busy market to be fairly noisy.

Finally, don't neglect sound. More shots are lost, more sequences reshot, more programmes abandoned because of poor sound than because of poor pictures. Viewers will stay with a programme if the pictures are less than perfect; if they have to struggle to hear what is being said, they will switch channels.

Time code

Time code is an eight-digit numbering system that gives a number to each picture on your videotape. The digits are grouped in pairs; reading from the back, the right-hand pair shows the frames (o to 24), the next pair shows seconds and the next pair shows minutes. The front pair is free – most people use it to number the cassette or note the date.

You may be asked if you want 'time-of-day' time code. This means that the numbers will show time-when (when you made the recording) instead of time-how-long (how much tape you have used). Time-of-day is useful if you are recording a long interview or a long stretch of unbroken

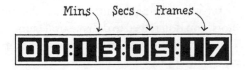

Mins Secs Frames

00:13:05:17

action (for example, a football match). If you note the time
when the interviewee said the bits you want or when the
goals were scored, you will know exactly where to find
them on the tape, provided your watch was synchronized
with the clock in the recorder. Some directors use time-of-
day time code for all their shooting because they usually
remember roughly when they did a shot ('It was after the
coffee break and before lunch') and so can guess what the
time code for a particular shot will be. With time-how-long
code they have to refer to a detailed shot list.

user bits
What happens if you shoot at the same time on several
days? Time-of-day code would give you the same numbers
each day; this could create confusion for the edit. To make
sure all your pictures have a unique number you have to use
another set of four pairs of two digits known as user bits.
These can be displayed on the editing screen exactly like
time code; the only difference is that you can enter letters
as well as numbers.

Run-up time and control track

One problem with time-of-day code is the jump in the
numbers between shots (the clock doesn't stop when you
stop recording). The editing machines can cope with this
jump if you do a run-up or pre-roll before each shot – that
is, run the camera for eight to 10 seconds before the start
of the action that you want to record. This makes sure that
there is enough control track before the action for the
editing machines to get into step with each other before
they do an edit. (If you are used to film terms, you are
putting down a leader of electronic sprocket holes which
the editing machines can use to lace up before each edit).
If there isn't enough control track, the picture after the edit
may flicker for a moment or the machine may have to use
the beginning of the action as pre-roll, which means you
won't be able to use it in your programme.

If you use the pause button to stop the camera between
shots, you don't need to do a pre-roll before each shot.
The record head stays in contact with the tape; there is no
gap in the control track and you can start the action as soon
as you have unpaused the camera. It's so straightforward,
there has to be a snag.

Unfortunately, there is.

The record head is spinning around at several thousand revolutions per minute against the same bit of tape and will damage the tape if it stays in contact. To protect the tape, pause will automatically switch itself off after a few minutes, disengaging tape and record head and putting a break in the control track. It's easy to miss that the camera is no longer in pause when you start to reshoot and easy therefore to carry on without putting down enough control track for a satisfactory edit. The pause button is a seductive habit. On the whole, don't use it unless you have good reason – for example, you are grabbing shots of a demo for the news.

A clapperboard?

Think about using a clapperboard, even if it's not strictly necessary, for synchronizing video sound and picture. The advantage of the clapper is that it labels a shot visually. This makes shots easier to find during editing, as you can spot a clapper even when you are spooling through your material at speed. 'Twenty-one take two' is easier to remember than 00.13.26.17. And 21/2 is also a convenient label to use when you display your shot in the 'gallery' of rushes which is a feature in non-linear editing systems. You don't have to put a clapper on every shot but you will find it very useful to have one handy to mark – for example – six takes of the same shot, when clapper-less crews have to resort to gesticulating with their fingers.

See Briefing 8 for more about clapperboards

Lighting

The other thing you have to watch during shooting is lighting. Setting up lights can be time-consuming, so try and restrict the number of setups that need it.

Your job – in consultation with the cameraman – is to decide what you want the lighting to do; his or her job is to decide how to do it. You should ask yourself not just 'Is there enough light for this shot?' but also 'Can we improve this shot with lighting?' Lighting is not just a technical requirement for recording pictures. Use it to improve them, not just to light them.

Thoughtful cameramen will avoid double shadows

Some cameramen will put every available light on a dark scene unless they are given specific preferences by the director. So it's best to try to say what lighting you have in mind for each shot. For example: 'I'd like this scene brightly lit with not too many hard shadows, please' or, 'Could you light the face gently to show those interesting lines and also keep the light on the wall behind rather low so as not to distract attention from the face?' Thoughtful cameramen will avoid double shadows from the nose and get rid of the big black shadow on the wall behind an interviewee by moving him or her away from the wall.

Make sure the lighting draws attention to the main object that you want to see in the picture. You don't have to flood every corner of the background as brilliantly as if it were a snooker table – lighting isn't spread as evenly as this in real life. And those interesting areas of shadow that you would find in real life have the advantage of not distracting the viewer's attention from the main object.

checking lighting

The way to check that lighting is in the right place is to look at the scene through half-closed eyes. Brightly lit things will then stand out in the picture; areas where there is less light will appear dark. If the things which become more prominent through half-closed eyes are the things you want to emphasize in your shot, all well and good. If they aren't, discuss possible changes with the cameraman.

Finally, be specially careful when you are doing a shot containing both very bright and very dark patches. The television system finds this strong contrast between light and dark difficult to cope with even though your eyes may have no problem. Try and film against backgrounds where the light is more even if you possibly can.

See Briefing 5 for more about lighting

Using the monitor

One of the advantages of video is its immediacy. On the whole this is not something you should exploit too much by asking for instant replays on location. Far better to use the monitor to check that you are getting what you want when you line up each shot with the cameraman. While the shot is being recorded, you watch the monitor. If it's not right, you can suggest improvements and then reshoot. If you are not sure if it's right, don't ask for a replay; air your doubts and shoot it again – it's quicker, gives you more material to take back to the cutting room and saves batteries.

The monitor gives you a chance to build up a relationship with the cameraman quickly – after the first few shots both of you are tuned into each other's way of looking at things. It's a partnership that takes longer to arrive at with film, where there is an unavoidable gap between shooting and viewing. To bridge this gap many film productions routinely offer the director a video monitor on location.

What should you look for on the monitor? Check where the main thing that you want to see is in the frame – is it too far away or lost in a jungle of other detail? (Television screens are small and so close-up shots tend to work better than long shots.) Check round the edge of the frame: can you see anything you don't want to see, like a camera box or half an interested bystander who shouldn't be in shot? Check the lighting and the shadows. Check that cables are tucked away out of the shot. Check that people don't have plants growing out of the tops of their heads or lines through their ears (the camera flattens scenes).

**camera's
view of
the world**

Remember that the world you see on the screen differs
from the world you see with your eyes. The difference is
worth studying carefully. The camera offers a more narrow-
angled view of the world than your eyes; even at its widest,
the standard zoom lens excludes more than it includes.
The camera also has to squeeze a three-dimensional
world into a two-dimensional picture and so its view of
the world is flatter than yours. You have to compensate
by using lighting, sound and things in the foreground
(sometimes known as 'dingle') to give depth to the picture.
The camera also gives equal emphasis to everything in the
picture, unlike your eyes, which are directed by the brain
to concentrate on specific parts of your field of vision.

So your task as a director is to choose what you want
your viewers to look at. Then use shot size, camera angle,
lighting, sound, composition and action to direct viewers'
eyes to what you want them to see. Show them your vision
of the world.

*See Briefing 13
for more about
composition*

It sounds a bit frightening at first but if you bear in
mind that there is a difference between your view and the
camera's view of the world and get into the habit of viewing
things as the camera views them, you should avoid the most
obvious pitfalls. The video monitor is invaluable for this on
locations where it's possible to have one – obviously a
monitor is not a good idea if you are covering something
like a protest march.

If you are using film and don't have a monitor, you can
build up experience of the camera's view of the world by
asking to look through the camera when the cameraman
has lined up the shot.

Using the tripod

One final point for this chapter: the tripod. For serious,
professional programme-making the tripod is a necessity.
It should be used for all shots unless there is a reason
for doing them handheld (shooting a riot where speed
is essential, doing a walking shot and so on). Some
cameramen will insist that they can hold any shot rock
steady. Don't believe them: it's difficult with long shots;

more difficult with mid-shots; impossible with close-ups, or if you're panning or zooming; and absolutely awful if you are shooting something that isn't moving, like a poster or a building.

Tactfully say to the cameraman, 'You may be able to handhold as steady as a rock, but please use the tripod anyway. I don't want to tire you out ...' It may slow down shooting a little if you use a tripod, but the extra time will give you extra quality.

There's also a psychological gain from using the tripod: it concentrates everyone's mind on the picture. Handholding often seems an end in itself – all that balletic footwork, panning and zooming are so satisfying for the cameraman to do that the performance becomes more important than the pictures. When you get to the cutting room you realize it's the picture that counts and the prancing around doesn't help the quality or the cutting.

a tripod on wheels

If you are working somewhere like a factory where there is a reasonably smooth floor, it's a good idea to use a tripod on wheels (also known as a 'rolling spider', or 'rolling spreader', or – my favourite – 'legs on wheels'). Your station probably has one; if not, suggest they buy one.

Don't accept Totter-style 'wobbly vision' (in San Totta the cameramen don't even bother to take their tripods on location). Wobbly-vision is unprofessional. It's also unnecessary and avoidable.

There's no getting away from it – videorecording and filming are hard work. You have to keep thinking all the time, and a lapse of concentration can cause problems later when editing. Don't worry – it's unlikely that you will get full satisfaction on all the points I have made to begin with. If you get 75 out of every 100 of your shooting decisions right, you're doing well.

But if you plan your shooting, work from the finished sequence on your mental TV, and learn from your mistakes, you will soon be on the right lines. The best way to learn is to do it.

SUMMARY
LOCATION SHOOTING

The director must go on location with the crew.

Tell the cameraman about the programme (even if he doesn't want to know).

Shoot important scenes and exteriors first.

Finish all the shots in one setup before moving to the next.

Shoot appropriate alternatives to give your editor (and you) a chance to cut together something good. Shoot enough!

Don't shoot more than you can edit.

What you shoot is as important as how much.

Don't forget
- *to do your homework*
- *for longer films look through your treatment the night before shooting*
- *every shot matters*
- *to do a GV (General View), 'establisher' or geography shot*
- *to do an introductory shot for every interviewee*
- *to avoid jump cuts*
- *cutaways*
- *wallpaper shots*
- *insert shots (slow down the action)*
- *overlaps for sound and vision*
- *to hold each end of the zoom for 'three shots for the price of one'*
- *you can't rely on the library for shots you leave out*
- *not to cross the line.*

V

Sound

Keep the sound recordist informed for each shot.

Shoot sync sound.

Eliminate off-camera sounds as far as possible.

If off-camera sounds are loud and persistent, move the location.

Time code and run-up time

Decide between time-when and time-how-long time code.

User bits give you extra labelling power.

Do a run-up to ensure trouble-free editing; use the pause button only when you have good reason.

The clapperboard has advantages – even for video.

Lighting

Keep the number of lighting setups to the minimum.

Use lighting to improve pictures, not just to light them.

Avoid double shadows on noses.

Get rid of dark shadows on the back wall by moving the interviewee forward.

Make sure lighting draws attention to the main object in the picture.

Check lighting by half closing your eyes.

Beware high contrast scenes.

V

Using the monitor

Use the monitor to line up shots and watch them being recorded.

Replaying shots wastes time and batteries; if you have doubts, do the shot again.

Check
— the right things in the picture stand out
— the edges of the picture
— lighting and shadows
— cables are out of sight
— composition.

Remember the camera doesn't see the world as you do.

Show viewers your vision of the world.

Use a tripod (or tripod on wheels) whenever possible. Banish 'wobbly-vision'.

Don't worry if you make mistakes. If you get 75 per cent of your shooting directions right, you're doing well.

Interviews

What is the worst interview you can imagine?

Virginia Donna managed to produce one for San TTV's Sixty Minute Profile which would be the runaway winner if prizes were offered for awfulness.

The guest, a San TA General (San TA = San Totta Army), was very nervous. He read his answers from a script (in shot throughout the interview), ploughing doggedly through each page while the viewer counted how many more pages there were to go. To hide his nervousness, the General wore dark glasses and chain–smoked (lighting a new cigarette was a problem, as his hands were full of script). Virginia, who likes to do all the important interviews herself, had her own script and ploughed through the questions as methodically as if the General were applying for a job. What is your

Guest and interviewee mean the same thing. To reduce the number of long words starting with 'inter …' I have used guest for studio interviews. It's clearer but unfortunately doesn't seem right for location interviews.

name? Where do you work? How many people work in your office? The questions sounded as if they had come from an application form. She never followed up any points the General made and stuck robot-like to her scripted questions, even if the General had dealt with the question in his previous answer.

It takes talent to set up an interview as disastrous as this. But not all the credit should go to Virginia; part at least must be given to the General. It takes two to make – or muck up – an interview.

Scripted interviews

Scripted interviews used to flourish when broadcasting was in its infancy but happily are rare nowadays. They usually crop up when a guest is extremely important or extremely nervous or both. The assumption seems to be that the medium is so important that it would be wrong just to answer questions in a normal way; so every reply has to be composed as carefully as a welcoming speech for a VIP. The result is boredom for the viewer.

How can you convince your guest that reading answers from a script is unacceptable? There are several arguments you can use.

TV is intimate

Try reminding him or her that the point of the interview is to allow viewers to see him as a natural person expressing himself in a natural way, using language that they can understand. Television is an intimate medium. If you want to get through to viewers you have to talk to each person individually, not pretend you are making a speech to an audience of thousands. If you script your answers in advance, you lose this intimacy and distance yourself from the viewer.

drawbacks of written language

Reading scripts so that they come to life and sound natural is not easy; success requires an actor, not an interviewee. Furthermore, when people write things down – as opposed to just saying them naturally – they start using formal, more complicated language. The result is that many less-educated viewers get the message that this is not for them or – worse still – simply don't understand what is being said (this is a problem that many television stations pretend doesn't exist).

These arguments may work. If they don't, try another line of attack: look at the problem from the guest's point of view. Ask him why he wants to use a script.

There are probably two reasons.

First, he's frightened of forgetting what to say, of drying up. You can always assure him that you will remind him of what he's talking about, should his mind go blank at a crucial moment.

The second reason the guest will probably give for wanting to hang on to his script is that he's frightened of saying the wrong thing. If the interview is a recorded one, you can easily deal with this fear by offering to repeat the question – or to edit it – if the guest is not happy.

If the interview is going to be transmitted live, and the guest refuses to be parted from his script, you have three more possible lines of attack.

First, refuse to do the interview. This sort of shock tactic quite often works. But of course if, like Virginia Donna, you are dealing with a powerful VIP like the General and don't relish facing a firing squad, this isn't a realistic option.

So try another argument. Suggest your guest makes notes on a card of the important points he wants to get across and does the interview with these notes only.

If this doesn't work, try suggesting that since scripted interviews are so ineffective with the television audience, he might like to put his message across in the form of a statement to camera. This may well be the neatest solution of all since it forces both producer and guest to decide exactly what needs to be said and how to say it. And it's also over more quickly. But remember the point about using formal written language which people may not understand. Keep to the simple words.

Dark glasses

You know how irritating it is to have anything beyond the briefest of conversations with someone wearing dark glasses. On television dark glasses are even more irritating.

Viewers are already deprived of most of the information they normally pick up from a person's body and hands because the most usual shot for interviews is the 'talking head'. Now the dark glasses deprive them of the information from the eyes as well. And it's the eyes which are by far the most interesting part of the face: if eyes aren't visible, a face conceals more than it communicates. So you should use all your powers of persuasion to get the interviewee to take off his shades.

Remember also, when interviewing outside, that bright sunlight can cast deep shadows under the eyebrows which will hide the eyes as effectively as dark glasses; on screen there will be just two black holes where the eyes ought to be. You can reproduce the effect by looking through half-shut eyes at a face lit by a midday sun high in the sky.

To avoid this, put your interviewee in front of a darker background or – if the sun is directly overhead – you may have to record with the interviewee looking slightly upwards (have the interviewer standing and the interviewee sitting).

Smoking

Warning: cigarettes can seriously damage your interview as well as your interviewee. And the damage to your programme – like the damage to health – only shows up later.

cigarettes

At the time of the recording, smoking may seem a good idea. It relaxes the interviewee, gives him something to do with his hands, and makes him look natural. The snags only show up when you try and shorten the interview by dropping a section. Invariably you find that the two shots won't cut because in one shot your interviewee has a cigarette in his mouth and in the next shot he hasn't. Or vice versa.

You also discover that a burning cigarette in shot acts like a clock for viewers: it gives them a way of measuring the passage of time in your picture. So as the cigarette grows shorter (or longer) with each edit viewers start thinking more about what you've left out than what you've left in ...

pipes   Pipe-smoking is safer for your programme, as well as for your health. At least viewers can't guess the passing of time from a pipe. Though you can bet that if you want to edit the interview, the pipe will be in different places in the two shots you want to join together.

cigars   Cigars are a sort of half-way house – less trouble than cigarettes (they burn more slowly) and more trouble than pipes (they are in and out of the mouth more often).

Of course, all these problems arise only if you want to edit the interview.

Questions

Let's assume that like Virginia you are asking the questions yourself. On the whole it is better to ask a presenter or reporter to do this for you, particularly if you are a new producer. You will find that you have more than enough to do organizing and directing the interview without asking the questions as well.

The first point to think about is what do you want from the interview? Interviews are good for reactions, opinions, anecdotes and reminiscences; they are bad for putting over complicated information and lists. So if your interviewee has done something, or has an eyewitness account or a good anecdote, or you are asking for opinions – fine. But if he or she is merely summarizing a report or giving you something second-hand, it might be more effective to put the information into a piece to camera or commentary.

If you decide that an interview is appropriate, think carefully about what you can get from it for your programme. Then write out a list of questions. If you are doing, for example, a short interview about a new tyre-making machine, your list might go something like this:

– why is the new machine needed?
– reaction of the factory workers
– benefit for motorists?

You need write out only your first question in full. Keep the rest in note form. You will find as the interview progresses that your mind automatically rephrases the questions to take into account what the interviewee has said, so that your

questions sound natural and spontaneous. Having the
questions in note form also stops you rehearsing the next
questions to yourself when you should be listening to the
interviewee's answers. This in turn avoids another bad
mistake (which can happen all too easily if you aren't
listening) – the mistake of asking a question which the
interviewee has already answered. It's this sort of mistake
which makes people wonder if you know what you are
doing.

supplementary
questions

It's worth following up interesting points in the
interviewee's answers (even if they take you into areas
which you haven't foreseen on your list) by asking extra
or supplementary questions. But beware of straying too
far from the planned course of the interview.

foresee likely
answers

It's a good idea while preparing for the interview
to think about the sort of answers you might get to your
questions. My first question about the tyre-making
machine ('Why is it needed?') is designed to get the
interviewee talking. He can't really answer the question
without first telling the viewers something about the
machine it is replacing, what the drawbacks of that
machine were, the advantages of the new machine and so
on. In short, he has to explain a lot about the background
to the change before he can answer the actual question in
a way that makes sense to anyone who isn't an expert in tyre
production. (If he doesn't do the explaining required, you
should ask a supplementary to make sure that he does.)

So the question 'Why is the new machine needed?' is
likely to produce an informative answer. Questions like:
'Will the machine be good for your business?' and 'How
much does the machine cost?' are not likely to produce
answers of any interest. It would be a stupid businessman
indeed who introduced a machine which he thought
would be bad for his business. Similarly, the actual price
of the machine is just a figure which means nothing – unless
it is unexpectedly high or low. 'About as much as you would
expect' would be an accurate – if rude – answer.

A better question about the cost might be: 'This machine has cost you one million dollars. With tyres dropping in price and lasting longer than ever, are you likely ever to get your money back?' Questions like 'How much does the machine cost?' are 'How long is a piece of string?' questions. The answer by itself is of no interest unless it is unexpected or makes a comparison.

how do you feel about … ?

Another type of commonly used question which it is better to avoid is the 'How do you feel about …?' question. 'How did you feel when you saw your granny falling over the cliff?' The question is so unfeeling that the nation would cheer to hear the interviewee bat the question back with 'How do you think I felt?' or 'I feel with my mind, body and emotions? How do you feel?' A politer interviewee might embarrass the questioner by answering it. 'How do

Don't ask 'How do you feel about …?' questions

you feel about having your life savings stolen?' 'Er … upset.'
'How do you feel about …?' produces something
interesting only if the interviewee ignores the question
and answers one you haven't put.

It is far better to ask questions which help the
interviewee through his story. For example, 'Did your
granny know there was a cliff there?' Or 'Why did you keep
your savings under the bed?'

It is easy to slip into using the 'How do you feel about?'
question because it's such an all-purpose fishing net for
people's opinions and feelings. But when you find it
springing to mind, stop and think. A more closely defined
question will get a better answer.

**questions
to avoid**

Other questions to avoid are questions which are too
general ('Has your grandmother's death changed your
views on the meaning of life?'); double questions ('How
did the thief get into your house and do you think the police
will catch him?'); questions which go on so long that they
sound more like answers; and questions which are really
answers in disguise and leave the guest with nothing to say
('This accident to your grandmother – obviously a terrible
shock and surprise – must have left you drained of emotion.
How has it affected you?')

**getting self-
contained
answers**

Finally, with a location interview you often want
answers that can stand alone without the question in the
finished programme. This means answers that include the
subject of the question and don't start with 'Yes' or 'No'.
This can be difficult to explain to interviewees, and can
make them nervous, since it feels stilted and unnatural
to answer a question like 'Is the machine working well?'
by saying 'The new machine is working well'. 'Yes, it's
fine' sounds far more natural, but wouldn't make sense
if used without the question.

There are two ways of getting self-contained answers
that don't start with 'Yes' or 'No'. The first is to use Who,
What, When, Where, Which, Why, or How; none of
these invites a 'Yes' or 'No' answer.

The other way is not to ask a question at all. Instead, use the formula 'Tell me ...' For example, 'Tell me how the new machine is working'. The answer is almost bound to be self-contained without a 'Yes' or 'No'. And if your interviewee answers, 'It's working well' instead of 'The new machine is working well', it will almost certainly be clear from the context in the finished programme what he is talking about.

Two other useful variations of the 'Tell me' formula are
1. To state the subject in advance. For example, 'The new machine, tell me how it's working'.
2. Use the formula 'Let's talk about ...' For example, 'Let's talk about your new machine and how well it's working'.
You can no doubt invent your own ways of getting answers in self-contained statements.

Before you start
Your interviewee has agreed to throw away his script, take off his dark glasses and stop smoking. You too should do all these things – except for the first. Don't let go of your list of questions.

keep your list of questions

It might seem inconsistent to advise interviewers to hang on to their scripts and interviewees to drop theirs. But the situations are really quite different. Interviewees should be familiar enough with the subject to answer questions without notes; it's far more difficult for interviewers to remember all the questions. Furthermore, questions prompt answers. Answers don't necessarily prompt questions.

he run-through with the interviewee

Before recording an interview, you should run through the list of areas you want to talk about and discuss each briefly with the interviewee. Let him or her think for a moment about the answers he would like to give. In some cases he might even suggest a different point to raise and there is no reason why you shouldn't accept this if it seems sensible. This run-through is not a rehearsal. It's a quick recce of the field of discussion so that the interviewee knows which way he's going. He's more likely to perform effectively if he's got his bearings than if he's lost. Unless of course you are trying to expose the interviewee's weaknesses ...

Let me emphasize that this run-through must not turn into a word-by-word rehearsal of the whole interview. If it does, you'll find that when you and the interviewee repeat it for the camera your second efforts will have lost the freshness of the first.

nervous
interviewees

The one exception to this rule is a trick you can play on interviewees who are particularly nervous. If the cameraman and sound recordist are ready, quietly tell them to start recording. Then tell the interviewee that you'll do a complete rehearsal with him so that he has nothing to worry about when he does the 'proper' interview. This 'rehearsal' is probably the best interview you'll get out of him. If you think you can do better there's nothing to stop you shooting the 'proper' interview as well. Even with an interviewee who's not particularly nervous there's nothing to stop you going over parts of the interview again if you think that he can improve on his first answers.

Now take up your interview positions, if you aren't already in them. Remind the interviewee that he should talk to you and ignore the camera. The sound recordist will want a few words from both of you to adjust the voice levels (if he or she hasn't done so already). The traditional way of getting the interviewee to talk for a voice test is to ask him what he had for breakfast. A question about some other subject (not the subject of the interview) may relax the interviewee more and give you a better idea of how your interviewee will talk and behave on camera. Then switch off portable phones (the crew's as well) and take any nearby telephones that are not in shot off the hook so that they don't ring in the middle of your interview. Start the camera and you're off with your first question ...

Interview shooting techniques

The thing to avoid in interviews is the profile. Profile shots (those where only one of the interviewee's eyes is visible) look and feel awkward. The viewers soon feel deprived, as if they had bought the cheapest seat in the theatre and have only a restricted view of the stage. You should put your viewers in the best seats in the house. So the thing to aim for is shots of both the interviewer and guest which show both their eyes.

There are two distinct techniques for getting these shots. Which one you use depends on how many cameras you have available.

1. The single-camera technique

It is impossible to get two people talking to each other in one shot without one of them being in profile. The only way it could work would be if both of them talked without looking at each other. But people can't do that for more than a few minutes without strain (try it with a friend). In most situations people face each other when they talk.

It follows therefore that if you have only one camera, you can successfully film only one person at a time. So you should of course start with the interviewee. Place him or her in front of the camera. Then – and this is the crucial point – place the interviewer next to the camera. The interviewee will naturally look at him while he (the interviewee) is talking and the camera will have a nice comfortable shot of the interviewee's face with both eyes showing.

over-the-shoulder two-shot

If the interviewer takes a step forward from his position next to the camera and the camera widens its shot a little, you have a useful two-shot showing the interviewee's face (as before) and the back of the interviewer's head and shoulder on one side of the picture. This shot is known as the 'over-the-shoulder two-shot' and is often used as an opening shot for an interview: the camera zooms in to a mid-shot of the interviewee as he starts his first answer. I don't like this opening much (it's used too often and the timing frequently goes wrong), but you may want to try it.

2. The multi-camera or studio technique

If you have more than one camera for an interview (as you do in the studio) the positioning of your interviewer and

Single shot   Over-the-shoulder
                     two-shot

guest is quite different. This time they both sit in front
of the cameras, slightly apart with chairs at right-angles
for most interviews, and directly opposite each other for
confrontation interviews. The cameras then 'cross-shoot'
– that is, each camera takes a shot of the person who is
furthest away so that the fields of vision of the two cameras
appear to cross (hence the name 'cross-shoot'). If the
cameras don't cross-shoot they will be getting profile shots.

Both cameras can also get an over-the-shoulder two-
shot if they move round slightly but cutting between two-
shots from each camera can be unpleasant – the jump isn't
smooth, even if both shots are well matched. So use only
one two-shot at a time.

If you have a third camera (not really necessary) you
can position it half-way between the other two and a little
the third behind them, so that it gives you a long two-shot with
camera interviewer and guest evenly balanced on either side of the
picture. This is the shot you should set up first in your studio
rehearsal time, as it determines the position of the chairs
more than the shots from the other two cameras. It's
probable that when you try this shot you will find your two
people are sitting too far apart and you will have to move
their chairs closer together to get them into one shot and

Interviewer   *Guest*

Position of 2nd camera mirrors position of 1st.

Single shot   *Over-the-shoulder two-shot*   *Single shot*   *Over-the-shoulder two-shot*

to trim the space between them for the screen. They may in fact have to sit closer together than feels natural, in some cases with their knees almost touching. Unnatural though this may feel to them, it usually looks all right to the viewer. For this two-shot the participants will be in profile, but this is acceptable for a short time.

You can also put your third camera next to your first or second one to give you an over-the-shoulder two-shot favouring either guest or interviewer. Opinions differ about whom it's best to favour. Normally, one would say it's better to favour the guest but the cut from two-shot favouring the guest to single-shot favouring the guest isn't very attractive. On the other hand the two-shot favouring the interviewer is useful for questions and cuts well with the single-shot of the guest answering.

Other points, mainly for studio interviews

1. Make-up
Both interviewer and guest should wear make-up for studio interviews. At the very least they should have a dusting of face powder to stop any perspiration glistening under the lights.

2. Nerves

Being interviewed in the studio is far more frightening than being interviewed on location. The guest finds himself on strange territory away from familiar surroundings. The studio lights glare down from the ceiling; he or she is surrounded by cameras which look none too friendly. He is also the only person who can't hear what's being said on the talk-back. It all makes him feel like the chief victim at a sacrifice.

So he needs especially friendly attention. If you are the only person in the production team whom he's met before, make a point of going to the studio floor and showing him to his seat. Remind him of the interviewer's name (in case he's forgotten) and introduce him to the floor manager. Tell him that the interviewer and floor manager will look after him when you have returned to the gallery and remember to ask the floor manager to keep him informed about what's happening when the inevitable delays occur.

I have already mentioned the trick of recording the 'rehearsal' if your guest is very nervous. Sometimes nerves may take the form of an inability to stop talking, in which case the interviewer must firmly and politely interrupt the guest to get him back to answering the question.

It is important that the interviewer always keeps his temper under control and behaves politely, even if he has a guest who isn't controlled and well-behaved. The interviewer should also avoid bullying his guest. If he doesn't, he will lose the sympathy of the viewers.

3. Restarting an interview

Many guests – even those who aren't particularly nervous – start off badly and then visibly improve as they relax, forget about the cameras and start concentrating on what they are saying. If you notice this happening and the interview is not going out live, stop the recording after the first two or three answers and start again from the beginning. You will almost certainly find yourself with a much improved interview.

This idea is also worth trying for interviews on location.

4. Swivel chairs

Some television problems are foreseeable and therefore avoidable; some are not. Swivel chairs belong to the first category. So refuse to have them in the studio. If you don't, you will one day be caught in a live broadcast with a guest who nervously jiggles to and fro. The jiggling will attract more attention than the words and your irritated viewers will remember little else.

5. Jumping flowerpots

Think for a moment about the area between the interviewee and interviewer. It will appear in both their shots – on the left of one shot and on the right of the other. If you have something eye-catching in this area (like a vase of flowers), it will appear to jump from one side of the screen to the other if you cut between wide shots. Avoid this unpleasant effect by moving the object to one side (so that it appears on only one of the shots), or by removing it completely from the set.

6. Close-ups of objects

If the guest has brought something to the studio which you want to show in big close-up, you must decide during the rehearsal which camera should take the shot. The most usual arrangement is to position the third camera next to the interviewee's camera and do the close-up on that. If you have only two cameras, ask the interviewer's camera to move during the interview. Try not to use the guest's camera for the close-up; if anything goes wrong, you may not be able to show the guest – who is, after all, the most important person – for an uncomfortably long time.

You must rehearse this close-up before you start the interview, as the cameraman won't be able to get a good close-up unless he or she knows exactly what is going to happen. So ask your guest to hold the object exactly how he intends to hold it during the interview. Then try and get a close-up on your chosen camera. You will almost certainly have to ask the guest to move the object slightly before you are satisfied. Once you are, make it clear to him (through the floor manager) that it's very important that he holds it in exactly the same position during the interview. Remind him also (if you feel it's not too much to ask) to make all his gestures round the object slow and clear. Then pray that he remembers these points – guests often forget.

Your guest may have problems holding the object steady for the close-up. If so, ask him to rest the object on the desk or table. If you don't actually need the guest's hands in the close-up, the safest solution is to place the object somewhere out of his reach and convenient for the camera.

On location, of course, there are fewer problems with this close-up. You do the close-up after the interview and as you already have the sound, you can direct the interviewee to handle the object as required while you are shooting. Or you can ask the guest to talk you through the close-up again. You then have a choice of two sound tracks when you insert the close-up during editing.

7. Cutting and shot sizes

In studio interviews it's tempting to change shot more often than necessary simply because you have two or more cameras. Resist this temptation. As a general rule, stay with the interviewee's shot and use the optional shots at your disposal only if the interview will be improved by them, not just because they are there. This means that you don't have to cut back to the interviewer for every question. You also don't have to cut to a long two-shot in the middle of an interesting answer just to show that you can. This doesn't mean you should do the whole interview on one shot. By all means make full use of the shots you have available, but make sure that they serve the content of the interview. Technique is the servant, not the master.

The way to do this is to listen to what your artists are **match shot size** saying. If the conversation is becoming interesting, move in **with mood** to close-up; if it's amusing, show a quick reaction shot of the

interviewer being amused. Mid-shots for relaxed answers,
medium close-ups and close-ups (the most useful shots)
for more important answers, big close-ups if the subject
is confessing something or under pressure. The more
fascinating you find the answer, the closer-up the shot
should be. And the closer-up the shot, the fuller face
it should be. Close-up profiles are contradictory: you are
cutting closer to show the viewers more, yet the profile
shows them less. The exception is if you have a verbal
battle in the studio. Then two close-up profiles in quick
succession can be effective.

    You can develop the sensitivity to match shots with
moods by observing people talking in normal life where
the way they look (or don't look) at each other is always
changing to suit the mood. Lovers tend to exchange
sweet nothings in close-up. It would appear very odd if
you bought a newspaper in the same way. Unless of course
you were being hunted by the police and were desperately
scanning the paper seller's face to see if he recognized you.

    The shot of the interviewer should be roughly the same

avoid size as that of the guest at any one time. Zooming in to
zooming out a person talking is perfectly acceptable. But zooming out
while a person talks is not: it looks like you are walking out
on him in mid-sentence. If you want to go to a wider shot,
cut to a two-shot or to your interviewer for a reaction shot
or question; then cut back to a wider shot of your guest.

8. How to avoid late cuts
It's easy when you are cutting between interviewer and
guest to miss the first few words of a question and the first
few words of an answer. The trick here is to watch the
monitor of the person who isn't speaking while listening
to the person who is. People normally wind themselves up
before they speak. So if, for example, you want to cut to the
interviewer for the next question, look for the tell-tale signs
(the back stiffens slightly, the jaw drops a fraction) that give
you a moment's warning that a question is coming. It seems
odd at first watching the person who isn't speaking and it
requires a deliberate effort but with practice, it becomes a

habit. Of course, there is no reason why the vision mixer shouldn't take the cuts for you during an interview, with you setting the course of the proceedings: for example, 'Stay with the guest for the next question' or, 'Take the next question on (camera) two'.

9. *Recording insert interviews*

If you are recording an interview in the studio for later use as an insert in a magazine programme, it's a good idea to start and end the interview with a shot of the guest and not the interviewer. This is specially helpful if the interviewer is also presenting the magazine programme since it avoids potential horrors such as the presenter (live) introducing himself (recorded) in the next shot. The same unpleasantness can occur if you end your interview with a shot of the interviewer and he then has to introduce the next item live from the studio.

10. *Cutaways*

If you expect to edit a recorded interview, it's worth doing listening shots of both interviewer and guest before the main interview. These can be done unobtrusively while the interviewer is talking to the guest to put him at his ease, and while the guest is answering a couple of questions about something other than the topic for the interview to give the sound supervisor a chance to balance voice levels. Listening shots done after the interview always seem to be a bit of a chore for the participants. So it's worth getting them out of the way first. But make sure the interviewer and guest are sitting as they will be for the recording – people often flop in their chairs for the rehearsal and then sit up for the recording.

Other points, mainly for single-camera interviews

1. *Shot sizes*

If you are doing a one-camera interview, you should discuss the shot size with the cameraman before starting the interview. Tell him or her which part of the interview is likely to produce answers most suitable for close-ups but let him use his own judgement about when to move

in close during the interview. It's best also to ask him to
change shot sizes during the questions so that you can edit
the answers without worrying about camera movements.

Changing shot sizes may seem to offer advantages when
you are shooting; in the cutting room the changes often
present more problems than plusses. The zooms fall in the
wrong places. The different sizes look messy when edited
together. The cutaways don't match. The safest and simplest
way to avoid all this is to shoot all your interviews in
medium close-up, with the bottom of the picture cutting
just below the arm-pits. You then know the shots will
cut together and the cutaway singles (medium close-up,
of course) will match. You can rely on the two-shots to
give viewers a feel of the wider setup.

2. Cutaways

If you want to edit one-camera interviews you will need
cutaways. There are two types of these: listening shots
(sometimes known as 'noddies') and cutaway questions.

The easiest cutaway to do is the over-the-shoulder
interviewee's   two-shot described on page 87 which you can use
listening shots   as a cutaway over a question. All you have to do is ask the
interviewer to talk to the interviewee (about anything
which doesn't make the interviewee laugh). The
interviewee just has to listen. Don't ask him to nod
as he will probably overdo it.

In fact, when you take cutaway shots of the interviewer
interviewer's   it's a good idea to ask him also not to nod too much.
listening shots   Too many nods can look silly. All that is required is that
the interviewer should not stand or sit as motionless as
a waxwork; a slight movement of the head or eyes or a
shifting of weight from one side to the other is all that is
needed for a usable listening cutaway.

The way to shoot a listening cutaway of the interviewer
shooting the   is to put the camera in the opposite position you had it for
interviewer's   the interview – in other words, position it so that this time
cutaways   the interviewee is next to the camera and slightly in front.
From this position you can shoot the interviewer listening
and then you can also zoom out for an over-the-shoulder
two-shot. For the two-shot it is best to ask the interviewee

Interview cutaways

Interviewee

Interviewer

Interviewer in shot sizes used for interview.

Basic shot of interviewee.

Over-the-shoulder 2-shot favouring interviewer.

Over-the-shoulder 2-shot favouring interviewee.

Wide 2-shot.

to speak, even though you can't see his face. If he doesn't, the absence of head and jaw movements will make the cutaway less convincing.

cutaway
questions

With the camera in this position (next to the interviewee) you can take shots of the interviewer repeating the most important questions, in single or in two-shot as you wish. Discuss with your interviewer which questions are best. You don't need to repeat all of them and should try and choose ones at points where you think you will want to edit. Then keep the recorder rolling while he goes through them one by one (with you prompting if necessary). If the questions during the interview were a bit loose and rambling, this is a good opportunity to make them shorter and more effective.

a quicker way to do interviewer's cutaways

For a short interview you don't of course have to do all these cutaways each time. Often the two-shot with the interviewee listening while the interviewer talks, some listening shots of the interviewer and a few cutaway questions will be more than enough. If you can remember to record all your cutaways on a different cassette (not the interview tape) you will save yourself a lot of spooling forwards and back during editing.

If you want only single-shot cutaways of your interviewer you needn't go to all the trouble of moving camera and lights to face exactly the opposite direction. Instead just move or pan the camera slightly so that it shows a different background – who is to know if it wasn't the

A quicker way to do interviewer's cutaways

Interview setup

Cutaway setup

Interviewee

Interviewer

Interviewee looks camera RIGHT.

Guest's chair moved to change background for cutaway shots.

Interviewer looks camera LEFT.

interviewer's actual background during the interview?
Make sure that the interviewer is looking to the right of
camera if the interviewee was looking left (or vice versa).

**the long shot
as cutaway**

You can also use a long shot of the interview as a cutaway
provided it is far enough away to prevent the viewer seeing
if the shot is in sync or not. This is usually possible only
when you are doing an interview outdoors. Sometimes
for very relaxed interviews a change of camera position can
also give you opportunities to edit without breaking the
flow of the talk with a cutaway.

3. Eyelines

Generally speaking, for interviews the camera lens should
be level with the eyes of the person in shot. If interviewer
and guest are roughly the same size and are sitting at the
same height, this is straightforward. If size or sitting heights
differ, the camera should try and reflect this by adopting the
point of view of each participant and looking up or down
on the person in shot as appropriate. But beware. Looking
down on people makes them look inferior (that's what
the word means); looking up makes them look superior.
You may want to introduce these slants for dramatic effect,
but before you do, ask yourself if they will help or hinder
what is said in the interview. Remember also that looking
up at ladies rarely flatters them; it tends to make their
jawbone look unattractively large and they won't thank
you for drawing attention to their double chins – if they
have any! Ladies should also be advised not to wear off-the-
shoulder evening dresses without straps when appearing on
television, as close-ups will give the impression that they
have no clothes on.

SUMMARY
INTERVIEWS

Scripted interviews

Avoid at all costs – they aren't natural and many viewers won't understand the formal, written language.

With recorded interviews assure nervous interviewees that they can repeat the interview (or parts of it) if they forget what to say or say the wrong thing.

With live interviews try
– *refusing to do the interview (risky, but often works)*
– *suggesting the interviewee uses notes instead of a script*
– *suggesting (if all else fails) a short statement to camera (at least it's over quicker).*

Avoid
– *dark glasses and smoking.*

Questions

First ask yourself if you should be doing an interview at all. Would commentary or a statement to camera be more effective?

Write out the first question but use only notes for the others.

Don't be frightened of supplementary or follow-up questions.

Foresee likely answers.

Avoid
– *'How long is a piece of string?' questions*
– *'How do you feel about …?' questions*
– *questions that are too general*
– *double questions*
– *overlong questions*
– *questions that are answers in disguise.*

V

For self-contained answers (which don't start with 'Yes' or 'No') start questions with Who, What, When, Where, Which, Why or How.

Or use the formulas 'Tell me ...' or 'Let's talk about ...'

Before you start

Run through the possible areas of discussion with the interviewee. But don't rehearse the interview word by word.

With nervous interviewees perhaps record a full-scale 'rehearsal'.

Remind interviewee to talk to the interviewer, not to the camera.

Let the sound recordist check voice levels.

Switch off phones and mobiles.

Start the recorder. You're off!

Interview shooting techniques

Single-camera technique – interviewer next to the camera.

Multi-camera technique – cross-shoot.

Other points, mainly for studio interviews

Don't forget make-up.

Interviewees find television studios strange and frightening. Reassure them.

Interviewers should always be firm, polite and never bully – even when provoked.

If the interview starts badly, start again after the interviewee has settled down by answering two or three questions.

∨

Swivel chairs and jumping flowerpots: avoid.

Close-ups of objects: use the third or the interviewer's camera.

Motivate your cuts. Match shot sizes with mood.

Avoid zooming out from people while they are talking.

To avoid cutting late, watch the monitor of the person who isn't talking.

Start and end insert interviews with a shot of the guest.

Record listening cutaways before the interview if possible.

Other points, mainly for single-camera interviews

Let the cameraman use his own judgement during the interview but tell him which part is likely to need close-ups. Ask him to change shot sizes during questions.

There are two types of cutaways: listening shots ('noddies') and cutaway questions.

Do over-the-shoulder two-shot for interviewee's listening shot.

Put camera behind interviewee for interviewer's cutaways – or just move or pan camera to show different background for interviewer. Record some cutaway questions (better expressed than the originals if possible) and listening shots.

Record cutaways on a different cassette to save editing time.

You can also use long shots or changes of camera angle to edit interviews.

Don't shoot from above or below eyeline height without good reason.

Avoid shooting ladies from low angles.

Off-the-shoulder evening dresses without straps can give an unfortunate impression in closer shots.

Editing

The everyday word for editing is 'cutting'. But the best
way of approaching this stage of the programme-making
process is to think of it as 'selecting'. When you edit, you
are selecting the best shots, and the best parts of the best
shots for telling your story.

finding the
natural life span
of a shot

The key to editing is finding the precise point at which
a shot starts being interesting and the precise point at which
it stops being interesting. All shots have a natural life span.
You should learn to identify this by looking at each shot
and asking yourself, 'Which bit works best?' With static
shots in which nothing much is moving – for example,
a shot of an oil tanker on the horizon – the cut-off point
comes quite quickly. You can lengthen the life span of
this shot by drawing attention to some aspect of it in the
commentary – for example, by saying something about
oil slicks on the water. But if you want to continue to talk
about oil slicks you will need a close-up of them; your first
shot has reached the end of its natural life span and it will
become boring if you prolong it.

With moving shots the natural life span may be
considerably longer. For example, you have a car filling the
shot and the viewer sees that the car is big, expensive and
very clean. He notices a flag fluttering from the bonnet and
then sees the shadowy outline of what looks like a VIP sitting
behind the driver. The shot begins to widen and he notices
the scenery which the car is driving through. The camera
continues to pull out and he sees that the car is stopping at a
petrol station. Obviously this shot will hold the interest of
the viewer for a lot longer than the static shot of the tanker,

because at each stage of its development it offers the viewer something new to look at.

The life span of a shot is also affected by the neighbouring shots. Clearly, following the long shot of the tanker on the horizon with a close-up would affect how long you keep the long shot on the screen.

Putting your shots in the best order to tell the story is also an important part of the editing. Try and distance yourself from the problems and priorities of the shoot and rethink how best to put the shots together. The best order is unlikely to be the order you shot them in.

Preparing to edit

is anything missing?

Make sure that everything you shoot arrives in the cutting room; you can't edit material that isn't there. Totta programmes are frequently 'cut' by a third before they get near the edit room because the cassettes aren't clearly labelled and go missing.

shot list

When you have everything, sit down and view it. You may prefer to make a shot list as you view or you may prefer to view everything first and then go through again to list it. No matter, the important thing is to make a shot list – the

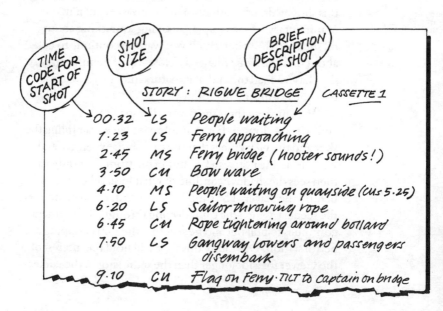

TIME CODE FOR START OF SHOT

SHOT SIZE

BRIEF DESCRIPTION OF SHOT

STORY : RIGWE BRIDGE   CASSETTE 1

00·32	LS	People waiting
1·23	LS	Ferry approaching
2·45	MS	Ferry bridge (hooter sounds !)
3·50	CU	Bow wave
4·10	MS	People waiting on quayside (cus 5·25)
6·20	LS	Sailor throwing rope
6·45	CU	Rope tightening around bollard
7·50	LS	Gangway lowers and passengers disembark
9·10	CU	Flag on Ferry · TILT to captain on bridge

time code where the shot starts, the shot and take number (if any) and a brief description of its contents. The list can be very simple. Don't bother with the last two digits of the time code (which count the frames); the minutes and seconds are sufficient. It's also a waste of time noting where each shot ends. The precise end point doesn't matter and common sense will tell you that it has to come somewhere before the beginning of the next shot.

CUTTING ORDER   RIGWE BRIDGE

3.50	CU	bow wave
1.23	LS	Ferry approaching
4.10	MS	People waiting on quayside
6.45	CU	rope tightening
10.17	MS	Captain on bridge
7.50	LS	Gangway lowers and passengers disembark

cutting order

The next step is to work out the order in which you want to assemble your material. This cutting order (or assembly order) is your editing plan. It's simply a written list of shots with enough information to identify them (time code plus an identifying word or two) in the order you think they will go together. If you have difficulty working out a cutting order shot by shot, just list the sequences with a few key shots thrown in, leaving the detailed decisions till later.

'Ah,' you may ask, 'why not use the order in the treatment?'

The reason is that it is extremely rare that your shots turn out as expected. Shots that you slaved over while filming can turn out lifeless and ordinary; shots you did as an after -thought can turn out marvellous. So it's important to look at all the shots with as unbiased an eye as possible, forgetting

the behind-the-scenes problems of getting them – the only
thing that matters for the viewer is what is on the screen.
Your editor can be a great help in this at whatever stage
he (or she) becomes involved. He is your first viewer. He
also offers you the bonus of seeing your shots with eyes that
are at the same time experienced and come fresh to the
story. So listen to what he has to say. If he is a good editor,
he's worth his weight in gold as a judge of your material.

cut first,
write later
The unpredictability of shots is also a good reason for not
writing your commentary first and using it as your editing
plan. This technique was once used only by news reporters
on location who didn't have the time or opportunity to
cut the pictures first. In the hands of someone who knows
how to write to picture it works reasonably well but the
results are never as good as when you cut first and write
later. There are many reasons besides the unpredictability
of shots. The most fundamental is that words and pictures
don't work at the same speed – try putting pictures to each
name as you say it in a list like 'London, Paris and Rome',
or illustrating each object in 'Oranges and lemons, say the
bells of Saint Clement's'.

Although you should think about the commentary
while you are cutting, don't let it dictate the order or the
length of the shots. Films are not illustrated commentaries.

picture
problems
The first viewing is also the time for unwelcome shocks.
If you are unlucky, some of your shots may be unsteady
or awkwardly composed or have the wrong exposure or
unusable sound. These disasters may come as a shock
to you, but don't retaliate by making a savage complaint
about the cameraman (certainly not if you are still a new
producer). Remember that the crew's mistakes all show
up in the picture; your mistakes aren't as faithfully recorded.
If you couldn't make up your mind about a shot on
location, the cameraman probably made up your mind
for you. If he couldn't make up his mind, there is almost
certainly a fault to show for it.

The careful viewing, the shot list and the cutting order
are essential preparations to help you get the best possible

edit when you start cutting. They will also impress the editor, who will be able to give his or her best because you are well-prepared.

Editing video – overview

The way you edit depends on the equipment and time you have to do the job. This section gives an overview of the various ways of editing video: a more detailed discussion follows. Film editing is discussed in Briefing Four: Processing and Editing Film.

The most straightforward – and fastest – way to edit video is to do it on the same format you shot on and intend to transmit from (Beta, D3 or whatever). This is known as on-line editing.

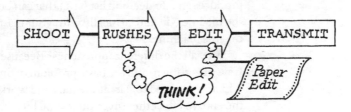

On-line editing

Video editing is a dubbing process: you dub or copy the shots you want in the right order and at the right length, from the playback tape on to the record tape. This means that you have to start with the first shot in your programme and work through to the last shot – an inflexible way of working that allows little scope for second thoughts.

So it's a good idea to do some form of pre-edit. The simplest pre-edit is to view your material and do a cutting order or paper edit. Or you could copy your shots on to a cheaper non-broadcast format (like VHS) with matching time code and use this for your pre-edit. This frees an on-line machine and also frees you to work away from the editing suite, either in the office or at home. If you have access to off-line edit machines, you can go one better with your pre-edit and do a full off-line edit, with or without an editor to help. Some off-line setups have a computer that

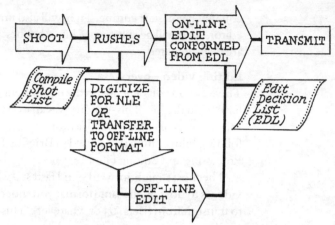

Off-line editing

produces an edit decision list (EDL) that can be used to repeat the off-line edit automatically with your master tapes on an on-line machine.

Why all the different approaches? Because they are all ways of getting round the basic problem of linear editing, which is the need to start at the start and work through to the end. In effect they give you several bites at the cherry – they make linear editing a bit more like film editing, where you can make changes in any order at any point. The true video equivalent of film editing is non-linear editing (NLE). There are several non-linear systems; they give you all the freedom of film editing, and more.

Editing video – details

On-line editing is the most straightforward way of editing **on-line** and if you are in a hurry for news or a fast turn–around **editing** programme, it's the only way of editing. You simply dub the bits you want from your playback (or source) tapes on to the record tape. You can rehearse each cut by previewing it. If you don't like it, you change the cut and then preview it again. Then, when you're happy, you press the record button and the machines reset themselves and transfer the shot from the playback to the record tape. Then onwards to the next shot: find it, decide where to cut, preview, record.

Editing like this is more difficult than it sounds. The problem isn't the cuts; you can preview them as often as you wish and have time for. The problem is the shots. Are they the right ones? Are they in the right order and at the right length (remember the natural span)? And most importantly, how do they relate to each other? And how do they affect each other? These questions are the difficult ones, because the answers change as you proceed through the programme and see the shots actually working together. On-line editing gives you only one go at the answers. It's like using a typewriter; the only word that's easy to change is the one you have just written.

video generations What happens if you have second thoughts about a sequence in the middle of an half-hour programme that you have just finished editing? If you decide to shorten one of the shots you will have to reassemble everything that follows. Why not get another tape and copy everything up to the offending cut on to the new tape, trim the shot and then copy everything that follows? Because you will end up with a copy of a copy of your original shots – a third-generation copy – and the picture quality is likely to be much reduced. Your original shots were first generation, the edited programme is second generation, the copy of the edited programme is third generation. Don't forget that you are likely to add further generations as you put in graphics, make copies for keeping in the library, selling to other stations, showing to contributors and so on. These fourth-or-more generation copies will really begin to show their age, with faded colours and fuzzy edges, like a disintegrating painting.

Of course technology can come to the rescue. Digital recording makes it possible to copy and recopy as many generations as you like without losing quality because digital systems copy the specifications for producing the picture, not the picture itself. Or you can avoid losing a generation by getting the on-line machine to do a computer-driven repeat of all your cuts before and after the change(s) you want to make. Or you can do some form of pre-edit.

pre-edit

You should do the simplest form of pre-edit – a cutting order – even if you are doing an on-line edit only; or rather, especially if you are doing an on-line edit only, when you need all the help you can get. Doing a cutting order makes you look at your material and think about the best ways of using it – preparation that will give the editor the chance of doing a better job for you faster.

The cutting order is sometimes called a paper edit. It collects your thoughts but can't take them further, because it doesn't let you see your shots cut together. An off-line edit does.

off-line editing

The original idea behind off-lining was to do a rough assembly of your programme on a cheaper video format like VHS. This gave you (a) the chance to see the whole programme up and running on screen; (b) time for your thinking to develop; and (c) the chance to make changes and see how they worked. You didn't have to worry about generations since the off-line edit was only a guide for the proper edit on the on-line machines.

conforming

All this is still true, except the tendency now is to expect you to take all the editing decisions during the off-line and not just do a rough assembly. In effect, the off-line is the edit; the on-line is a technical tidy-up. The computer on your off-line machines produces an EDL (edit decision list) by logging the time-codes for all your picture and sound edits in its memory. This log is then used to make a computer-driven copy of your programme from your original first-generation master tapes, a process known as conforming. You can also grade the colours, add graphics and dissolves and lay sound tracks to prepare for the dub at this stage.

assemble or insert?

One question you have to answer before starting to off-line – or do any video edit – is 'Do I assemble edit or insert edit?' The procedure for both is the same except for one crucial difference. With assemble editing the control track is assembled as you go along. With insert editing the control track is put on the record tape in advance.

What is the control track? Why should you record it in advance?

control track

The easiest way to understand the control track is to think of it as electronic sprocket holes (the holes along the edges of film). The control track is recorded as a continuous unbroken signal on the edge of a blank tape in a procedure known as 'black and burst' or 'b and b'. The playback machine uses this signal to synchronize itself with the record machine when you are doing an edit. An irregularity in the signal can cause a problem (in the same way that missing sprocket holes can cause film to jam or snap), so 'b and b' has to be recorded in one unbroken sweep. It also has to be recorded in real time (a 30-minute tape takes 30 minutes to do); so make sure it's recorded before the editing session. A competent editor will always have a supply of 'b and b' tapes handy.

If your record tape has 'b and b' on it, you can insert edit; if it doesn't, you have to assemble edit.

assemble
edit

Assemble editing is fine if you are just doing a cheerful slap-together of your material. If you are doing anything more, it has a couple of disadvantages. The main one is that it doesn't allow you to split picture and sound. This means that you can't take the sound a little earlier or later to disguise an awkward picture cut or improve a sound cut, and you also can't go back to do a picture-only overlay (unless you remember to switch to insert editing). The other disadvantage is that the first few frames after an assemble join may be unstable because the join in the control track is not quite right (remember, there's no control track on the record tape so the machine has to assemble one as it goes along).

insert
editing

Insert editing, on the other hand, gives you complete freedom to edit picture and sound separately, a facility you definitely need if you want to make the most of your material. It also, of course, allows you to do an insert. This means that you can change a shot anywhere in a tape without repeating everything that follows, provided that you put in exactly the same duration of picture as you took out. Remember to give the record machine an out point as well as an in point when you do inserts – with other edits it's sensible to dub over more of each shot than you need and determine the out point when you do the next edit.

digital

Doing an insert is a straightforward process from the technical point of view. From the creative point of view, however, it's less than satisfactory, because the shot you want to put in is rarely the same duration as the one you want to take out. The technology is driving the creativity and it should be the other way round. This is the problem of linear editing – the machines are always telling you what you can and can't do. A digital format such as D3 or D5 is one way round the problem. Digital machines trade in numbers, which don't change their value, no matter how often they are traded; analogue machines (the usual kind) deal in signals, which lose a little with each transfer. So when you are editing on digital you can make changes wherever and whenever you like and copy the rest of the edited programme without worrying about generations – all digital pictures are effectively first generation. Digital coding also offers other benefits, such as excellent sound, and picture dissolves in two-machine suites (a nice trick). The only snag is that copying can't be speeded up: copying time equals running time.

Like rearranging letters into anagrams, non-linear editing allows you to change whatever, whenever, wherever

Non-linear editing

Non-linear editing, on the other hand, goes one better. It offers the freedom to change whatever, wherever,

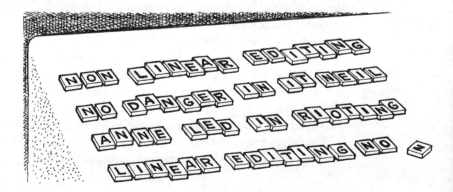

whenever, without having to copy the edited part of
the programme – just like film editing, which was non-
linear long before the term was invented. If linear editing
is like typewriting, non-linear is like word-processing.

The keys are speed, digits and random access.

how does   A powerful computer can find and transform digits into
NLE work?   pictures so fast that it doesn't need to store shots in the order
you want them. When you do an edit, the computer simply
records the in and out points. Then when you want to view
your edited material, the computer whizzes round the
memory where the digital codes of the rushes are stored,
finds the pictures you want and does an instant assembly
on the screen. It's like a word processor which instead
of storing words in the order you write them, stores the
instructions for retrieving them and retrieves from the
library every time you want to read them.

The first stage in non-linear editing is to stock your
digitizing   library. This is done by transferring your rushes to
the editing machine's random access memory store, a
process known as digitizing. (Random access means you
can retrieve things in any order. A computer disk drive is
random access memory; video tape, which is also memory,
is linear access.)

There are two problems with the digitizing process.
First, it can't be speeded up; it has to be done at normal
speed. Secondly, you probably won't be able to transfer
everything you shot because the amount of data needed to
record a picture is so hefty that the computer soon runs out
of memory. The technology eases this problem by storing
only about two per cent of the information needed for a
broadcast quality picture. This two per cent gives you the
equivalent of VHS quality on the screen, which is more than
adequate for editing. You can ask for better quality pictures,
but if you do, you may have to pay for extra memory.

The way to economize on time and memory is to
transfer fewer rushes. If you list the time codes of the usable
material on a word processor and feed the list to the editing
machine via a floppy disk, the machine will transfer only the

shots you want. You can always go back and transfer
more material during the edit if you find that you missed
something.

Once your shots are in digital form on the hard disks
you can do anything to them that a computer can do. You
can call up any shot at any time, instantly. You can display a
palette of rushes on the screen with labels for each shot (put
in the labels when you select the rushes for transferring).
You can play, shuttle or jump through shots, forwards or
backwards, instantly, by a whole menu of methods. You can
edit and lay up to 24 sound tracks independently from the
picture. You can flip shots (reverse right and left), freeze
frames and add mixes, wipes, fades and graphics. You can
access other computers to show shot lists, cutting orders,
archive listings and so on. You can have your pictures and
sound laid out in strips (in 'timelines'), with an indicator to
show where you are in each bit, and use these strips to edit
on. Everything you do is recorded in a list that can be used
by on-line machines to produce a transmission copy of your
programme from the original rushes. With many non-
linear systems it's possible to play the programme directly
into the transmission chain from the edit machine so the
on-line conforming process is becoming obsolete.

**checking
your edit**

But let's get away from the technology and back to the
programme. In the end the only thing that matters is what's
on the screen and you are responsible for that. If a cut
doesn't work, you can't blame it on the machines.

**the overall
shape**

Let's assume you have done an off-line or first assembly
and are sitting down with the editor to view it. First of all,
look through the programme non-stop without worrying
about details. This will give you an idea of the programme's
overall strengths and weaknesses; discuss these with the
editor and think about ways of strengthening the weak
points and making more of the strong points. Is the overall
pace of the programme too even (and therefore a little
boring)? Are the fast and lively sequences distributed to
their best advantage? Does each sequence add something
new to the story? Do you have a strong sequence at the start
and a strong sequence to end with?

After considering the overall impact you should go over each sequence with the editor, looking carefully at every shot and every cut and seeing if they can be improved. The easiest way to do this is to stay in the cutting room while the editor is reworking the first assembly. Many directors, however, prefer to discuss changes with the editor and then leave him or her to get on with it. Of course it depends on you, the editor, and your preferred ways of working but the fact remains – there is no better place to learn about programme-making than in the cutting room. If you want to direct well, you have to know how pictures work together and the only place to learn that is in the cutting room. My advice is: stay with the editor. You will realize how well your time was spent when you next go out directing.

Whichever way you decide to work, here are some details to look for:

1. Check the length

Check that you have found the best possible length for each shot. Would it do its job as well if it were shorter? If so, trim it. Most films and shots suffer from being too long rather than too short.

2. Are the cuts smooth?

Does each shot join up smoothly with its neighbours? The eye concentrates on only one point of the screen at a time – usually the brightest point, or the point where there is something moving (for example, the fly crawling up the newsreader's jacket). You can often make a cut smoother (and therefore better) by making sure that the points which attract the eye in neighbouring shots are in the same section of the screen. Often jump cuts between locations (your reporter is inside the building in one shot, outside in the next) can be made to look acceptable by following this principle. But make sure the shot sizes are different, as cutting between the same size shots of a person or thing is frequently ugly.

If you have an awkward cut and all else fails, a trick you can use is to introduce a sudden, sharp noise on the sound track just before the offending cut – something like a car horn or a door slam. The viewers will blink involuntarily and miss the cut!

3. Trim interviews

Trim the first question from interviews; you can almost always set up what the interviewee is talking about in fewer words in the commentary. Often you will find that your interviewee doesn't really start answering the question till about the third sentence in. If this is so, drop the first two sentences.

It's common too that the middle of the interviewee's answer contains the meat of what he or she wants to say and everything thereafter is a bit of trimming, or even a repeat of what he has just said. Do you need this extra bit? I am not suggesting you cut all interviews to shreds. But your programme will benefit enormously if you use only the meat of the interviews and trim the fat.

4. Shots with camera movement

With camera movements trim off the static bits at each end and just use the moving part of the shot, unless there is a definite reason why you should keep both in. It looks odd, for example, if you hold a static wide shot of a street scene for two or three seconds and then suddenly zoom in to a close-up of a poster and there is no apparent reason why you started to zoom at that point. It's much better to start the shot at the beginning of the zoom. Or (if you have remembered the three-for-the-price-of-one technique) perhaps use the static long shot first and then cut to the static close-up of the poster. Beware keeping too many zooms in your film; they can make it look very sloppy.

5. Cutting into wobbles

As a general rule you shouldn't cut a shot while it is actually panning or zooming. But with zoom or pans that wobble, try using the static point of the wobble as the beginning of the shot (there is always a static point – often extremely short – where a wobble changes direction). You may also be able to cut early if there is a wobble at the end.

6. Cut on action

If a shot is moving, don't cut. If a person or thing moves and you have the action covered by two shots of different sizes, cut on the action, if a cut is appropriate. A person sits down, a telephone is picked up – movements like these disguise cuts most effectively.

7. Don't cut unnecessarily

Don't use shots just because you have them. Every shot should move the story on; there's no point cutting to a shot if it adds nothing new.

8. Don't be hopeful

Don't be hopeful about your shots. Some shots simply won't be good enough to get into your film and you should drop them. Don't put them in hoping they aren't as bad as they look. They are.

9. Mixes (or dissolves)

Few programmes are improved by mixes; many look as if they have caught a disease from them. Don't use them as a general substitute for cuts as they tend to reduce everything to visual mush. Save mixes to make a specific point. In the right place – and there won't be many right places – they are very effective.

10. Using interviews as voice-over

Using an interview as voice-over – in other words, as commentary over shots illustrating what the interviewee is saying – can throw up the same problems as trying to fit pictures to a pre-recorded commentary. If you film a person's daily routine and also ask him to talk through it in an interview, the pictures and words won't give equal time or emphasis to the same incidents – they may not even cover the same incidents. The best way to proceed is to edit the pictures first and use them as the clothes line on which to hang passages from the interview. If you use the interview as the clothes line, you will find the shots more difficult to fit in and will be able to use fewer of them. You will also be making an illustrated interview when you should be making a film.

clean up the soundtrack

Whichever way you choose, remember that when you use interview as voice-over you have an opportunity to make the sound flow really smoothly. So cut out all the 'ums' and 'ers' and repetitions and pauses from the sound track, always bearing in mind that your interviewee's style should remain recognizable, even if it has acquired a strange fluency.

11. Remember the sound

The sound in your completed programme will convey at least as much information as the pictures, so don't neglect it. Listen to what is on the tracks and drop non-synchronized distractions where possible, such as car horns, passing aircraft and interpolations from the director or crew. Then copy acceptable sound from the same location on to a separate track to cover the gaps. Make sure the replacement sound is longer than the sound you took out so that you can mix smoothly between the tracks during the dub.

You should also record sound on different tracks to overlap the joins between sequences. Then, when you have finished editing, you can combine the tracks either in the editing suite or in a dubbing theatre to produce one high quality sound track with all the levels properly balanced. You may end up spending a lot of your editing time on getting the sound right – it's time well spent. Viewers will accept poor pictures more readily than poor sound.

Finally, don't be frightened of working really hard at editing. You may have to go through some sequences five or six times viewing, listening, editing, re-viewing and re-editing before you get them right. Don't be discouraged. Films are shot on location but made in the cutting room.

SUMMARY
EDITING

Editing is selecting – selecting the best shots at the best length and in the best order for telling your story.

Preparing to edit

Make sure everything you shot arrives in the cutting room.

View all the material and make a shot list.

Work out a cutting order (unlikely to be the same as the order in the treatment).

Don't let the commentary dictate the order or length of shots. Films are not illustrated commentaries.

Editing video

On-line editing is fast but making changes can be difficult unless you are willing to lose a generation.

Digital copying transfers the code for the picture, not the picture itself. So copies are the same quality as the original.

The off-line edit gives you time and opportunity to sort out editing problems on a cheaper format. The results can be recorded as an edit decision list. On-line machines can use this list to produce an exact copy of the off-line edit.

If you assemble edit your programme, the machines transfer control track as they perform each edit. The main drawback is that picture and sound can't be handled separately – a serious limitation for good editing.

If there is a control track already on the record tape you can insert edit. This allows you to handle picture and sound separately. Use insert editing whenever possible. The control track should be dubbed on to the record tape before the editing session.

∨

In non-linear editing the computer stores the details of each edit and does an instant assembly on the screen when you want to view your work. This means that you can change whatever, wherever, whenever (just like film editing!).

Check your edit
First check the overall shape of the programme, then each sequence, then each shot and each cut.

Things to look for
1. Are the shots the right length?
2. Are the cuts smooth? Are points of interest round each cut in the same part of the screen (vital if you want to make jump cuts work)? Cuts between same-sized shots of the same person or thing are ugly – have you avoided this?
3. Trim the first question from interviews. Identify the meat of the interview; trim the fat.
4. Trim the static bits at both ends of pans and zooms. Don't keep too many zooms in the programme.
5. Don't cut in the middle of camera moves. Wobbles in pans and zooms can often be used as cutting points.
6. Cut on action – if a cut is called for and you have different-sized shots of the same action.
7. Don't cut unless you have to. Every shot should move the story on.
8. Drop poor shots. Don't hope they are better than they look. They aren't.
9. Use mixes (dissolves) sparingly.
10. When using interviews as voice-over, cut the pictures first and fit the voice-over to the pictures, not vice versa. Clean up the sound track whenever the speaker is off-screen.
11. Don't neglect sound. Viewers will accept poor pictures more readily than poor sound.

Work hard at editing. Films are made in the cutting room.

three words a second for current affairs programmes. You
should check with someone experienced if you aren't sure.

The first line of commentary is often the most difficult
the first line to write. If you don't have a good line in your notes and
can't think of one, go on to the next section; you'll probably
hit on a good idea while you are worrying about something
else. If you find writing difficult – as most of us do – it can be
helpful to get a rough commentary on to paper quickly and
then go back and revise. You may be one of those people
who find editing easier than writing.

Count the words of each section as you finish it, adding
counting or dropping words till the passage fits its allotted duration
words exactly. If you find it a nuisance to count words while you
are writing, it's a useful tip to write on graph paper with a
ration of six words per line, with the words set out in

columns	like	this.	You	can	then
tell	at	a	glance	that,	assuming
your	speaker	reads	at	three	words
a	second,	you	have	written	enough
for	about	ten	seconds	of	picture.

If you don't have any graph paper, you can fold an ordinary
don't use a piece of paper into columns. Or you can train yourself to
stopwatch start a new line every six words. Whatever you do, don't
use a stopwatch to time your words. The reason is that it is
unlikely that the speed you read to yourself will be the same
as your reading speed (or that of your commentator's) in
front of a microphone. Stopwatch timings can cause grief
– and panic – during the recording.

The first section of commentary (each section is usually
script layout referred to as a 'cue') should not start earlier than two or
three seconds into the programme to reduce the risk of
words being lost if the opening of the programme is clipped
off by mistake during transmission. To help the reader,
write out all the numbers and dates as words rather than
figures. Make sure also that the last cue on a page doesn't
run over onto the next. You are making things
unnecessarily difficult for the reader if you ask him or her
to start a new page in mid-sentence without rustling the
paper and give a good performance – all at the same time!

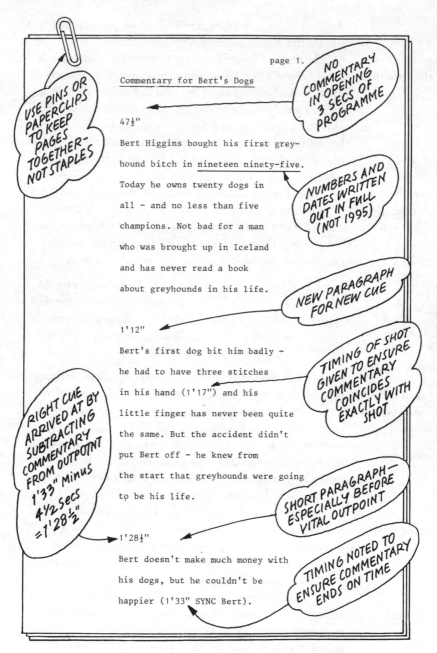

page 1.

NO COMMENTARY IN OPENING 3 SECS OF PROGRAMME

Commentary for Bert's Dogs

USE PINS OR PAPERCLIPS TO KEEP PAGES TOGETHER— NOT STAPLES

47½"

Bert Higgins bought his first grey-
hound bitch in nineteen ninety-five.
Today he owns twenty dogs in
all - and no less than five
champions. Not bad for a man
who was brought up in Iceland
and has never read a book
about greyhounds in his life.

NUMBERS AND DATES WRITTEN OUT IN FULL (NOT 1995)

NEW PARAGRAPH FOR NEW CUE

1'12"

Bert's first dog bit him badly -
he had to have three stitches
in his hand (1'17") and his
little finger has never been quite
the same. But the accident didn't
put Bert off - he knew from
the start that greyhounds were going
to be his life.

TIMING OF SHOT GIVEN TO ENSURE COMMENTARY COINCIDES EXACTLY WITH SHOT

RIGHT CUE ARRIVED AT BY SUBTRACTING COMMENTARY FROM OUTPOINT 1'33" minus 4½ secs =1'28½"

SHORT PARAGRAPH— ESPECIALLY BEFORE VITAL OUTPOINT

1'28½"

Bert doesn't make much money with
his dogs, but he couldn't be
happier (1'33" SYNC Bert).

TIMING NOTED TO ENSURE COMMENTARY ENDS ON TIME

Script layout

If you want words in the middle of a cue to hit a specific picture, you should note the start of the picture in brackets (1'17" in the illustration). The same goes for commentary that must be finished by a certain point (1'33" in the illustration). The starts for these cues should be worked out by counting backwards from the crucial word(s). Keep the lead-ins short, as the longer they are, the more likely it is that the commentary will overrun or fall short of its target.

In fact, all your cues should be kept short. If you are writing more than three or four sentences for a cue you are probably trying to say too much and making too little of the pictures. Leave a pause for music or sound effects; let the pictures (and the viewers!) breathe by keeping an interesting piece of action or a close-up clear of words. The best television commentary is simple, clear and brief.

checking commentary

When you have finished writing and counting, read the commentary out loud to yourself to take out the flaws (flaws itself is one of those words that can't be broadcast, as it sounds like floors). Listen to yourself. Do the words sound good? Do they make sense? Would you – could you – say the same thing face-to-face to anyone? Many statements in programmes are so pointless or pompous that the speakers would blush to repeat them away from the microphone.

Did you misread some of the sentences? Work out why. Was it because you lost the sense of them or misjudged the emphases? Your speaker and viewers may have similar problems. See if you can make improvements.

When you are satisfied, check the commentary against the pictures to make sure it works and fits as intended. You will almost certainly have to make a few more adjustments.

The finished commentary should be typed or printed out on paper that won't make a noise when handled in the recording booth. Use a paper clip rather than a staple to keep the pages together; the reader will want to handle each page separately and a paper clip is easier to remove.

writing the commentary first

Writing the commentary before editing is almost a contradiction in terms – you can't commentate on something that isn't there yet. If you must write before editing (probably because you work for news), view the pictures that are available, work out how they might be cut together and then keep them constantly in your mind's eye while you are writing. You may then produce some text that gives the editor a chance of getting the pictures to work roughly in time with the words.

The problem with writing before editing (or shooting) is that words have almost instant impact; pictures – particularly moving pictures – take longer. It's therefore easier to fit words to pictures than pictures to words. To write successfully for pictures that haven't yet been cut together, you first need to know how to write for pictures that have. You will then know that it's relatively easy to move words and swap sentences round to fit the picture – and very damaging to pictures to force them to fit words.

screen fillers

Of course, you may be writing for one of those events that don't take place on camera or lend themselves to illustration. There are a lot of them, especially on the news: an announcement or decision about the economy or schools or railways or hospitals or air travel. Before you send someone to take yet more shots (or dig out the stock shots) of cash registers, playgrounds, trains, hospital exteriors or the airport, ask yourself whether they will add anything to the story. In some cases they may hinder more than help: planes, in particular, are so photogenic and – given half a chance – so noisy that they often distract from the words.

If you decide to give the old favourites another airing, do take the trouble to look at them first and see if you can highlight any aspect of them with your words to make them contribute to the story. If you don't make this effort, the pictures become mere screen fillers. If you make a habit of writing without viewing, your writing becomes less and less sensitive to the needs of pictures. You stop looking for shots and situations that make the point or tell the story. You end up using slag heaps to illustrate coal surpluses and shots of passing trains to illustrate rail strikes (two recent examples). You end up not caring about pictures at all. It's not an effective use of television.

SUMMARY
COMMENTARY

Keep a list of commentary points for each sequence during editing.

DO *make the commentary fit the picture – by planning, taking timings and counting.*

DON'T *describe the picture. Add to it.*

The first line is often the most difficult. Leave it till later if you are struggling.

Counting – write six words to a line. Then each line is two seconds. Don't use a stopwatch.

Script layout – don't start the first cue earlier than three seconds into the programme. Don't let a cue run over onto a new page. Write out dates and numbers as words. Where words must hit a specific picture, put timings in brackets.

Keep cues short. Let the pictures, sound (and viewers!) breathe. The best commentary is simple, clear and brief.

Check commentary by reading it aloud. Then check against the pictures.

Edit first, write later. Words are easier to manipulate than pictures. If you must write before editing, view the pictures first and then highlight some aspect with the words so that the pictures contribute to the story.

Dubbing

It's difficult to write about dubbing as practices vary so much in different TV stations. Some stations have fully equipped dubbing theatres with a library of music and sound effects; others improvise in the edit suites; and some use the studio – live, during transmission – to cover all the pictures with wall-to-wall words and soapy music.

San Totta of course employs the last method. The commentary and soapy music often run into the recorded interviews and it's not unknown for the programme to finish before the commentator.

The safest way to make sure that the commentary fits the picture is to write it at the end of the off-line, record it wild (without the pictures in front of the reader) and lay it as a track during the on-line. The editor can then make the minor adjustments that are needed to ensure a perfect fit between pictures and words and you have one less thing to worry about in the dubbing theatre.

It's important to think hard about whom you want to **choosing** read the commentary. Discuss the choice with your picture **a voice** and programme editors. You need someone who can make the words live without taking on a life of their own, away from the pictures they are supposed to be complementing.

When you have chosen, show him or her the programme before you go to the recording and work hard together to get the right tone of voice, the best speed of delivery and to make the most of the interplay between words and pictures. A badly-judged commentary can ruin your programme; a well-spoken one can contribute hugely to its success.

recording
commentary

On the day of the dub it's usual to start the session by recording the commentary, if you haven't already done so. Do a rehearsal before you start recording. The reader takes his or her cues from a green light (the 'cue-light') which is operated by the producer. The cues should always be given about a second before the timing in the script, depending on how long it takes the commentator to draw breath and start (the time varies).

When you have dealt with any problems thrown up by the rehearsal, record the commentary. Although you will be able to stop at any point to return to the last cue and begin to record again from there, don't stop too often or you run the risk of harming the flow of the piece. You should be able to get through fairly quickly by this stage (remember, you've had a rehearsal), stopping only occasionally to ask the commentator to read faster or slower or fine-tune an emphasis.

the dubbing
chart

After the commentary the dubbing mixer (the technician in charge) will start work on building the music and effects track (also known as the M&E or international sound track). The editor will have prepared a dubbing chart listing the exact timings for the in and out points of all the commentary, music, dialogue and effects (each will have at least one track to itself); the dubbing mixer will work from this chart to combine all the different components into one M&E track. While this is going on, you should listen hard and think. Would this sequence be improved by having the music or effects come in earlier? Or later? Would it help to drop some? Or add some (possible, even at this late stage, provided you can find them)?

When the M&E is ready, the mixer will run through the programme one last time to combine the M&E with the commentary. This is called the final mix and you should pay attention to the relative levels of the M&E and speech. Allow for the fact that the loudspeakers in dubbing theatres are usually far better quality than the speakers in home television sets. One result is that sound effects which can be heard clearly but softly in the dubbing theatre may be

completely inaudible to the viewer at home; if you suspect
this might be happening, discuss it with the dubbing mixer
and ask him or her not to keep the effects too low. Dubbing
mixers are often so used to their high-quality speakers
and have such finely tuned ears that they forget about the
relative insensitivity of viewers' speakers (and ears).

It's worth paying close attention to what's going on
in the dubbing theatre, as a good dub can add a lot of polish
to a programme. Carefully chosen sound effects can quickly
create an atmosphere which gives viewers that exciting
feeling of being there themselves. Dull shots can be brought
to life by adding a distant dog bark or birdsong or the sound
of insects buzzing. The fit between commentary and the
beginning of an interview can be improved by moving
the commentary track a fraction forwards or backwards.
A picture can be given depth by letting viewers actually
hear something from that ship on the horizon. The touches
you add may seem tiny and the viewers may not even notice
them consciously, but they are still worth making because
they all contribute towards the total impact of the
programme.

If you are using the studio to dub or transmit your
dubbing in programme and therefore haven't prepared a formal
the studio dubbing chart, it's important that your commentary script
includes all the things you intend to do and a stop-watch
timing for each of them. For example:

  49" Super title
  1'23" Go grams 'Marches' Side 2 Band 3
  1'54" Lose grams
  3'15" Run tape – birdsong
  3'55" Lose tape
  7'06" Super caption: General Hiro

These instructions can be written into the commentary
script, or if the script is a long one, it might be more
convenient for them to be written on a separate sheet
for distribution to the studio team. You should do a full
rehearsal before recording or transmission so that everyone
knows exactly what to do.

sound effects

A word about music and sound effects to end this chapter. Sound effects should be the normal accompaniment to your pictures; I have already stressed the importance of recording them with the picture and editing them in sync. Without effects the impact of your pictures is halved: imagine, for example, the arrival of a helicopter – first without sound, and then with it. Sound effects can give the beginning of a sequence an enormous boost if they are left free of commentary and played loud. They can be used to bring drawings or still photographs to life. Mixed with music or taking over after a sequence with music they can be magical.

music

Music is also something to conjure with. It has this marvellous power to get through to people's feelings in a few seconds. But you must use it sensitively; don't for example, cut it abruptly in full flow just because the sequence has ended (fade it out gently instead). Use it like commentary (and sometimes instead of commentary) to add meaning to the picture: a love song played over the shot of a naval vessel leaving its home port can say more about the feelings of the sailors and the families waving them goodbye than the best written commentary. You can also use music ironically; for example, wedding music played over a scene in a divorce court. And of course cutting pictures to music is an effective technique.

When you want to use music as commentary, it's a good idea to drop a hint in the commentary leading up to the music section so that the viewers know what to expect. There are many ways of doing this: a line like 'It's a time for private thoughts' would do for both the examples above.

Whatever you do, don't use music as audible chewing gum. The music you use must have a definite flavour to communicate to the viewers. So having it gently playing in the background to hide the absence of sound effects, or simply because the sound track is a bit quiet, is a waste. If, for example, you have a person in a studio telling a children's story illustrated by drawings, it's perfectly acceptable to have the narrator's voice on the sound track

and nothing else. If you think that music would help the
story, that's fine too. But don't just have a record churning
away in the background because you are worried that the
background is a bit quiet. Choose instead a few points in
the story where music would really add something to the
pictures – where a person feels sleepy, or is excited or in
danger. Then make a big effort to find the right music to
heighten each moment – it's unlikely to be the same for
all of them.

SUMMARY
DUBBING

*Choose the voice with care. Show him or her the script
and programme in advance.*

Procedure in a dubbing theatre
1. *First rehearse, then record the commentary. Cue the
   reader with the green light.*
2. *Build up and record the M&E (or International Sound
   Track). Look for improvements.*
3. *Do the final mix (of commentary plus M&E). Monitor
   relative levels and make sure music and effects are not
   held too low.*

If dubbing in a studio
1. *Prepare a sheet listing everything you want to do (or write
   it into the commentary script). Distribute to studio team.*
2. *Rehearse before recording or transmitting.*

*All pictures should have sound – without them their impact
is halved.*

*Never use music as audible chewing gum; it's far too powerful
to waste on covering up the absence of proper sound effects.
Use it like commentary to add meaning to pictures.*

Studio

The studio at San Totta is the heart of the station. It's also
the place where the producers and directors are most likely
to have a heart attack.

The reason is pressure. Pressure to make things happen.
Pressure to brief and rehearse everyone and to sort out all
the things that go wrong. Pressure not to miss vital cues.
Pressure to keep to time, to meet the deadline, to make
instant decisions, to avoid mistakes, to keep one step ahead
… it's not a relaxing environment. Get it wrong and you
may need intensive care.

On the other hand, if you prepare well and know what
you're doing, directing a studio can become addictive,
an exhilarating drug, driving you to a 'high' that takes hours
to come down from.

For a stress-free time in the studio you have to remember
one basic fact: nothing happens in the studio unless you
arrange it to happen. So you the producer are in charge of
everything that goes on. You have to think of and organize
everything, from the positions of the performers to the
colour of the set.

Happily you don't have to do this all by yourself. The
various technical departments are there to help and advise.
But the push has to come from you.

The first thing is to decide what you want in your
programme. That's what the earlier chapters in this book
are about and any studio producer who has turned to this
chapter first, hoping to save himself some reading, would
be well-advised to turn back. Ideas, research and treatments
are as important for studio programmes as for any other.

It's only when you have decided on the contents of your programme that the procedure is different.

book a studio early

Book yourself into a studio as early as possible, in fact as soon as you are sure that you have a programme worth doing. Totta producers tend to treat the studios as casually as the canteen, and drop in when they feel like it; you should approach the studio as carefully as a parent who orders a wedding feast, worrying about each detail of the decor, menu, music and cost.

the set

It makes sense to start with the items that take the longest to prepare. This almost always means the scenery or set. So start by going to your designer and telling him about your programme (what it's trying to achieve, how many artists are involved, what they will do, how big your budget for design is, and so on) and also what sort of set you are thinking of. So – what should you look for in a set?

It's difficult to advise about this since the design of the set must answer the demands of the programme. But if you find yourself asking for a massive, complicated set full of the sort of features that are in the houses and countryside all around you, be careful. Perhaps you shouldn't be doing your programme in the studio at all. Wouldn't you be better off on location?

Don't forget the virtues of a simple set brought to life by effective lighting and one or two carefully chosen props. A few rostra (platforms) to break up the flat expanse of the studio floor and a few patches of colour or pattern can work wonders. Remember TV is most at home with mid-shots and close-ups and the chances are that the viewers won't see all that much of the set. Anyway, what the people on the set are saying and doing should be holding the viewers' attention more than the set itself. But don't go overboard for the simple (and cheap): if a set is too skimped, it draws attention to itself and away from the people on it, and that of course defeats its purpose.

If, on the other hand, you've invested a lot of money in a set – for a quiz or entertainment show perhaps – it makes sense to cut to wide shots fairly often, just to show how

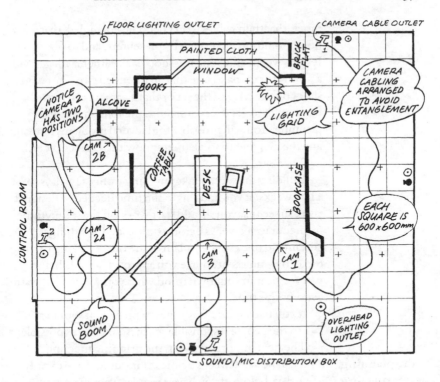

Floor plan   much money you've spent (big bucks heighten the
showbiz glitter). Use these wide shots to make the most
of particularly hilarious moments or as a punctuation mark
for the proceedings.

the floor plan   The designer will need some time to work on his or her
ideas. He will draw them on a floor plan (this is a printed
diagram of the studio marked with a grid that can be used
to pinpoint any position on the floor). When you receive
the design, go through your script or treatment for the
programme, 'placing' it in the set and imagining what it
will look like, thinking about where the cameras will be,
what they will see, where the performers will stand and sit,
where they will come in and where they will go out. Do
this systematically from the beginning to the end of the
programme and pencil in all the main positions on the floor
plan, checking that there is enough room for the cameras to

move, that their cables won't become entangled, that
floor monitors can be seen by presenters, and so on.
It's also worth checking the shots each camera will get with
a protractor to make sure that an intended two-shot won't
shoot off the edge of the set or that a camera can move back
far enough to get everything into the long shot you are
planning. You will probably find several problems for you
and the designer to solve (better now than on the recording
day).

Building the set can take anything from a few days to
a few weeks. If you add this to the time needed to design it,
you can see that you should start work on the set anything
from four to six weeks before studio day. One thing is
certain: no one ever complains that you are talking to them
too early – unless of course you approach people before
you are clear in your own mind what you want. That wastes
everybody's time.

If you need special costumes or props you should also
talk to the people responsible for these as early as possible.

The next important date is the planning meeting.

**the planning
meeting**
This can be a few weeks before your studio day – or only
a few days before, if you have a regular weekly programme.
The planning meeting is usually attended by the designer
and senior members of the studio technical crew who will
be on duty on the day of your programme – the technical
manager, the lighting supervisor and the sound supervisor.
It might be useful to have the floor manager and a
representative from the workshop there as well. You should
bring to this meeting the floor plan marked with the camera
positions and all positions and movements of everyone in
the programme. You should also have a running order (the
contents of your programme written down in note form),
especially if the final script isn't ready. If you can send those
concerned the script and running order a few days
beforehand, so much the better.

The best way to conduct a planning meeting is to start
by giving a quick outline of the programme and asking the
designer to explain the main points of the set. Then run
through the programme explaining all the movements,

positions and actions of the participants and cameras at each stage. The technicians won't want you to read the script to them, but they will want to know things like – where is the presenter at the beginning of the programme? Is he or she standing or sitting? Is he in position when the programme

Camera script   starts or does he walk in? If he walks in – where does he walk

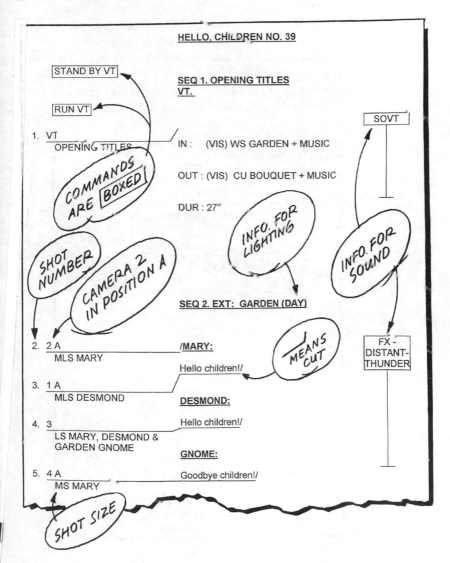

HELLO, CHILDREN NO. 39

STAND BY VT

RUN VT

SEQ 1. OPENING TITLES
VT.

SOVT

1. VT
       OPENING TITLES   IN :   (VIS) WS GARDEN + MUSIC

                             OUT : (VIS) CU BOUQUET + MUSIC

                             DUR : 27"

COMMANDS ARE BOXED

SHOT NUMBER

CAMERA 2 IN POSITION A

INFO. FOR LIGHTING

INFO. FOR SOUND

SEQ 2. EXT: GARDEN (DAY)

2. 2 A   /MARY:
       MLS MARY
                             Hello children!/

MEANS CUT

FX -
DISTANT-
THUNDER

3. 1 A   DESMOND:
       MLS DESMOND

4. 3   Hello children!/
       LS MARY, DESMOND &
       GARDEN GNOME   GNOME:

5. 4 A   Goodbye children!/
       MS MARY

SHOT SIZE

in from? Which camera will he be looking at? And so on. All these details are vital to the technicians. Without them they cannot give you the lighting, sound and pictures you want.

camera script

The next stage after the planning meeting is to finish the script, if you haven't already done so. This should then be typed out in the form of a camera script, containing not only everything that will be said in the programme, but also the details of all the shots, camera movements, sound coverage and so on. You should keep to the layout normally used in your studios if it differs from the one shown in the illustration. The important thing about the layout is that everyone should be used to it and understand it.

Camera cards

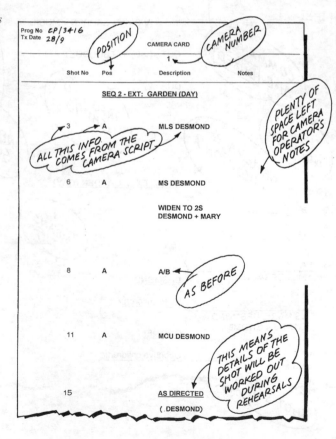

camera cards

When the script is finished the next job is to prepare camera cards. These are cards given to each cameraman listing all his or her shots; they are in fact individual scripts for each camera. It is best to have them typed out with lots of space between each shot so that the cameramen can make their own notes during the rehearsal.

script for live programmes

For news and current affairs programmes it usually isn't possible to prepare a detailed camera script and camera cards in advance – too much of the programme is unscripted, items are added or dropped or come in late. For this sort of programme, it's best to put each item on a separate page, noting the title of the item, the words of the introductory link from the studio, the opening and closing words of any inserts and their duration. For longer inserts it's also useful for the script to include one or more optional out points so that the studio director can leave the insert early if the programme is overrunning on transmission. The pages for all the items are then assembled and a running order put in front. This layout makes it easy to drop or add items while

Running order   the programme is on air (just drop or add pages).

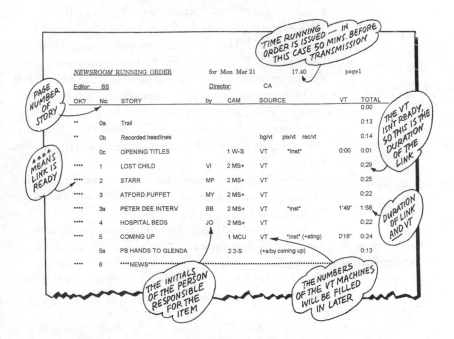

The closer you are to the day of your studio booking, the more there seems to do. You have to check that everything and everyone involved with the programme is organized, briefed and knows when and where to come. Don't forget to ask your performers to come early if they need special make-up, or if there are a lot of them needing make-up (in both cases make-up should be warned). Scripts, props, costumes, music, sound effects, graphics – everything needs to be checked by you personally. Pay particular attention to the spelling in the graphics; misspellings are easy to miss until they are on air.

Time passes very quickly on the day itself and there are always a few emergencies which you can't foresee (like technical breakdowns) which will eat into your rehearsal time. So make sure as many snags as possible are sorted out in advance: the more things you know are right, the more time you will have for coping with the unexpected.

Studio day

Then comes the great day itself – studio day. Make sure you arrive at least half an hour early to give yourself time to talk to the technicians and familiarize yourself with the set. Walk round the set and check the details. Is it clean and freshly painted? Has it been damaged or marked while being put up? If the set is regularly used, is it showing any signs of wear and tear (usually noticeable at the edges)? Are the cables in the back of the set out of sight? Are there any cigarette stubs, sweet wrappings or chalk marks from the last programme on the floor? If you find any of these, speak to your designer about it. The studio camera can't turn a blind eye to a grubby set – nor should you.

When it's time to begin your rehearsal, ask the technical manager if everything is ready. If it is, get down to work without delay.

Start by going through the programme, shot by shot. Line up each shot, look at it, tell the cameraman what's wrong if it's not what you want and then when you are satisfied, confirm the shot to the cameraman. Then move on to the next shot and do the same. This shot-by-shot line-

run through
shot by shot

up should never be skipped. It's the only chance you have of telling the cameramen exactly what you want from each shot. If you don't do it, they are left to guess your intentions from the notes on their camera cards. Be precise, but don't waste time by being too pernickety: ('... left a teeny, teeny bit to see one more book on the shelf, now tighten up a tiniest smidgen ...'). A trained cameraman will offer you the right shot more often that not without having to be coached, provided he or she understands the point of the shot. If it isn't the shot you want, explain what you want, not how to get it. 'Zoom out' or 'Pan right' are unhelpful directions: how far should the cameraman zoom or pan? 'Zoom out to include the lamp' or 'Pan right to lose the chair' are more precise.

When you have lined up the shots for a tricky sequence – one with lots of captions, for example – interrupt the line-up for a moment and try and put the sequence together. It helps break the ice in the studio. Everyone concentrates to get the sequence right and when it is almost right (it doesn't have to be perfect at this stage) it's reassuring for everyone to know that it works and that they can function effectively as a team. It's worth putting a sequence together like this early in your rehearsal time.

The shot-by-shot line-up may show up all sorts of problems, some of which you may have to get round by adding or dropping shots. Announce any shot changes clearly on the talkback so that everyone in the team can make adjustments.

adding shots If you are adding a new shot, it should be given the number of the previous shot followed by a letter – 'Add shot 27a – camera 3 – close-up: presenter's hands'. Give everyone time to note the change on their scripts.

By the way, this lining-up process can be started before the set and lighting are completely ready: there's no point holding things up because a table or flower-pot hasn't been put into position. You also don't need to wait until all your participants have arrived – you can always line up the shots using someone else as a stand-in. But make sure you use stand-ins who are about the same height and size as your participants – this is important for lighting as well as cameras.

rehearsing

When the shots are all lined up, rehearse any tricky bits you didn't stop for the first time. Run the beginnings and ends of any inserts (if you don't have time to view the whole insert) to make sure that everyone knows where you are going to cut in and out. Then go through the whole programme at the correct speed without stopping, if possible. If you have any time left after this, use it to rehearse again (a) the sections where things went wrong, (b) the closing of the programme, and (c) the opening.

When the rehearsal is over there may be a short break for the technical line-up. The studio crew need this time (usually it's half an hour) to check the cameras and other equipment; your participants can use it to rest and have their make-up refreshed. You can use the time to do a little fine-tuning with your participants but, please, only on a few points. This is not the time to introduce major changes to the programme.

Sometimes the line-up can be done earlier (it depends on the type of equipment and how long it's been in use since the last check) and so the rehearsal is followed immediately by recording or transmission. If you have prepared well, you should need to say very little while this is going on. Your time is better spent keeping one eye on what is happening on screen and one eye on what is going to happen. Check that the next shot is ready, the next graphic is in place, the next insert is right and the next participant is standing by. Make sure also that the shot you're cutting to isn't the same size as the shot you are on. If it is, change the size of the waiting shot – or don't cut. Don't relax during the recorded inserts; use the time to check that everything is ready for the next section of the programme.

See Briefing 1 for more abour directing in the studio

Good luck!

Further points

1. Sound at the opening

At the beginning of a programme it looks neater if you
bring up the sound a split second before the picture;
bringing up the picture first gives the impression that the
sound department is asleep. Bringing up the sound first
doesn't for some reason make the picture department look
bad, perhaps because it doesn't feel as if the programme has
really started until you see the picture. Anyway, whatever
the reason, sound should lead.

2. Cut-off

Anything that is within two or three centimetres of the edge
of screen in the studio probably won't be seen by viewers
at home. This is because on most sets the part of the screen
carrying non-picture information is hidden behind the
casing (engineers say the picture is 'overscanned'). So make
sure that important bits of information are not too near the
edge of the screen in cut-off. Words in particular can easily
lose a letter or two if you aren't careful. If you ask, the
technical manager can show you the extent of the cut-off
on the preview monitor.

3. Preview monitor

Don't forget the preview monitor. In many studios the
monitors for each of the cameras are black and white,
with only the transmission monitor (often labelled 'TX'
for short) and the preview monitor in colour. You can ask
for any picture from the other monitors to be shown on the

preview monitor. This gives you a chance to see if any
colours are clashing; or to check how a name caption will
look when superimposed over a shot of an interviewee
whose knees are showing at the bottom of the picture
— it's usually better to tighten the shot so the caption misses
the knees.

4. Small studios

Don't be put off if you have only two cameras (or even one)
at your disposal. After all, when you are on location you will
have only one camera to work with 99 per cent of the time.
In studio programmes where you can't stop between every
shot, one camera only is of course limiting (try recording
in chunks and using caption scanners and pre-recorded
inserts to give variety). If you plan carefully, two cameras
are adequate for all but the most complicated programmes.
Here again you can work wonders by pre-recording
complicated bits of the programme and playing them in.

5. Studio marvels

Even the most unambitious studio has a surprising number
of technical tricks built into it. Most of them are hardly
used because producers simply don't know they are there.
So take time one day (not on your studio day, of course)
to ask a friendly technician to show you what the studio can
do: electronic colours, fancy wipes, black and coloured
edging, cut-outs, electronic letters, numbers and arrows,
chromakey, flashing coloured lights, different lenses and
filters, sound echoes, reverse phasing and so on. You'll be
surprised how many effects are available.

6. Vision mixing

Vision mixing is a specialist activity. A skilled operator takes
a huge amount of work off your hands, freeing you to look
ahead and sort out problems before they become serious.
Come transmission or recording time he or she will be able
to do most things without a cue from you, but the argument
is sometimes heard that when you do need to give a cue, the
vision mixer will always be a fraction behind. The reply is

that a good vision mixer will foresee your intention and
will cut at almost exactly the same time as your cue.

7. Studio crews

Remember that crews are human beings. So telling them
who you are at the beginning (they may not recognize
your voice over the talkback even if they have met you),
a word of appreciation for a difficult shot well done and
a ten-minute break for refreshment are all welcomed.
But don't say 'please' and 'thank you' for every command
(it becomes irritating); an occasional courtesy is enough.

8. Studio discipline

If you have problems with members of the crew (the
sound supervisor, perhaps, doesn't seem to be listening
to your instructions, the lighting men are having a loud
conversation which is disturbing your concentration),
don't try and solve them yourself. Ask the technical
manager to speak to the crew; he is their direct boss.

If observers in the gallery are making a noise it's up to
you as director to ask them to be quiet. Should they be there
at all? If your boss is in the gallery and like Magnus Vision,
Totta's General Manager, makes a habit of interrupting with
suggestions at crucial moments, ask him to keep them for a
convenient break in the rehearsal. If (like Mr Vision) he still
keeps on interrupting, there comes a point when you have
to consider giving him your chair and asking him to direct
the programme ... but this of course is a drastic step. Mr
Vision fancies himself as a sportsman and so often turns up
in the studio for Caesar Andante's *Sports Round-Up*. One
day when Mr Vision had made one too many suggestions,
Caesar turned round and asked him to take over the
programme. Pause, while everybody waited to see what
the GM would do. 'No,' he said, 'you carry on, Andante; if
I did it, the change of style would be much too noticeable.'

Not for nothing is Magnus Vision the General Manager
of San TTV.

But he stopped making suggestions after this, and a little
later went out of the studio. So Caesar had made his point.

9. Breakdowns

If the studio isn't ready on time to start the rehearsal
and there are technical breakdowns which eat into your
precious time, it's useful to make a discreet note of how
long you have lost as the result of each incident. You are not
entitled to have this time made up to you as a right. But
as it is not unknown for technicians to say the programme
got into difficulties because the producer wasn't properly
prepared, it's just as well to have a few facts available on your
side of the argument.

SUMMARY
STUDIO

Preparing

You are in charge of everything. Nothing happens in a studio unless you arrange it.

Make sure that the studio is booked for you on the right day at the right time.

Get design and construction departments working on your set as early as possible. Use the floor plan to visualize your programme in the set to identify problems before the design goes off to be built.

Order costumes and props early.

Invite the designer, technical manager, sound and lighting supervisors and other interested parties to the planning meeting. Bring the floor plan with positions for the cameras and participants marked on it. Run through the programme explaining all the positions and movements.

Finalize the camera script and prepare camera cards.

Check everything and everyone in the programme personally as studio day approaches. Do they know where and when to come? Allow time for make-up when telling participants what time they should turn up.

Everything you can get right in advance, you should. This will leave you with more time to cope with the unexpected.

Studio day

On studio day arrive at least half an hour early. Check the set for damage, cleanliness and signs of wear.

Run through the programme shot by shot, so that everyone knows what you want. Rehearse tricky sections. View all programme inserts.

V

Then go through the programme without stopping. Note any problems and use any time remaining to eliminate them. Then rehearse again the closing and opening of the programme.

During the technical line-up give last-minute instructions (as few as possible) to the participants. Leave time for make-up and relaxing.

During recording or transmission keep an eye on what's happening, but also check ahead on the next shot, graphic, insert and participant.

Further points
1. For a sound opening, sound should lead.
2. Allow for cut-off on home screens when framing shots.
3. Use the preview monitor to check colours and captions.
4. All but the most complicated programmes can be successfully made using only two cameras if you plan carefully and use pre-recorded inserts from VT.
5. Arrange a demonstration of studio marvels.
6. Don't do your own vision mixing.
7. Technicians are humans. Treat them accordingly.
8. Studio discipline: let the technical manager look after the crew. You look after the rest.
9. Keep a discreet note of time lost through technical breakdowns.

Outside broadcasts

Outside broadcasts are the reverse of studio programmes. Studio programmes put the location in the studio; outside broadcasts put the studio in the location.

Because that is what a traditional OB unit is: a studio on wheels complete with camera, vision mixing desk, sound and videotape machines, talkback and a graphics generator. Everything that is found in the standard studio except for those rows of lights hanging from the ceiling (and if anyone could think of a cheap way of hanging them from the sky, they would come in handy).

It follows, therefore, that to do an OB you use a mixture of location filming and studio programme techniques. The main thing you borrow from your location technique is the recce (refresh your memory of the Recce chapter). But for a first-time OB in a new location the recce is not just advisable – it's essential. Even if the location is one you've used before, you should go back for a survey. Things can change, and you may have to change your plans.

the OB recce
The OB engineer must come along with you on the recce. The traditional, full–scale OB unit needs a great deal of technical support and the engineer is the one who has to organize it: a nearby source of mains electricity (or a mobile generator), telephone lines and microwave links back to the studio (if you're transmitting the programme live), raised platforms for the cameras if you want them to look down on the action (and you almost certainly do), slings and gantries to get the cables across roads without obstructing traffic, approval from local safety officers about any structures you build, and so on. If you are taking a large OB to a remote area

the engineer may even have to check the strength of the
bridges on the way: full-size OB units need support below
the ground as well as above it. Of course if you have a lightweight OB unit you won't have to worry about things like
bridges, but most other points about OB planning still apply.

On the recce the engineer will first want to know
the basic details of the programme: the nature, time
and duration of the event, the location of prize-giving
ceremonies, interviews and any other action.

The thing to decide then is the position of the cameras.

camera
positions

These positions are extremely important – for you, because
the success of your shots depends on them; for the engineer,
because he probably has only a limited length of cabling and
will have to juggle around with the placing of the OB van to
give you the positions you ask for. So once you have picked
the positions you probably won't be able to change them.

The engineer will also want to know which lenses you
want on which camera; there is usually a selection of wide-
angle and short or long zoom lenses on offer. You should
ask the engineer's advice if you find it difficult to decide
what should go where on your first OB. There may also be
one or more remote cameras available (cameras that don't
need to be connected to the OB van with cables). These are
obviously useful to cover areas where you want shots from
lots of different angles (which you won't be able to get from
a fixed camera).

So where should you put your cameras? The following
notes will give you a rough guide for the more standard
events covered by OBs. Remember in each case to avoid
'crossing the line'; use your mental TV to check that the
action as seen by each camera will go in the same direction
on the screen. Your aim should be to put your viewer in the
best set in the grandstand for wherever the action is – and
then keep him there.

Football

Put two cameras as close to the halfway line as you can.
They should be high enough to give a clear shot of the far
touch-line, and far enough back to see the near touchline;
if you put the cameras too near the pitch they won't be able
to see play directly below them. Ask one cameraman to
follow the play in long shot and the other cameraman (the
one with the longest zoom) to follow the play in close-up.
You can cover the whole match quite adequately with this
long shot/close-up pair of cameras.

If you have a third camera, put it on the near touchline
for ground-level shots; if it's a remote camera and can move
along the touchline, so much the better. This camera will
also come in useful for interviews and award ceremonies
after the match.

If you have a fourth and fifth camera, place them at
ground level or slightly raised behind and on the nearside
of the two goals. This position is ideal for dramatic close-
ups of the frantic thrashing about which often comes before
a goal or an attempt at goal. If you have only four cameras,
you will have to decide which is the better end, taking into
account things like the position of the sun when making up
your mind. Then position the fourth camera about 15-20 m
behind the near goal and 15-20 m high. This gives the
camera a clear view of both goals, and you can then record
its output separately for slow-motion replays. Also

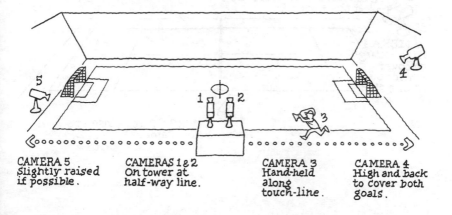

CAMERA 5
Slightly raised
if possible.

CAMERAS 1 & 2
On tower at
half-way line.

CAMERA 3
Hand-held
along
touch-line.

CAMERA 4
High and back
to cover both
goals.

remember to check that at least one of the cameras can get
a good close-up of the scoreboard.

This arrangement of cameras will work for hockey
and polo but needs to be adapted for rugby and American
football where the whole try line, rather than just the goal,
is important. Find out what colour shirts the teams will
be wearing – if they are at all similar or won't contrast well
in black and white, try and persuade one side to change.
The home team will probably find it easier to do so.

Tennis

Games played across nets such as tennis, table tennis,
badminton and volleyball, tend to have smaller playing
areas than games with goals. So the two-cameras-at-the-
halfway-line technique won't work; the cameras won't be
able to pan fast enough to follow their play. Instead put the
main camera at one end high enough up to be able to cover
the whole playing area in one long shot. Another camera
can go next to it to give close-ups of play at the far end.
A third camera can be placed on the ground to cover play
at the end below the other two cameras and also the players'
resting positions between games. Don't forget the
scoreboard. The same camera positions are also suitable for
games which have small playing areas, like snooker.

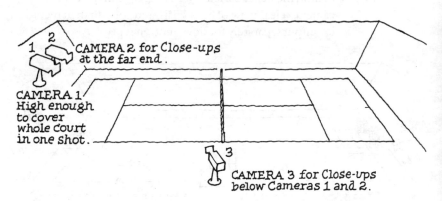

CAMERA 2 for Close-ups at the far end.

CAMERA 1 High enough to cover whole court in one shot.

CAMERA 3 for Close-ups below Cameras 1 and 2.

Races

Camera positions for races on a straight course are as you might expect: a camera slightly in front of the start, a camera at the finish and a moving camera travelling alongside the course, if the course is at all long. If the course is short (not more than about 200 m) a camera placed at a safe distance behind the finish showing the contestants coming straight towards camera can be very effective.

A version of these arrangements will cover running, walking, swimming, horse, donkey, dog, camel, and most other races you can think of. For rowing races it's effective to have a camera on a boat travelling alongside or behind the racers. With races round a circular track use your mental TV to check that the shots you get from each camera position maintain the continuity of direction and don't cross the line. Concentrate your coverage on the start, the final bend and the finish.

Boxing and wrestling

Pugilistic sports like boxing, wrestling, judo and karate don't involve defending territory and so the direction you approach them from isn't as important as for other sports. One or two cameras mounted high to give long shots and close-ups are all that's needed, but make sure they are both more or less on the same side of the ring. A camera low, near the ringside, can give excellent close-ups, but you have to be certain that the position is safe. Fighters sometimes make unscheduled flying exits that can damage camera and operator as well as themselves.

Golf

To cover all the holes on a complete eighteen-hole course you may need as many as four or five OB units. With one full-scale OB unit you will be lucky to get partial coverage of four holes – but four holes are better than nothing. Where you put your cameras depends wholly on the course layout. Try and find positions that give coverage of more than one hole.

Long route events

Events such as processions, rallies, long-distance running, Grand Prix motor racing, and cycling that take place over a long route create special problems. First of all you have to decide which bit of the route to concentrate on. Obviously the start, the finish, saluting bases, pit stops and tricky and photogenic bends (motor racing) are bits which you should go for. But once again you may find yourself severely limited by the length of cabling and the number of cameras required. A mobile tracking camera mounted on a vehicle can help with long-distance running and cycling but getting a continuous signal back to the main OB can be a difficult technical problem. A camera in a helicopter or airship can also be effective, but a communications engineer is essential if you are to get the full benefit of the shots from these moving cameras. Check the flying restrictions in the area before you opt for aerial shots.

'Buffer' shots

You may also find in this sort of event that it is impractical to keep all your static cameras on the same side of the route; an interesting portion of the route may run alongside a cliff, for example. The trick here is to do a 'buffer' shot with a third camera which shows the action coming towards or going away from the camera. This buffer should be used to separate the two shots which are reversing the continuity of direction.

If you haven't got a spare camera to give you a 'buffer', you can achieve almost the same effect by panning one or both of your cameras and holding a shot of the action travelling nearly straight towards or away from the camera before cutting to the next shot. Another trick which you might use is to cut to a close-up of something like a road sign or a flag and then ask the cameraman to zoom out to show what's happening on the route. The close-up then acts as a buffer shot, but obviously you can't use this trick too often unobtrusively.

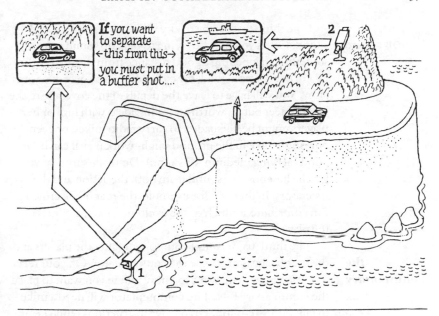

If you want to separate ←this from this→ you must put in a buffer shot....

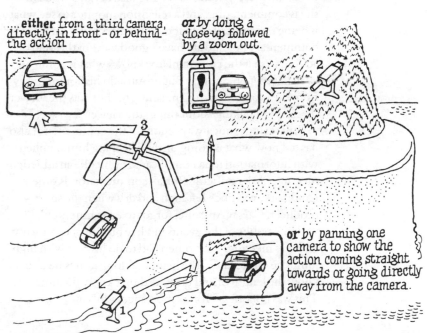

....**either** from a third camera, directly in front - or behind - the action

or by doing a close-up followed by a zoom out.

or by panning one camera to show the action coming straight towards or going directly away from the camera.

OB sound

One thing that can be tricky with OBs is getting good sound. Often you may be trying to pick up sound from something happening a good distance from the mike – the far corner of a polo field, for example, can be over 200 yards away. You will have to leave the details of the coverage to the OB engineer but it's worth swapping ideas with him or her: players might be persuaded to carry radio mikes, or even burying a mike in the ground might work (earth can be a good carrying medium for sound). Do make sure that you get the best possible sound from both the action and the spectators. In football, for example, the roar of the crowd can contribute as much to the excitement as the efforts of the players.

the commentary box

The third major sound component (after the players and the spectators) is of course the commentator. On your recce the OB engineer will want to know where you want to place the commentary box. The commentator will need a mike to talk into, ear-phones to receive instructions while he or she is commentating, and a television monitor to see what is being transmitted. A pair of binoculars is also useful. The commentary box should have a good view of the field of action, so that the commentator knows what is going on even if it isn't on camera. But he must do his commentary from the monitor, adding meaning to the shots the viewer sees and not talking about things the viewer can't see.

But seeing is not always enough; the commentator also has to know what is going on, and keeping him supplied with information for a complicated event like an athletic meeting can be difficult. Totta's commentator, Romeo Landmark, was once left high and dry when the sports producer, Caesar Andante, forgot to keep him supplied with the results of the events in a live broadcast of an army athletics meeting. So Romeo had to do his best with high jumps he didn't know the height of, long jumps he didn't know the length of and races he didn't know the times of. This was not one of Totta's most successful OBs!

SUMMARY
OUTSIDE BROADCASTS

Recces are essential for OBs. The OB engineer must go with you.

The engineer will want to know
— *date, time and duration of the event you want to cover*
— *where you want to do prize-giving ceremonies and interviews*
— *where you want the cameras*
— *where you want the commentary box.*

Remember to take into account where the sun will be when deciding where to put the cameras.

Make sure that none of your cameras has 'crossed the line' (the action as seen by all cameras should flow in the same direction).

Where it's impossible to avoid placing a camera on the wrong side of the action, arrange 'buffer' shots of the action.

OBs need a script and rehearsal just like studio programmes.

Make sure you can get good sound from the action and spectators.

The commentator should work to a monitor, but should also be able to see the action directly from his box. Work out how to keep him supplied with times, scores, statistics, judges' decisions and so on.

Publicity

You have now finished making the programme, but the
work isn't quite over. You still have to consider: is the
programme worth publicizing? The answer for all except
the briefest of magazine items should be 'Yes'.

A telephone call or note saying when the programme
will be shown is always appreciated by everyone who took
part. A feature article or at least an extra paragraph in the
listing magazines together with a photograph should not be
difficult to arrange. There is little to lose (and possibly a lot
to gain) in contacting the local newspapers and offering
them an interesting fact or two and a photograph but clear
it with your boss and/or station press officer. Or even
better, write a little item about the programme yourself
(they can always change it if they want to).

Of course the most powerful advertising medium of all
is right there in your own television station: make a short,
snappy trailer. And don't forget radio – they can be
surprisingly helpful, even though you might be considered
a competitor.

How to make better programmes

1. Don't skip too many of the chapters in this book, particularly the early ones: Ideas, Research, Recce, Treatment.

2. Make lots of programmes. Gain experience. Learn from your mistakes.

3. Watch other people's films and programmes and compare their approach with the way you would have tackled the same problems. Analyse their techniques: did they work or not? Why? Remember nothing happens in a programme which wasn't made to happen by someone. Could it have been done better?

4. Work hard at programme-making. There are so many things to do and so many ways of improving your final product that you can never afford to stop trying.

5. Enjoy making your programmes, and the chances are the viewers will enjoy watching them.

Briefings

You should now be familiar with the procedures set out
in the Basics part of this book and so have at your disposal
a plan of action for producing and directing a programme.
These Briefings take you a step further by looking at a
selection of topics in more detail.

Some of the material here could have been included
in Basics but wasn't because of the risk of overloading the
new producer with information. Some is of interest only
to those who already have a few programmes to their credit;
some of it is designed as a handy reference.

Use these Briefings in much the same way as you did
Basics. First skim through to get an overview – each
Briefing has a summary. Then go through in detail when
you are ready to explore a particular topic more fully.

Shot sizes

LONG SHOT
shows the whole body

MEDIUM LONG SHOT
cuts at the knee

MID–SHOT
cuts just below the elbow

MEDIUM CLOSE–UP
cuts at the armpits

CLOSE–UP
cuts just below the collar

BIG CLOSE–UP
*loses the top of the head and
often the chin*

The right words

The right words are important when you are talking to other television people. A camera, for example, can move in 12 different ways; it can also move as many as four at the same time, though this would be unusual. It's important therefore that the cameraman is given something more specific than 'Can you – er – point it over there?'

Let's start with the shot sizes.

1. The right words for shots
In addition to the standard shot sizes shown opposite, there is also a Very Long Shot (VLS) which, as the name implies, is even looser than the Long Shot.

These shot sizes vary slightly from place to place and change with time. Shots today are probably tighter than they used to be; if screens become larger, they may become looser again.

The shot sizes reflect the way we look at and talk to people. Lovers murmur sweet nothings in BCU. You might discuss a difficult problem with a colleague in MCU – but in MS with your boss. What happens if you change the sizes and have lovers conducting their affair in LS and you talking to your boss in BCU? Choose your shot size carefully; they convey a lot about relationships.

2. The right words for camera moves
Camera moves fall into two groups: moves over the ground and moves in the same position (see illustration on the next page).

The right words all end with 'to …' (except for 'elevate' and 'depress'). This is to remind you that it is important to

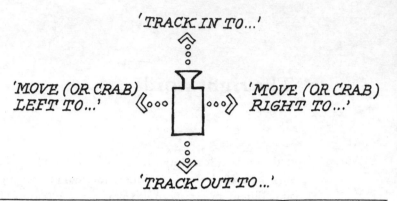

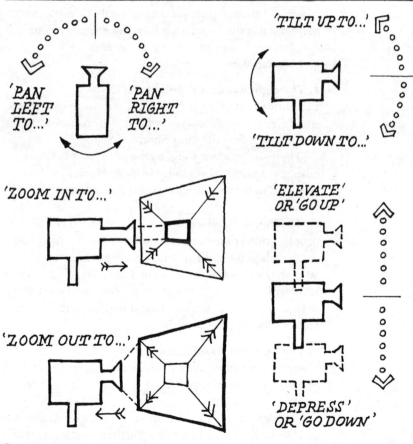

Camera movements

tell the cameraman the aim of the move ('Pan right to the photograph', 'Move left to bring the interviewee's head away from the flowers', 'Zoom in to a close-up of the statue'). If you don't specify what he or she should move to, the cameraman has to guess your intentions, and this is not a good way to direct. Of course you need only specify the aim of the move during rehearsal: during recording or transmission a reminder ('Pan right' or 'Zoom in') is all that is needed. If you want a camera move to stop, say '... and steady' or 'Steady it there'; the move will stop but the programme will continue. If you want everything to stop say 'Hold it' – not a good idea during recording or transmission, for obvious reasons!

'camera right' and 'camera left' If you are standing in front of a camera and facing it, your right and left are the opposite of the camera's. To avoid confusion, always use the camera's right and left and make it clear you are doing so by prefacing 'right' and 'left' with 'camera'. So you say 'Please clear the cable camera left' or ask an actor to 'Move camera right, please'.

3. The right words for sound

It's a good idea to let sound take their own cues during recording or transmission; it gives you one less thing to worry about. Obviously for this to happen, you have to explain what you want during rehearsal and also ask them to agree to take their own cues.

go sound If you do need to cue sound, the key word is 'go' – 'Go grams', or 'Go tape'. If you want something to come up gradually, say 'Fade up sound' and specify the speed during rehearsal: 'slowly', 'quickly', or 'very gently'.

At the beginning of a programme it always looks better if the sound comes up slightly before the picture. So start the sound first ('Go tape'); then bring up the picture ('Fade up 2'). If you want sound to stop whatever they are playing back, say 'Fade down sound', or 'Stop sound', or 'Lose sound'. At the end of the programme say 'Fade sound and vision'; once again it looks good if the sound goes first and the picture fades a fraction later.

4. The right words for VT and TK

run pictures

The key word is 'run' – 'Run VT' or 'Run TK' (TK stands for telecine, which is the machine used for film inserts). Don't mix up 'run' and 'go'. Picture operators react to 'run' and sound operators react to 'go' and using the wrong word leads to confusion.

If you have more than one machine allocated to your programme, you can mention the number of the machine ('Run VT3'), but in practice the operator will know from the rehearsal which machine you want. You should also have mentioned the number of the machine when you (or your assistant) asked the operator to stand by: 'Stand by VT3'. The operator replies to this and any other request by pressing the buzzer once for 'yes', twice for 'no'; obviously with this system he can't answer more than one question at a time. Acknowledge any message on the buzzer with 'Thank you, VT' (or TK). You don't usually have to stop VT or TK (they take their own cue) but if you do, just say 'Stop VT', or 'Stop TK'.

If you want the operator to go back to the beginning of his or her insert(s), say 'Reset VT' (or TK), specifying the insert if there is more than one. If you don't need TK or VT for part of the rehearsal, tell them so that they can relax – it's a strain staying alert over a long period in a noisy machine room.

5. The right words for lights

'Up lights', 'Down lights', 'Dim lights', or just 'Lights' (the lighting man should know what to do from the script and the rehearsal).

6. The right words for the floor manager

The floor manager is the director's representative on the studio floor: use him or her to convey instructions to staff who aren't on talkback, to show contributors to their places and pass on instructions to them, to organize props where you want them and so on. Resist the temptation to go onto the studio floor yourself. Your place is in the director's chair in the gallery, where you can keep in touch with everyone via talkback and they can speak to you.

cue and cut

During recording or transmission most of your instructions to the floor manager (usually known as the FM) are to do with cueing contributors. The words for this are straightforward: 'Cue Jack' or 'Cue Jill'. If you want to cut to someone as they start to speak, always say 'Cue and cut' in that order; the floor manager and speaker will take far longer to react than the vision mixer will take to cut and so there is no danger that you will miss the speaker's first words. But if you are mixing instead of cutting, say 'Mix and cue'. A mix takes time and you could miss the first words if you said it the other way round.

To close an interview you or the assistant usually say 'One minute to go', '30 seconds to go' and, with 15 seconds to go, 'Wind him (or her) up'. The floor manager signals this to the interviewer. Be careful not to cut to the interviewer while the floor manager is signalling to him or her.

If you want the floor manager to stop everything on the studio floor, say 'Hold it'. Once again, don't use this term to halt a camera move.

7. The right words for the vision mixer

By the end of the rehearsal the vision mixer should know as much about the picture cuts as the director. So for scripted programmes you don't need to call the cuts. For unscripted programmes and interviews you may need to call some of the cuts but – more important – you need to warn the vision mixer of what you have in mind. So get into the habit of saying which camera or what you want next ('Two next' or 'VT next' or 'TK next') followed, if necessary, by 'and ... two', or 'and ... VT', or 'and ... TK'. The 'and' should be a bit drawn out; the 'two', 'VT' or 'TK' should be said crisply, as that marks the point at which you wish to cut. This system also works with mixes, wipes, supers and so on. Simply say 'Mix to two next (pause); and ... mix'.

Some directors like to say 'Coming to two', instead of 'Two next'. Fine – as long as you are consistent. If you usually say 'Coming to two ... two', and then suddenly start saying 'Two next', you might get a cut on the 'Two'!

checking
ahead
You'll find the warning words – whichever formula you use – help you the director as much as they help everyone else. That's because saying 'Two next' reminds you to look at the monitor to check that camera two's shot is as you want it. You should get into the habit of checking ahead, even when your assistant is saying 'Two next' for you, as he or she would in a drama or any scripted programme. The monitor-checking habit will save you from many embarrassing mistakes: for example, cutting to a camera with the same size shot of what you already have on the screen, or cutting to a shot before it is in focus.

8. The right words for everyone
Some general points:

1. Who – what – when
There are at least a dozen people listening to you over the talkback and so when giving instructions you must always say first whom you are speaking to. 'Camera three – close-up on the hand, please', 'Sound – can we have the effects louder, please?'

Who – what – when is the order to follow when directing.

2. Stand by
'Stand by' are the words to alert people: 'Stand by TK', or 'Stand by studio'. But don't overuse it. Think how irritating it is for someone who has heard your first 'stand by' and is standing by to have to listen to you saying 'stand by' several more times. If it's TK or VT, they will have given you a buzz after your first 'stand by'; if it's a cameraman you are asking to stand by, he will be offering you the shot on his monitor or will nod his camera up and down in acknowledgment (shaking it from side to side means 'no'). One 'stand by' is enough! Repeating the order raises people's blood pressure, not their alertness.

3. Mark up your script
When you are directing you don't want to waste time looking for the next shot in the script. So write over the typewritten camera numbers and other instructions with

a pencil, using large letters that stand out. The vital information you need to stay in control of the programme should then catch your eye instead of you having to search for it. Another tip to help you keep your place in the script: don't follow it word by word as it is being read. You will never keep up.

Mark up your script Instead, put your finger on the words that cue the next shot change, memorize them and then carry on checking ahead on the monitors. When you hear the cue words, give the appropriate command (if any) and then slide your finger to the next cue words.

Telling you how to mark up your script and where to put your finger may seem unnecessarily bossy. Surely the typed script and common sense will be enough to see you through successfully? The answer is: they will – provided nothing unexpected happens. When something unexpected does happen, a director shows his worth, and a marked-up script and a finger in the right place show theirs: you always know exactly where you are on the page.

4. Breaks

If you interrupt a rehearsal for refreshment announce clearly the length of the break and the time for restarting. 'Ten minutes break, everyone. Restart at eleven.'

5. Starting the recording

When you have finished rehearsing or have run out of rehearsal time (usually the latter!), there's a procedure for starting the recording, which goes something like this (write it on your script):

'Stand by, everyone. We're going for a recording.'
'Start the recording.'

Wait for confirmation that the VT machine has run up to speed. The floor manager and the assistant in the gallery then start counting 'Ten, nine, eight …' The floor manager stops at 'three'. The assistant in the gallery continues 'Three, two, one, zero'. At 'three' the vision mixer cuts to the first shot if the recording is an insert, or to black if it is a complete programme. Just before the assistant says 'zero', the director starts the action with 'Go grams', or 'Take VT', or 'Cue Bess', or whatever.

You're off!

6. 'Please' and 'thank you'

A reminder about 'please' and 'thank you'. No one expects you to say them during the recording or transmission. Use them occasionally during the rehearsal, but not too often.

7. Ending the recording

At the end of the recording say 'Fade sound and vision. Stop the recording and check it, please.' Wait till the technical manager confirms that all is well with the recording. Then if there is no unfinished business (such as retakes or trailers), 'Thank you, everybody'. This is the signal for everyone to pack up and go. Don't forget to congratulate your contributors and everyone who has served you well before you go to the edit or start celebrating.

SUMMARY
THE RIGHT WORDS

For shots
- *very long shot*
- *long shot*
- *medium long shot*
- *mid-shot*
- *medium close-up*
- *close-up*
- *big close-up.*

For camera moves
- *track in/out to ...*
- *move (crab) right/left to ...*
- *pan right/left to ...*
- *tilt up/down to ...*
- *zoom in/out to ...*
- *elevate (go up)*
- *depress (go down)*
- *camera right/left (to identify sides)*
- *... and steady (programme continues)*
- *hold it (everything stops).*

For sound
- *go grams/tape or fade up sound*
- *fade down sound or stop sound or lose sound*
  fade sound and vision (at the end of the programme).

For VT and TK
- *run VT/TK*
- *stop VT/TK*
- *stand by VT/TK (one buzz means 'yes'; two buzzes, 'no').*

Don't mix up 'run' and 'go'.

For lights
- *lights*
- *up lights*
- *down lights or dim lights.*

∨

For the floor manager
- cue Jack
- one minute to go, 30 seconds to go, etc.
- wind him (or her) up
- hold it.

Always cue before cutting — say 'Cue and cut'.
But 'Mix and cue'.

For the vision mixer
- two next ... and ... two
- coming to two ... and ... two
- mix to two next ... and ... mix.

For everyone

When directing in the studio always follow the order
who — what — when.

One 'stand by' is enough.

Cameras nod up and down for 'yes', and shake sideways
for 'no'.

Write direction notes on the script BIG.

Keep your finger on the next cue words.

The occasional 'please' and 'thank you' are welcome.

Write procedures for starting and stopping the recording
on your script.

Technology for the non-technical

Some brains seize up at the thought of anything technical. Television technology is complicated, so the attitude is understandable. But the basic ideas that make television possible are straightforward enough to be grasped even by the most untechnical of people. At best you will begin to appreciate some of the satisfying ingenuities in the system. At the very least you will realize that not everything the technicians say and do has to be a closed book.

A first look at the system

Television is light. For colour television you need just three colours of light: red, green and blue. These are known as the primary colours; by mixing them together in different proportions you can create almost any colour you wish. The three colours together appear as white light; black is the absence of light.

chip cameras   Video cameras break up light into the three primary colours and focus each colour on to a CCD chip (CCD stands for *charge coupled device*). The chips convert the light from each element in the picture (from each pixel – the word is derived from *picture* + *element*) into an electrical charge. The charges from all the pixels are in effect a charge image of the scene before the camera. This charge image is passed to a storage layer in the chip, which is then read out to produce the television signal.

phosphors   The television set in each viewer's home receives the encoded signal and breaks it down into three separate signals, one for each primary colour. The screen is made up of many thousands of clusters of three phosphors, again one for each primary colour. These phosphors glow when they are struck by the beams from the electron guns in the tube, with each phosphor reproducing the same amount of primary colour that the camera found at that point in the original picture. Because the phosphors are so small and close together, the viewers' eyes blur them together into one picture, a picture almost identical to the one in front of the camera.

Encoding the signal

Let's start again with the camera.

Think of the camera as a device for converting light variations into electrical variations or signals. The colour camera then has four jobs to do: it has to produce a signal for red, a signal for green and a signal for blue. It also has to produce a signal for viewers in black and white – they couldn't just be abandoned when television began its move to colour in the '60s. In theory there is no reason why each of these four signals shouldn't be conveyed to the receivers separately – you could have four wavelengths, four cables or four cassettes each feeding one signal to the receiver. Plus an extra wavelength, cable or cassette for the sound.

It's easy to see that such a system would be cumbersome and expensive. It would also drastically reduce the number of channels that could be broadcast. The broadcasting part of the electromagnetic spectrum, which ranges from long waves (low frequencies) to UHF (very short waves and ultra high frequency), can only be divided into a finite number of bands and television has to compete with other telecommunication systems for its share.

How can you cut down the number of wavelengths – or bandwidth – five channels would need? One way of reducing it makes use of a peculiarity in human vision: our eyes are good at discerning detail in black and white but less effective when the detail is in colour. So we see the edges of blocks of colour as slightly blurred, which is why they look sharper if they are given a black edge. Blurred colour vision is one of the reasons that the dots of primary colour on the TV screen merge so easily into a complete picture.

So the camera converts the picture into two sets
of electrical signals: a black and white signal known as
luminance to convey all the detail, and a chrominance
signal to convey the colour information. Because of our
blind spot for colour detail the chrominance needs only to
be low definition – which makes it easier to combine with
the luminance signal. In fact television works like a careless
comic book artist. First it draws a detailed black and white
picture and then it roughly fills in the colour. If you freeze
an uncluttered picture on the screen and look carefully at
something with a hard outline like a nose in profile, you
can see this slapdash approach to colour at work: the colour
often visibly overlaps the outline.

luminance and chrominance

So four signals have been reduced to two: luminance
and chrominance. But how do you get a black and white
signal (the luminance signal) out of a camera with three
colour chips? The answer is to go back to first principles.

Red, green and blue light, as we have noted, appears
as white light. To produce the luminance signal the camera
adds up the output from its three chips, taking 30 per cent
from the chip dealing with red, 59 per cent from the green
chip and 11 per cent from the blue chip. The amplitude of
the signal varies with the brightness of the picture. A very
bright area of picture will produce a high luminance signal
(white); a dark area of picture will produce a low luminance
signal (dark grey or black). In this way the camera produces
a signal that defines all the shades of grey between white and
black. This is the signal we see on black and white receivers.
It is also the signal that defines the detail for colour viewers.
Engineers say the signal is compatible, which means that it
works for both black and white and colour receivers.

luminance signal

How does the camera arrive at the chrominance signal?
Not – as you might expect – by encoding the three colour
outputs separately. This would duplicate information that
is already in the luminance signal (red + green + blue =
white). Instead the camera produces signals for just two
colours, red and blue, chosen because they account for only
30 per cent and 11 per cent of white light and are therefore

chrominance signal

easier to include in the complete signal. The proportion for the third colour, green, can be worked out in the receiver by subtracting the values for red and blue from the luminance signal – in effect any brightness in the picture that isn't accounted for by the red and blue signal must come from the green. Red and blue are encoded as the values remaining after the luminance signal has been subtracted from the output of each colour chip. In other words they are encoded as two colour difference signals, which together make up the chrominance signal. It sounds complicated when written out in words but if you consider it as a set of equations it is easier to understand.

Encoding colour

- The camera adds the output of the three primary colours to produce the luminance signal: Y (luminance) = $0.3\,R$ (red) + $0.59\,G$ (green) + $0.11\,B$ (blue).
- It calculates $R - Y$ and $B - Y$.
- The receiver receives $R - Y$ and $B - Y$.
- It uses Y for black and white and detail and decodes $R - Y$ and $B - Y$ by adding Y: $(R - Y) + Y = R$, $(B - Y) + Y = B$
- Then $G = Y - R - B$

encoding

So the camera has reduced the four signals needed for colour television to two: luminance and chrominance. The next stage in the compression process – getting all this information into one video signal – is known as encoding and involves squeezing a reduced version of the two colour difference signals into the same space as the luminance signal. This usually works fine but in some circumstances the colour and luminance signals overlap and the receiver confuses the two signals. This is why you sometimes see oddities like strobing or false colours in tweed and herringbone materials, or patterns of dots in the coloured parts of the picture where the colour is most saturated. This coding system is designed to minimize these defects but they can sometimes still be seen.

All this information about brightness and colour will fail to reproduce a picture if the camera and receiver aren't

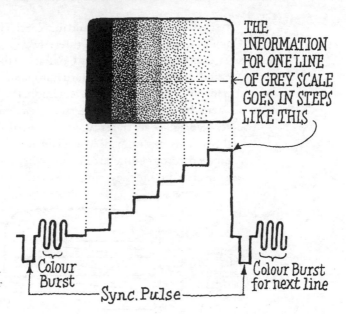

THE INFORMATION FOR ONE LINE ←OF GREY SCALE GOES IN STEPS LIKE THIS

Colour Burst

Colour Burst for next line

Sync. Pulse

The signal for one line of television picture

working exactly in sync with each other. So the signal for each line of a TV picture starts and ends with sync pulses, which give the signal the characteristic shape you may have seen on the technical manager's oscilloscope in the studio. The sync pulses cue the electron beams to fly back to begin a new line. With 625 lines being refreshed 25 times a second, there are 15 625 pulses every second.

There are three different systems of encoding in use: PAL, NTSC and SECAM. PAL stands for Phase Alternating Line. NTSC refers to the United States body that set the standard in 1953 – the National Television System Committee – and SECAM comes from the French initials for Sequential Colour with Memory (SECAM was devised in France). PAL and SECAM are normally 625 line systems; NTSC normally uses 525 lines.

PAL, NTSC, SECAM

The above is a very simplified version of how colour is encoded in the NTSC and PAL systems but it gives you an idea of their beautiful ingenuity. The PAL system is a refinement of NTSC and reproduces colours better because it averages out transmission errors over two lines. NTSC, the American and Asian standard, does not and therefore needs a hue control, with the result that the colours are far more variable

– NTSC is sometimes said to stand for Never The Same
Colour. PAL is blessed with Pictures Always Lovely and
SECAM with System Essentially Contrary to the American
Method. SECAM is used in Eastern Europe and the states
that formerly made up the Soviet Union. It works on
a system that is different from NTSC and PAL – its colour
difference signals are transmitted on alternate lines. None
of the systems are compatible so if you don't have the right
equipment, programmes from other systems will have to
be converted before they can be viewed.

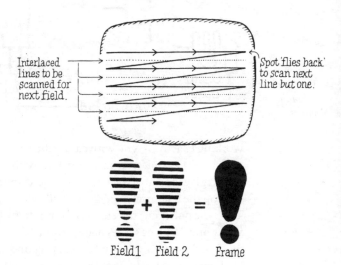

Interlaced
lines to be
scanned for
next field.

Spot 'flies back'
to scan next
line but one.

Interlacing

Field 1   Field 2   Frame

Two fields make a frame

Moving pictures are an illusion; video and film pictures
are in fact static. They appear to move because of a
phenomenon known as persistence of vision. Our eyes
continue to see a picture for a fraction of a second after it
has disappeared. If a second picture appears before the first
has faded, the brain merges the two. So the movement we
see on the screen is made up of a rapid succession of stills.

interlacing   The scanning rate of 25 frames a second is fast enough
to fool the brain into believing it is seeing movement on the
screen. But not fast enough to stop the eye seeing a flicker
between each frame. Film gets over this problem by

showing each frame twice. Television eliminates flicker
by a process known as interlacing: the picture is scanned on
alternate lines, first all the odd lines, then all the even lines.
Each alternate line scan is known as a field and is scanned in
one fiftieth of a second (half of a twenty-fifth); in the US it's
one sixtieth of a second (half of a thirtieth).

Each field of 625 line television has 312½ lines. Two
fields make a frame. The brain blends the fields together
just as it blends successive frames into each other. So
movement appears smooth on the screen and the flicker
once every fiftieth of a second is too fast for the eye to see.
Fields have another advantage: they use up less bandwidth.
In effect they give you the illusion of seeing 50 pictures a
second while occupying the bandwidth of 25 a second.

teletext

In fact not all the 312½ lines in a field are used for picture
information. The scanning beam needs time to fly back
to the top of the screen to begin a new field; it also needs
time to settle down when it gets there. So the beam doesn't
actually carry any picture information till about line 25 of
the first field and line 336 of the second. These spare lines
at the top of the picture can be used to transmit the digitally
coded information known as teletext. You can see the signal
as a narrow twinkling black and white band at the top of the
screen if you adjust the vertical hold on an old-fashioned
television to let the picture slip. To display teletext your
television needs a decoder to unscramble the signal. You
need a keypad to select the page you want from the index.

Video recording

It is difficult to think of television without videotape, but
for the first two decades of its history (from 1936 onwards)
there was no satisfactory way of recording electronic
pictures. Pointing a film camera at a picture tube was
the technique most often used. The telerecordings this
produced, however, were both expensive and poor quality.

The idea that you can record an electrical signal by
magnetizing a tape was developed into a practical device
for audio before the Second World War. It seemed an
obvious next step to develop this audio technology in order

to record the signal from a camera but the amount of information needed for pictures is so enormous that it proved a difficult problem to crack.

Magnetic tape is a plastic strip coated with millions of **writing and** tiny magnetic particles. If you pull this strip past the head of **reading** an electromagnet with a variable current passing through it, the particles are magnetized. This process – writing – turns the magnetic field on the tape into a record of the current that passed through the head. This copy can be read by reversing the process: in other words, using the magnetic field round the tape to re-create the variable current round a replay head. This is what happens when you play back the tape.

Using this technology to record the amount of information needed for pictures is not easy. Hi-fi audio needs a bandwidth of 20 hertz to 20 kilohertz. TV needs over 250 times this amount – an enormous range. This is reduced to a workable system by modulating the frequency on a carrier signal, which varies between about 5 and 15 million cycles per second.

Frequencies this high are difficult to record on tape. Its frequency response is limited by the speed of the tape past the head and by the size of the head, which has to be smaller than the wavelength or it won't be able to write or read each wave individually. You could increase the capacity of the tape by making the particles on the tape smaller and the recording head narrower, but again there's a practical limit: the magnets on the tape are already as fine as powder. So the only way forward is to make the tape pass the head more quickly – in other words, increase the writing speed. The arithmetic suggests that the tape needs to move past the head at a speed of at least 15m per second (54km an hour) to record information for pictures. The information for one hour of video therefore requires 54km of tape – about 1½ times the width of the Channel. It's clearly impractical to move that amount of tape that fast.

How do you get the tape past the head fast enough? **two-inch** First of all, you increase the width of the tape and record **format** the information across the tape (instead of along it). This

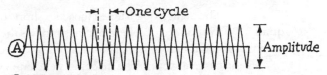

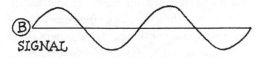

CARRIER WAVE
Unmodulated radio frequency (RF) carrier wave rising
and falling several million times (cycles) each second.

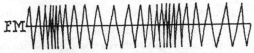

SIGNAL

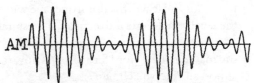

AMPLITUDE MODULATION
The amplitude of Ⓐ is modulated (changed) by Ⓑ.

FREQUENCY MODULATION
The frequency of Ⓐ is modulated by Ⓑ.

AM and FM

reduces the length of tape that has to be shifted. Then you
increase the writing speed by having more than one head
and moving the heads as well as the tape – this makes a
further saving on tape. The first practical videotape
(brought out by Ampex in 1956) had four heads mounted
on a drum spinning at 240 revolutions per second for 525
lines (250 revolutions for 625 lines). The 50mm (2 inches)
tape was drawn past the head at a speed of just over 38cm
per second – much easier to do than 15m per second.
This combination of tape speed and head speed produced
an effective writing speed of 137km per hour, just over
80 miles per hour. And an hour's programme would fit
comfortably on just 1400m of tape.

*Ampex's
memorable name
has nothing to
do with amps
but comes from
the initials of the
company's founder,
Alexander M.
Poniatoff, and the
first syllable of the
word 'excellent'.*

quad

The 2-inch quadruplex (quad for short) or transverse scan produced excellent pictures and was the standard format for professional broadcasting for 25 years. Only on base, however. The machinery and tapes were too large, heavy, and expensive for taking out on location (except in OB vans). Editing was also difficult and slow. Each cut took several minutes to do: the cutting point had to be located with a microscope and the tape had to be physically cut with scissors and then glued together again. It was unusual to do more than two or three cuts per programme!

C format

C format is the system that took over from quad. The tape on C format is wrapped round the drum containing the heads and leaves the drum one tape width higher than the level it first came into contact. This spiral-shaped path – or some variation of it – known as helical scan (after *helix*, the mathematical word for a spiral) is now standard for almost all video machines.

Helical scan made it possible for the designers of C format to simplify the transport of the tape and halve its width from 2 inches to 1 inch. The tracks are laid diagonally along the tape (quad tracks are laid across the tape) so they are longer and each track represents one complete field. This makes it possible to produce a still frame on screen even when the tape isn't moving – the two heads merely scan the same track over and over again. It's also possible to speed up or slow down action and/or show it backwards.

U-matic and Beta

C format 1 inch tape produced excellent quality but it was too bulky to be practical for use on location. Three-quarter-inch U-matic, which came in three versions – low band, high band and high band SP (Superior Performance), was the first format that made sense on location, but the real breakthrough came with the development of the ½ inch Betacam cassette, which was small and light enough to allow the recorder to be built into the camera. Enter the camcorder.

component and composite

Betacam also introduced component recording. In this type of video the luminance and chrominance signals are put onto the tape separately in parallel tracks. The chrominance signal, which carries the colour information, is compressed and recorded alongside the luminance signal and the two signals combined again on playback. This approach is radically different from previous formats, which used what is now known as composite recording, where luminance and chrominance signals are recorded as one signal already encoded in the appropriate standard (PAL, NTSC or SECAM).

digital formats The distinction between composite and component recording is a key one for the development of all formats since Betacam. When digital (see below) arrived, the first format, D1, was component. Component is better quality and easier to manipulate for compressing, graphic effects and so on. The snag is that the tape and hardware are more expensive and most existing devices in broadcasting are composite. So D2, the second digital format, is composite. D3 is also composite. The step forward is that it uses ½ inch tape (D1 and D2 are ¾ inch formats) which makes it suitable for camcorders and cheaper to manufacture and store.

There is no D4 – four is an unlucky number in Japan, (where most tape technology comes from), rather like 13 in western countries. D5 is component. In the long run, component is likely to be the universal standard. It is possible to decode composite into component and vice versa but you lose some quality – roughly the equivalent of going down a generation in an analogue format.

The pace of technical progress shows no sign of slackening. The latest wave of domestic and professional formats are all digital, recording on both ½ inch and ¼ inch cassettes. In due course the tape will disappear altogether and cameras will record directly on computer-style memories, as has already happened in non-linear editing machines.

Digital

The basic idea behind digital systems is not difficult. Take the illustration of the TV signal earlier in this chapter. The graph-like drawing at the bottom is an analogue representation of one line of the signal, a continuous line

being used to show something else, just as the hands on a
clock are a continuous representation of the passing of time.
If you wanted to describe the signal to a friend over the
phone you could ask him to get a piece of graph paper
and label the columns and rows with letters and numbers.
Then, if you arm yourself with similarly labelled graph
paper, you could phone through a value for each column,
thus enabling your friend to build up a picture of the signal
on his graph. The middle part of the signal, continuing
the colour information, wouldn't be a problem, but
the beginning and end of the signal, where there is more
detail, would be impossible to describe accurately
without splitting the columns into quarters or eighths.

**digital
characteristics**

You are in effect digitizing the signal. The important
features of this, or any digital system, are these.

1. The value for each column – each measurement or
sampling – stands on its own; it is what is known as discrete.
(Analogue is continuous).

2. The more frequent the sampling, the more accurate
the representation – as we saw when we had to split the
columns to convey the ends of the signal. Compact disc
(CD), which is a digital system, samples the sound it is
recording over 48,000 times a second.

**digital
copying**

Two advantages flow from these characteristics of a
digital system. The first is that copies are never more than
one step away from the master. This comes about because
digital systems reproduce not the master but the code for
the master. If you photocopy the diagram of the TV signal
and then photocopy that copy, each copy is a step further
from the original and the quality of the reproduction gets
worse every time it is copied. Your friend, however, could
pass on the numbers you gave him to another friend, who
could pass them on to another friend, and so on, as many
times as anyone cares to and everyone would end up with as
good a copy of the original as your friend. Representations
(analogue) get worse each time you copy them. A number
(digital) keeps its value, however many times you copy it.

The other advantage of a digital system is that it is all done by numbers and so is ideal for processing by computers. So you can use digital video effects (DVE) to manipulate the data for the picture in an infinite number of ways; or you can select the data for problem parts of the picture to alter or restore the colours.

megabits   Computers excel at performing great numbers of calculations on great amounts of data at great speeds. Digitally speaking, for each line of a standard picture you need 720 luminance measurements and 360 chrominance measurements for each of the two colour signals – that's 1440 measurements for just one line. To represent one frame (576 lines) you need – in round figures – 8 megabits (a megabit is a million bits). So for one second of moving colour picture (25 frames) you need about 200 megabits. The international standard transfer rate for digital TV is actually 270 megabits per second but this includes a lot of other information that is also needed.

The exact figures are complicated and vary but don't really matter for our purposes. What is important is the deluge of bit rate numbers you need for digital colour and the speed they have to be dealt with (the bit rate) – something over 20 million numbers a second. That's a lot of data to crunch, even for computers. The challenge is how do you compress the data without losing picture quality? Compression techniques take advantage of the fact that much of the information in a picture is either repetitive or predictable. So it is possible to reduce the bit rate very significantly. Digital Betacam works on a 2:1 compression ratio, which reduces the bit rate by about 50 per cent to about 100 megabits a second, with virtually no loss in quality. Videophones, which can get away with a far lower quality picture, use only a few kilobits a second (thousands as opposed to millions). Generally speaking, the higher the compression ratio, the lower the quality.

Unless you can improve the compression technique.

Compression

There are two approaches to compression. The first
approach, JPEG (Joint Photographic Experts Group), was
developed for stills and can offer high compression ratios
– but at the expense of quality. JPEG treats each picture as an
individual entity. This is important, because when it is used
for moving pictures, you can cut at any frame you want.

The other approach, MPEG (the Motion Picture Experts
Group) builds on JPEG techniques but reduces the bit rate
even more dramatically by using – among other things –
the fact that successive pictures contain very similar
information. If, for example, there is no camera movement,
the background in each frame of a shot will be virtually
identical. So instead of recording all the data for each frame,
the computer selects key frames and records only data
differences for the frames in between. The problem with
this is that you can't edit at any frame you choose because
the information for that frame may depend on a backward
or forward reference to a key frame. These problems apart,
MPEG compression makes it possible to broadcast hundreds
of digital channels via satellite and terrestrial transmitters
or cable.

SUMMARY
TECHNOLOGY FOR THE NON-TECHNICAL

A first look ...

All television colours can be made by some combination of the three primary colours – red, green and blue.

White is made up of 30 per cent red, 59 per cent green and 11 per cent blue. Black is the absence of light.

Cameras convert light into electrical signals, one for each primary colour. The signals are encoded in PAL, SECAM or NTSC and activate tiny phosphors on the viewer's screen to recreate the original picture.

Encoding the signal

The TV signal is encoded to reduce the number of channels – or bandwidth – required.

The luminance signal contains information for black and white and details; the chrominance signal (a combination of two colour difference signals) contains the colour information.

Twenty-five frames a second is fast enough to create the illusion of movement, but not fast enough to eliminate flicker. So each 625-line frame is split into two 312 ½ interlaced fields, sent at the rate of 50 a second. The fields create a flicker-free illusion of 50 pictures a second while occupying the bandwidth of only 25 pictures a second.

Teletext systems occupy unused lines at the start of each field.

Video recording

Recording pictures is much more difficult than recording sound because of the huge amount of information needed for pictures. Magnetic tape is designed to record and hold a magnetic pattern, which is written by the record head and read by the replay head.

V

Ampex's quad system used four heads on a spinning drum to record pictures across 2 inch tape. It was high quality but too cumbersome for location shooting.

C format recorders use 1 inch tape which is wrapped round a drum containing two heads (helical scan). The pictures are recorded diagonally across the tape. A field fits onto one track, making it possible to show a still frame.

U-matic formats, using ¾ inch tape, were the first practical location recorders.

Betacam recorders, using only ½ inch cassettes, are small enough to be built into the camera. Enter the camcorder.

Betacam also introduced component recording (luminance and chrominance are recorded as separate parallel tracks). Previous formats used composite recording (the signals are encoded before recording).

Component recording makes it easier to maintain the quality of pictures during post-production. The snag is that most existing machinery is composite.

Digital

Digital systems sample a signal thousands of times a second and record a separate value for each sample. The more frequent the sampling, the more precise the specification.

Numbers retain their value, however many times they are copied. So digital pictures don't get worse when they are copied. Analogue pictures deteriorate because their signals are continuous representations of — not specifications for — the original.

Computers excel at processing numbers very fast but the data needed for colour pictures is enormous. Compression systems (JPEG and MPEG) aim to make the job faster, easier and cheaper by taking advantage of the fact that much of the information in pictures is repetitive or predictable.

Chromakey

Have a quick look at the diagram on the next page. The
problem is: how do you put the person in the picture?
Answer: take a shot of the person, cut round the figure
and put the cut-out in the picture.

This, basically, is what you're doing when you use
chromakey (also known as colour separation overlay, or
CSO). You put the person in front of a camera in the studio
and colour the background blue – this is known as the
foreground shot. You superimpose this shot on a shot
of the picture (the background shot). This is done by
programming an electronic switch to cut from the
foreground to the background shot whenever it comes
across blue, thus combining the two shots into one.
And there's the person in the picture.

Let's look at the process in detail.

Basics

The background picture
This can be a painting, a drawing, a diagram or a set in the
studio. It can come from tape, film or an outside broadcast
camera or any source you want. It should be slightly out
of focus so that it looks realistic when combined with the
foreground shot; the best way to achieve this is to focus
on someone or something in the position where the
foreground person will be inserted.

The foreground person
This of course can be as many persons – or things – as you
like. The only limitation is that nothing you want in the
final, composite shot is blue because the chromakey switch

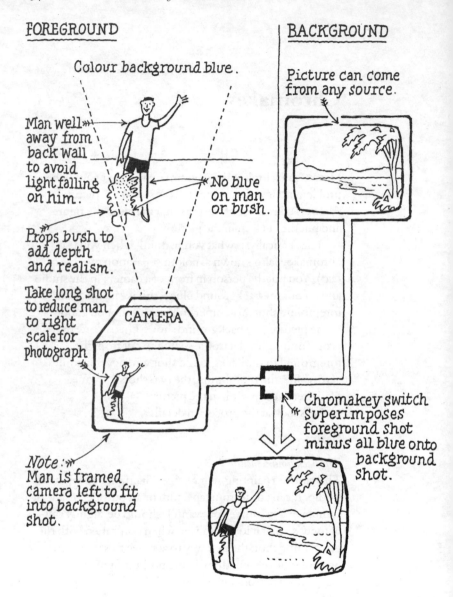

FOREGROUND

Colour background blue.

Man well away from back wall to avoid light falling on him.

Props bush to add depth and realism.

Take long shot to reduce man to right scale for photograph

No blue on man or bush.

CAMERA

Note: Man is framed camera left to fit into background shot.

BACKGROUND

Picture can come from any source.

Chromakey switch superimposes foreground shot minus all blue onto background shot.

Chromakey

will replace it with background picture. So warn people
not to wear blue shirts, suits or jewellery.

It can be difficult to get the lighting on the foreground
person to match the lighting in the background picture,
particularly if you are trying to light a person in the studio
to look like he or she is outside. Shadows in the foreground
shot are also a problem – both getting them to fall at the
same angle as the background shadows and getting them
to appear realistic in the composite picture.

It's a good idea to have props in the foreground set
to match things in the background picture: chairs, a vase
of flowers, a bush or tree for outdoor scenes. Positioned
carefully, these props add depth and realism to the
composite picture. Again, careful lighting is vital if
you want realistic results.

Blue

Blue is the colour most commonly used for the
disappearing bits in chromakey because the foreground
subject is usually a person and there is very little blue in
the various colours of skin. But there is no reason why you
shouldn't use yellow or green or any other colour as the key
to trigger the switch between foreground and background.
The key can come from paint, light, a curtain or a
combination of these. The important thing is to have a
strong, saturated colour that produces a good, clean signal,
making it easy to differentiate between the wanted and
unwanted parts of the foreground shot.

Let's assume you are using blue as your key. It's vital
then to keep all traces of blue out of the wanted parts of
the foreground. Blue reflections, for example, can cause
problems. Colours like magenta, which contains a lot of
blue, can also give trouble. If you are using coloured light
to supply the key, it has to be kept from spilling on to the
foreground subject, where it may produce a messy fringe
that is both noticeable and unattractive.

Vignettes

If you want the foreground subject to appear very small in the composite picture, you may have to move the camera a long way back and show more of the studio than can sensibly be covered with blue. In such cases it's possible to use an electronic wipe to produce a blue frame (sometimes known as a vignette) to hide the unwanted parts of the foreground shot. Getting the size of the foreground subject right in relation to the background can be tricky. If you are taking the background picture specially (and for a really convincing result you need to), plan the background and foreground shots before you do them, working out the exact camera positions, angles, height and the lenses. It's best to get specialist help to do this.

Beyond basics

Fringe problems

The most common chromakey problems occur at the switching point. The switch usually works fine if there is a hard, clean edge between foreground and background, but a hard switch can sometimes make the foreground subject look like it's pasted on to the composite picture when it should look part of it. A soft-edged transition between foreground and background may reduce the sparkly effect on the edges and produce a better result, particularly if there is fine detail at the transition such as wisps of hair. It may also be possible to get a more natural looking edge by using a device known as a fringe eliminator (or hue suppressor) which makes the fringes much less visible by replacing the blue areas in the foreground picture with black.

Linear key

Shadows, smoke and reflections are also tricky for chromakey because they contain a mixture of foreground and background and a switch must choose one or the other. In such cases it's possible to use a linear key, which instead of doing a straight switch between foreground and background uses the amount of blue in the foreground to control the amount of background in the composite

picture. In effect, the linear key performs a partial as
opposed to a complete switch. A linear key and a hue
suppressor can also be used together to produce convincing
results for transitions that are finely detailed or semi-
transparent (cigarette smoke) or insubstantial (a shadow).

Digital compositing
It's also possible to use digital technology to produce your
composite picture. This allows you to re-touch each frame
separately so that you get the best possible marriage of your
foreground and background material. But its scope is not
unlimited: you still have to make sure that the lighting,
perspective and focus in your sources will match when put
together. The technology is expensive and only available
as a post-production process, so you can't use it as live input
into a programme, as you can with normal chromakey.

There are a host of other ingenuities to extend what
you can do with chromakey, such as systems that link
foreground and background cameras so that you can move
them in unison, and techniques for making the foreground
person appear to walk behind something in the background
shot. Chromakey can get very complicated but don't be put
off using it. It's the standard method of putting a picture in
the screen behind the newsreader's shoulder. It's a cunning
way of transporting a presenter or actors to a location
beyond the reach of your budget. And it's also the basis
of most shots that make people wonder 'How did they do
that?'. To use it successfully you need three things: specialist
advice, careful planning, and plenty of time for each shot.

SUMMARY
CHROMAKEY

Chromakey (also known as colour separation overlay, or CSO) is an electronic switch that makes it possible to combine two shots into one.

The switch is triggered by a colour (usually blue) known as the key. The key colour in the foreground shot acts as a signal for the switch to select the background shot at that point.

The background shot can come from any source. The key colour can come from paint, light, a curtain, an electronic wipe or a combination of these. It's vital to keep the key colour out of the wanted parts of the foreground shot.

It takes skill, planning and time to match the lighting, shadows, scale and perspective in the foreground and background shots.

Most problems occur at the transition between foreground and background, particularly where the transition is finely detailed (wisps of hair), semi-transparent (cigarette smoke or glass) or insubstantial (a shadow). Given time and the right equipment these problems can be overcome.

Chromakey can tackle shots that appear to be beyond the limits of possibility, or beyond your budget. You need specialist advice, careful planning, and plenty of time for each shot to use it successfully.

Processing and editing film

In the early days of television everything outside the studio was shot and edited on film. There were two types of film: reversal and negative. Reversal was different from negative because the process didn't need copies. The roll of material you exposed in the camera was the roll you cut and used for transmission. You didn't make cutting copies and graded show prints as you do with negative, so reversal film was quick and cheap. But there were drawbacks: scratches acquired during editing were often visible on air, the joins sometimes snapped during transmission, and if you needed copies they were expensive and not very good quality.

Videotape has taken over from reversal. It needs no processing and it's probably cheaper (if you don't think too hard about the cost of all that advanced editing technology). You can copy it easily and   if it's digital – as often as you want without loss of quality. You can transmit it direct by satellite or cable. Scratches and join snaps are history.

Video, however, hasn't replaced negative, which can pleasantly reproduce a far greater range of contrasting light and dark on screen. Negative also scores on colours: the harmony and subtlety of the shades delivered by photographic chemistry (as opposed to video physics) keep film as the preferred medium for prestige productions.

Negative's path from camera to screen is illustrated overleaf.

Instead of following this path from neg to show print you can transfer your neg to video, edit your rushes on film and do the 'neg-cut' (as it were) on video. Or alternatively you can do all your editing on video, using a NLE (non-

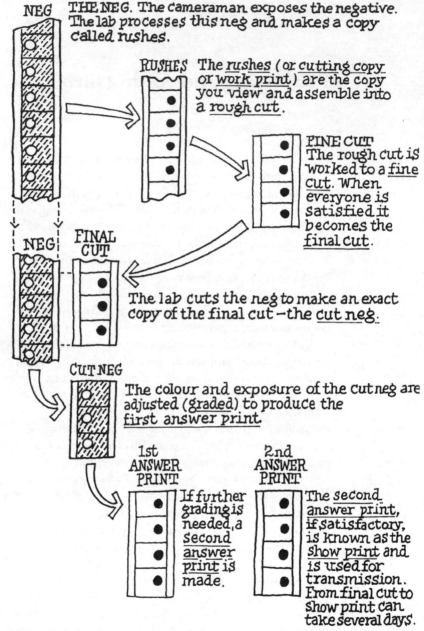

NEG

THE NEG. The cameraman exposes the negative. The lab processes this neg and makes a copy called rushes.

RUSHES The rushes (or cutting copy or work print) are the copy you view and assemble into a rough cut.

FINE CUT The rough cut is worked to a fine cut. When everyone is satisfied it becomes the final cut.

NEG **FINAL CUT**

The lab cuts the neg to make an exact copy of the final cut — the cut neg.

CUT NEG The colour and exposure of the cut neg are adjusted (graded) to produce the first answer print.

1st ANSWER PRINT If further grading is needed, a second answer print is made.

2nd ANSWER PRINT The second answer print, if satisfactory, is known as the show print and is used for transmission. From final cut to show print can take several days.

From neg to show print

linear editing) system to preserve the flexibility you have with film editing. Video editing was discussed on pages 103 to 120; the following section applies only to film.

Editing film: Preliminaries

the equipment

The equipment for editing film couldn't be simpler: a machine to view it, blades to cut it and some sticky tape to join it. Most cutting rooms have two viewing machines: a flat-bed called a Steenbeck, and a pic-sync that can take more sound tracks than a Steenbeck and is easier to

Joiner >

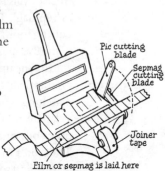

cut on. The blades and sticky tape are fixed on a gadget called a joiner; this has guide teeth that fit into the sprocket holes to hold the film in the right place for the cuts. Picture cuts are made at right-angles between frames; sound cuts slope to smooth the transition from one sound to another.

This simple technology has provided non-linear editing for decades – it's much older than the phrase. It offers total flexibility. You can cut picture or sound together or separately wherever and in whatever order you wish. As a result, film editing is an evolutionary process: you start with a rough assembly of shots and then cut, trim, reorganize and recut until you have a fine cut you are happy with.

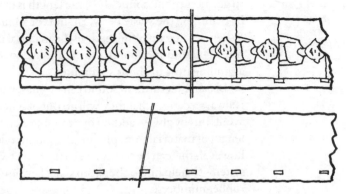

Picture is cut at a right-angle between frames; sound is cut at a slope to smooth the transition

sepmag

Before you can start cutting, however, your material has to be prepared. The sound is transferred from digital or ¼ inch tape on to a 16mm stock (the same size as the film stock) – this is the separate magnetic track, usually known as 'sepmag'. This track is taken from the transfer suite to the cutting room for 'syncing' (synchronizing) with the rolls of picture rushes from the processing laboratory.

syncing up

To sync up material the editor (or more usually, the assistant) lines up the sync mark on the picture roll with the matching sync mark on the sound roll. The marks may be a clap from the clapperboard, time code or an electronic blip. The editor marks the points on picture and sound with a wax pencil and then winds through to the sync marks for the next shot. The aim is to line up all the sync marks on both rolls so that each pair of marks goes through the machine at the same time and the complete rolls are therefore in sync. To do this

Pic-sync >

Spools for stock

Sound tracks

Picture

Viewing screen

the sound and picture for each shot have to be exactly the same length; this doesn't happen automatically because camera and sound don't switch their machines on and off at exactly the same time during the shoot. The adjustment to get picture and sound the same length is made either by trimming the waste between shots or adding spacing. When syncing up is finished, all the material is in matching rolls of picture and sound, usually about 2000ft each, giving a running time of about 50 minutes.

Because picture and sound can be cut separately there is always a danger that they will go out of sync. The editor avoids this by always adding or dropping exactly the same length of material from picture and sound rolls. At times, however, this can be tricky and so there are two other systems to help him or her keep sync: key numbers and rubber numbers.

key numbers

Key numbers are built into the edge of the negative – they are also known as edge numbers. They print through automatically when copies are made and so are there whether you want them or not. They are mainly used by neg cutters to match the master negative with the cutting copy.

rubber numbers

Rubber numbers are added later, after the material has been synchronized and before editing begins. The numbers are printed on the edge of the picture and sepmag and provide an accurate, easy way to get picture and sound back in sync if for any reason they have come adrift. Both

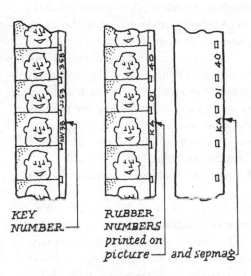

key and rubber numbers can be used to reunite short pieces of material with their neighbour, provided the short piece has a number on it. So don't throw away trims or bits of shots before you have finished editing – they can come in useful in surprising ways. I remember an out-of-focus shot of a surgeon leaning over an operating table that worked beautifully as the point of view of his patient drifting away under the anaesthetic.

KEY NUMBER

RUBBER NUMBERS printed on picture and sepmag

Editing film: Procedures

add overlays last

Look again at the chapter about editing. The sections that apply to both film and video are the opening, preliminaries and checking your edit. There's one point to add that applies specifically to film: when editing an interview, select the cutaways and any shots you want to use for overlay but don't ask the editor to put them in at once. The reason is that if he or she puts them in before you have finished editing and you decide later to shorten the interview, the editor has a lot of extra work unpicking the overlays and

then recutting to make them fit again. Remember also
– before the overlays go in – to make the non-sync or
out-of-vision (oov) sound flow as smoothly as possible by
shortening excessive pauses and cutting out 'ums' and 'ers'
and repetitions.

As with any editing, don't be frightened to review,
rethink and recut to make the best possible use of your shots
and produce the best possible programme. The work you
put in now will benefit both the film you are working on
and future programmes, because you are finding out what
you should have shot and what editing can deliver. You may
also be lucky enough to experience that satisfying buzz of
excitement when two shots – or a sequence, or the whole
film – mesh together and make an impact on screen.
Pictures and sound have huge power when the mix is right.

When you have finished editing you will probably have
to show the programme and read out a first draft of the
commentary to someone senior. You should accommodate
any suggestions for changes – how many suggestions you
take up depends on you, your senior and the relationship
between you. Then do a final check by viewing the
programme one more time. If all is well, you have arrived
at the final cut.

**laying
commentary as
a sound track**

It's now time to get to work on the final draft of your
commentary. The most reliable way of ensuring a snug fit
between words and pictures is to record the commentary
wild (without the pictures in front of the reader) and have
the editor lay it as a separate sound track. If you decide to
use this method. write the commentary in the normal way
so that it fits the picture, check it against the picture and
then show the reader the commentary and the programme
before the recording so that he or she understands how
words and pictures relate.

The editor lays the recorded commentary to the picture,
lengthening or shortening the pauses and occasionally
trimming the picture so that words and picture fit each
other exactly. But don't let this technique become an
excuse for writing the commentary first and then trying

to fit the pictures to it – 'painting' them in. For effective
programme-making the picture must always come first.

The adjustments to fit the commentary (if you have
recorded it wild) should be the last changes to the fine cut.
The editor still has a lot of work to do to get ready for the
dub: splitting the sound tracks, finding and laying extra
sound effects, checking the tape joins and so on. Don't go
back to the editor with ideas about changing sequences or
trimming shots or you will make his or her job impossible.
It's too late for second thoughts.

SUMMARY
PROCESSING AND EDITING FILM

Negative's path from camera to screen
- the neg is exposed in the camera
- the lab processes the neg and produces rushes
  (the cutting copy or work print)
- you edit the rushes into a rough cut, then a fine cut,
  then a final cut
- the lab cuts the neg into a copy of the final cut
- the lab then prints a graded answer print
- this print (or a second graded print) becomes the
  show print.

Editing film

Film editing is evolutionary: you cut and recut until
you're happy.

Sound is transferred to sepmag. Picture and sound for each
take are then put in sync and made up into matching rolls.
Key numbers and rubber numbers provide regular sync
points to help keep the rolls in sync.

Put cutaway and overlay shots in last. Edit OOV sound
to make it run as smoothly as possible.

To get a snug fit between words and pictures record
commentary wild and then lay it to picture as a separate
sound track. Make sure the commentary fits before you
record it.

Lighting

If you had to choose the single most important thing about pictures you would be well advised to choose light. Pictures are records of the way light falls on a subject; cameras are devices for capturing light; transmitters, cables and cassettes distribute particulars about light; television sets reproduce light. So as a programme-maker you have to be aware of light because that is the raw material of your craft.

It's a pity therefore – as light is so basic a requirement – that television is not happy with most of the light that surrounds us every day. Our eyes and brain focus on what we want to look at and we pay little attention to the lighting. You could say we see what we want to see and ignore the rest.

The camera can do no such thing. It records the lighting along with the action and on screen it's obvious if the lighting doesn't make a good picture. So lighting for the camera has to be more precise than ordinary lighting. Most indoor lighting, designed for the human eye, is disappointing on screen. Landscapes can also look flat and uninspiring; sunlight is not designed for the camera and you can't give nature a helping hand by relighting a whole landscape. When you are faced with this sort of problem, try speaking nicely to the cameraman to see if he or she wouldn't mind getting up early next morning for the shot – the dawn light will make the view so much more interesting on camera ...

For most indoor locations, however, you are very much in the business of modifying the light to make it look better on television. The situation you will come across most often is the basic single-camera interview. The simplest way to light the interviewee is to shine a light straight at him or her from the front, rather like the flash on a stills camera. The result is pure Totta: a washed-out face devoid of detail with a thick black shadow on the wall behind. News editors sometimes have to accept this sort of picture for their bulletins but they should do so only reluctantly and then ask questions. Other producers should never accept it at all.

No, there is more to lighting than just providing enough to record a picture. It's also an art, and it's very much the art of the cameraman. Not so long ago (before titles became inflated) directors of photography in the film industry were known as lighting cameramen – that's how important the top craftsmen think lighting is. So once you have decided with the cameraman where to do the interview and discussed the mood you want to establish, give him or her some time to light it.

lighting an interview
While this is going on, let's look at the usual approach to lighting an interview. This is to use three lights: a key light, a filler and a back light. The key light goes in front of the interviewee on the same side of the camera as the interviewer. It stands in for the sun, so it shines down on the interviewee at a 45 degree angle and is usually a hard light, casting distinct, hard-edged shadows that emphasize the features of the face. The side of the face furthest from the key will now be comparatively dark – this is where the filler comes in. Its job is to fill in the hard-edged shadow thrown by the key without producing a shadow of its own. So the filler is a soft light, casting a soft-edged, indistinct shadow. The back light is then placed to one side and behind the interviewee to make him or her stand out from the background and give a little extra sparkle to the hair.

This is the usual approach to lighting an interview but there are as many variations as there are cameramen and situations. Some cameramen use hard lights only, some like to bounce lights off the walls and ceilings, some take white umbrellas on location to act as reflectors. Most cameramen will try and base their setup on the lighting that's already on

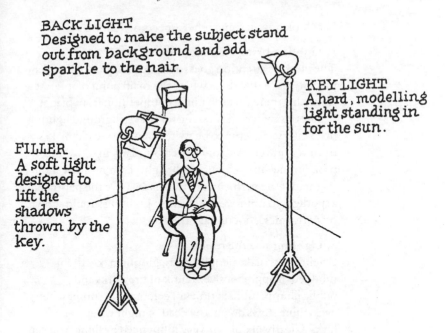

BACK LIGHT
Designed to make the subject stand out from background and add sparkle to the hair.

KEY LIGHT
A hard, modelling light standing in for the sun.

FILLER
A soft light designed to lift the shadows thrown by the key.

Lighting an interview   the location – using, for example, the daylight coming through a window as the key. All these approaches are related (some only distantly related) to the basic key/filler/ back combination.

Your job is to decide whether you like the lighting and whether it fulfils your requirements. Look at the monitor (if there is one) or ask the cameraman if you can look through the eyepiece. If you can't do either of these, look at the scene through half-closed eyes. The contrast between light and dark is emphasized and you will see bright patches and gloomy patches that you hadn't noticed before. Look in particular at the shadows on the interviewee's face. Are the eyes lost in pools of dark? Is the nose shadow reasonably unobtrusive? Do you want lines and wrinkles clearly defined or would something more flattering be in order? If the interviewee is wearing spectacles, do the shadows from the frames obscure the eyes? When you have considered the face, look at the background: is it interesting without being distracting? If you see anything you are not sure about, discuss it with the cameraman.

Let's look now at some other aspects of lighting.

1. Lighting brings out highlights

The viewer's attention goes to the lightest part of the scene first. So make sure that's where the main point of interest is and that there isn't too much competition from bright patches elsewhere. Try asking for the background lighting in an interview setup to be switched off to see if it makes the interviewee stand out better. Similarly in show-biz programmes an excess of bright lights flashing all over the set can put the performer in the shade. Give the performer a spotlight to improve the balance. Lighting should show off performers, not upstage them.

2. Lighting sets the mood

Bright lights make people happy, gloom makes them subdued or apprehensive. Think of fireworks and public illuminations at times of celebration, sunset when everything slows down, the dead of night when danger lurks. Clearly people are very influenced by light. You can profit from this, as it provides you with a second short cut to the viewer's feelings (the first short cut is music). So try and define what element in the scene you want to emphasize; in a location interview, for example, you may want to highlight an official's business-like approach to problems (brighter light called for) or his sympathetic consideration of the public's best interests (more gentle lighting would be suitable). Define the mood you want and light accordingly.

3. Lighting gives depth

The screen is two-dimensional; life is three-dimensional. Careful lighting helps restore the third dimension to television. If a set is lit evenly throughout with few shadows, there will always be enough light on the performers, wherever they move. But the picture will look flat, uninteresting and unnatural. In real life there is dark as well as light. Introduce some shadows and you give the scene depth, as well as interest.

4. The source of light

There are occasions when highlights, mood and depth seem fine but there's something that is still not right about the picture. This is the time to think about the source of light.

When you are outdoors, the sun is the source of light and you have one shadow. When you are indoors, there may be several sources giving you several shadows and if they all appear to be equally important, the effect can be messy. So discuss with the cameraman where the main source of light should be. If there's an obvious light source in the picture, like a window or a standard lamp, the lighting should appear to come from these visible sources; in other words, the side of the face farthest away from the window or the lamp should look less brightly lit. The viewer then sees that the lighting has an apparent source and it makes sense and will appear right. If you don't have an obvious light source in the picture, you are free to pick whatever direction you want for your apparent source of light.

5. Colour temperature *(See chart on following page)*

Daylight is bluish, artificial light is yellowish. We normally aren't aware of the colour of light because our eyes and brain smooth out the differences. The colour can be measured in degrees on a Kelvin scale, where 0 = absolute zero, or -273.16 Celsius. This number is known as the colour temperature. Daylight in the UK, for example, has a colour temperature of about 5600 degrees Kelvin.

6. White balance

Cameras, unlike the human eye, can't ignore the colour temperature difference between daylight and artificial light, which is why you need to do a white balance every time the type of light changes. This is a procedure for establishing the mix of red, green and blue needed to reproduce white – think of it as fine-tuning the camera to the prevailing light. If the fine-tuning is wrong, the colours that arrive on the screen will be wrong. You will be able to correct some – but not all – of the damage by electronic filtering but as always, it's better to get things right to begin with rather than rely on imperfect remedies.

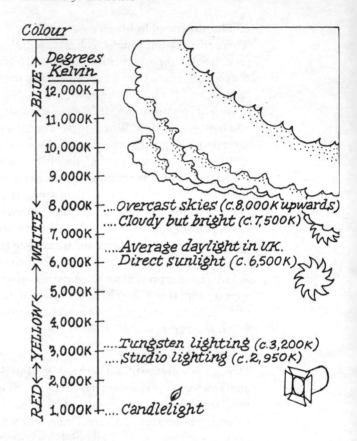

Colour
temperature

Colour

Degrees
Kelvin

12,000K

11,000K

10,000K

9,000K

8,000K ....Overcast skies (c.8,000k upwards)
....Cloudy but bright (c.7,500k)

7,000K

....Average daylight in U.K.
6,000K   Direct sunlight (c.6,500k)

5,000K

4,000K

3,000K ....Tungsten lighting (c.3,200k)
....Studio lighting (c.2,950k)

2,000K

1,000K ....Candlelight

BLUE ↑ ← → WHITE ← → YELLOW ← → RED

7. Mixed light

If you have a scene lit partly by daylight and partly by
artificial light, the camera can't be correctly adjusted for
both types of light at the same time. The way round the
problem is to put blue filters on the lamps so that the
artificial light matches the bluish daylight (your eyes won't
notice much difference, but the camera will). Putting filters
on lamps is not difficult to do, but it takes a little time. It also
cuts the amount of light coming from the lamps, which in
turn restricts the area you can light effectively. Alternatively,
the cameraman can filter the daylight by putting orange
filters on the windows, but this again takes time and lowers
the general light level.

So if you're in a hurry, it's a good idea to find a way round the mixed light problem. The most usual dodge is to draw the curtains or drop the blind, thus excluding direct daylight from the room and the picture. Or you can use an HMI light, which is a type of light with approximately the same colour temperature as daylight. (HMI are the catchy initials for the distinctly uncatchy name *hydrargyrum medium iodide*). Or you can move your scene into a corner of the room where there isn't a window.

8. Studio lighting

Studio lighting is at once easier and more difficult than lighting on location. It's easier because the average television studio has a large number of lights available (on location the usual problem is that you don't have enough). It's more difficult because most studio work is done in a continuous sequence and so you can't reset the lights for each shot.

Studio lighting therefore is usually a compromise between the demands of different shots. As producer you can help by keeping your performers away from the walls of the set and from overhanging bits of scenery (both features make it difficult to get lights behind the performers); by making sure the sets are not too cramped to be lit; by knowing what you want from the lighting, and, above all, by being able to tell the lighting supervisor at the planning meeting exactly where your performers will enter, where they will move to and where they will exit. Don't forget the sound supervisor: the most usual problem is finding a way of keeping the shadow from the sound boom out of shot.

Finally, get into the habit of looking at the light around you – outdoors and indoors, at dawn, dusk and noon, on sunny days and cloudy days and days which are not quite either. Half close your eyes to see how much detail the camera would miss. Think about what the light is doing to the scene in front of you and how the scene would change if the light changed. Don't forget to look at the light in other programmes and films, in photographs and paintings. And don't forget also to look at the shadows – they contribute creatively as much as the light. The art of lighting for the camera is also the art of shadows.

SUMMARY
LIGHTING

Normal everyday light is OK for eyes, not so good for TV. You usually have to accept normal light outdoors. Indoors you can and should modify the available light to produce attractive pictures.

Hard light has distinct, hard-edged shadows, soft light has indistinct, soft-edged shadows.

Interviews are usually lit using a
- *key light (hard) to bring out facial features*
- *filler (soft) to lighten the shadows on the side of the face furthest from the key*
- *back light (hard) to give depth and add sparkle to the hair.*

Check lighting by considering
- *highlights: does the lighting draw the viewer's attention to where you want it?*
- *mood: does the lighting hit the right note?*
- *depth: does the lighting make your picture 3D?*
- *source: does the lighting have an apparent source?*

Mixed light
Daylight is bluish, artificial light is yellowish. If you have mixed light in your scene the cameraman will have to fix filters on the lamps or over the windows. This takes time, cuts light output and restricts the area that can be lit. You can avoid this by drawing the curtains, using an HMI lamp or moving the scene away from the window.

Studio lighting
Studio lighting has to be planned in detail because there isn't time to reset the lighting between each shot. Help the lighting supervisor by
- *keeping artists away from walls and overhangs*
- *ensuring sets are not too cramped*
- *knowing where artists will enter, move and exit*
- *knowing what you want.*

Help the sound supervisor keep boom shadows out of shot. Learn to appreciate light by observing it – and the shadows it throws.

Sound

Close your eyes and listen to the sounds around you. First listen to the loudest noises and think where they are coming from. Then disregard them and listen to the most distant sound you can hear (birds? traffic? aircraft?). Then after a while come in closer and concentrate on the sounds immediately around you (radio or TV sets? people talking? rumbling pipes?). Finally, try and shut out all these sounds and listen to your own body. Can you hear yourself breathe?

You have just done what no microphone can do: discriminate between sounds. Your ears, like your eyes, can be directed by the brain to concentrate on some sounds and disregard others (think how you can single out one voice among many at a crowded party). Mikes, on the other hand, can't discriminate. They're more like fishing nets, hauling in all the sound that falls within their range. The shape and size of their nets differ; so choosing the right mike is important if you want a good recording. The choice is one of the responsibilities of the sound recordist, who knows what each mike can do.

Types of mike

There are four basic types of mike. One type will net sound from any direction: these mikes are known as omnidirectional. Another type will net sound from the front and the back of the mike (but not from the sides): the figure-of-eight mikes. A third type will cover a wide, heart-shaped area in front: cardioid. And the gun mike, the most common mike on location, accepts sound from the direction it is pointing and rejects all but the loudest noise from the sides. It belongs to the category known as hypercardioid.

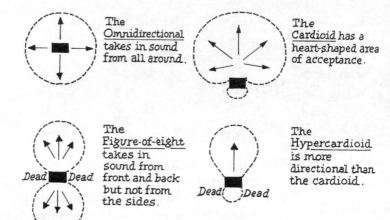

The Omnidirectional takes in sound from all around.

The Cardioid has a heart-shaped area of acceptance.

The Figure-of-eight takes in sound from front and back but not from the sides.

Dead   Dead

The Hypercardioid is more directional than the cardioid.

Dead   Dead

Four types of mike

gun mikes (hypercardioid)

Within these categories mikes have particular advantages and disadvantages. The gun mike is marvellous for excluding unwanted noise from the sides. But it is so narrowly directional that if it isn't pointed exactly at what you want to hear – your interviewee, for example – it will miss the target and give you a dutiful recording of the traffic in the background with your interviewee's voice featuring as an off-mike accompaniment.

The short gun mike is the one you see most often, but there is also a long version. This is more directional than the short, a specialist mike you can sometimes spot positioned at regular intervals round sports fields to provide close-up sounds of athletic effort or balls being kicked or hit. Long gun mikes also come into their own in wildlife programmes when you are filming animals that prefer to keep their distance.

personal mikes (omni-directional)

The personal mike, which clips on to a jacket or tie, is fine for static interviews. The mike itself is tiny and considered acceptable in vision but the accompanying cable is not so unobtrusive and is best hidden behind a jacket or inside a shirt or blouse. If it's impossible to hide the cable, or if you want your subject to be able to walk around while talking, it's better to use a gun mike on location and a mike on a boom in the studio. The personal mike will also have problems if clothes rustle or jewellery tinkles – or if the speaker goes in for breast-beating. Don't use it for histrionic confessions!

hand mikes (omni-directional)
Handheld mikes give performers more freedom to move around but you should let your performers rehearse with them before using them on camera. Hand mikes pick up sound from a small area only so they need to be held close to the source of the sound. It takes a few minutes' practice to find the best place to hold them and the best way of managing the cable.

radio mikes
Both personal mikes and hand mikes are often linked with a tiny radio transmitter that is strapped under the performer's clothing (usually in the small of the back). The hand mike also comes in a version known as a radio stick, where the transmitter is built into the handle. All these mikes allow the performer to move round freely; they also let the director use whatever shot he or she wants. There are no cables to worry about and the recordist can be a good distance away with the receivers and recorder. The only limitation is the range of the transmitter, which is usually several hundred metres. Radio mikes are equally effective in the studio or on location – provided there is no interference from radar installations, transmitting stations, nearby power cables or local transmitters on the same frequencies.

sound perspective
Radio mikes raise a topic that is worth thinking about – the perspective of sound. With a radio mike it's possible to see someone in long shot and hear their voice in close-up. If you are shooting someone climbing a cliff, this effect can be dramatic. But what do you do with a terrified fugitive looking for somewhere to hide in a deserted warehouse (close sound appropriate) who is then attacked and shouts for help? Do you want to hear his shouts close or echoing in the distance? There is no right answer to this question. But don't forget that whenever you do a long shot, you have a choice of perspective. If you have to make a choice on the spot and are not sure what to do, record the sound close. You can always make it sound more distant in the dubbing theatre.

mikes in shot

In practice a lot of the time you spend on sound will be taken up worrying about keeping mikes and mike shadows out of shot. Any appearance of a mike or mike shadow on screen in a drama programme will make the shot unusable. In other programmes the convention is that mikes on stands (either on tables or on the floor), hand-held mikes and personal mikes are acceptable in shot. Mikes operated by the sound recordist (boom mikes and gun mikes) are not. Making sure that the recordist can get the mike in close enough without getting it in shot can be tricky. Don't worry if the mike keeps dipping in and out of the picture while you are setting up a shot on location or in the studio. It's just the recordist establishing how close the mike can go without being seen on camera. But if the mike is still in shot when you are about to start recording, alert the recordist.

camera mikes

One mike that is never in shot is the mike that is on (or in) the camera. It may be good quality but with mikes, good quality is not enough. To get good sound, the mike must also be in the right position and a camera-mounted mike is only occasionally in the right position. If you are using it to record a person, for example, he or she should be reasonably near the camera, looking roughly in its direction and there shouldn't be too much surrounding noise – in other words, conditions should be ideal. If they aren't, you will get a less than ideal recording. This could make your shot useless, as viewers will tolerate poor pictures more readily than poor sound. Use camera mikes to record non-specific sound for general shots, sound that can be replaced if there is a problem. They can't be relied on to deliver high-quality recordings of the sync speech and effects you need for your programme.

One other problem with camera-mounted mikes: some of them pick up noise from the motor working the zoom. The cameraman can get round this problem by operating the zoom manually but this can be difficult to do if he or she isn't used to it and under pressure to get the shot.

wild tracks

The recordist will want to do a wild track of the background noise on each location – the editor needs this to cover any awkward gaps in the track. 'Wild' means non-synchronous: the sounds are not in sync with any picture. Every location has its own distinct background sound, sometimes no more than a hum. It takes far less time to record it on the spot than look for a matching sound on disc or concoct one in a dubbing theatre.

With film, where the sound is recorded on a separate piece of tape; you can run the recorder without running the camera and make a track that is truly 'wild'. With video you have to run the camera to record sound, so while the wild track is being done, it makes sense to record a picture anyway – a general shot of the view or a road or an interesting detail in a room. It's surprising how often these wild track shots come in useful during the edit.

Stereo

There are two approaches to recording stereo: A + B and M + S. For A + B two mikes fixed at right angles to each other record sound to the right and left with the overlap between them looking after the sound in the middle. The M | S approach also uses two mikes. The middle one is a directional mike (usually a cardioid) and picks up sound from the front; the side mike (usually a figure-of-eight) picks up the sound from the sides.

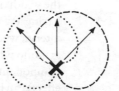

The A+B approach – usually two cardioids at right angles.

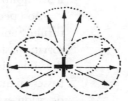

The M+S approach – usually M (the middle mike) is a cardioid and S (the side mike) is a figure-of-eight.

Stereo mikes > Both approaches produce a pair of signals that can be manipulated in various ways to produce a 'sound stage' for the viewer, where the sound coming from the television set seems closer to reality because it appears to be coming from more than one direction.

Which to use: A + B or M + S?

In theory A + B can do everything M + S can do and vice versa. In practice, however, A + B is used mainly in programmes (usually multi-camera programmes) where you don't want the sound perspective to change every time the shot changes – when you are recording an orchestra, for example. M + S is almost always the choice for single camera shoots and – for the non-specialist – it's easier to understand. M stands for middle and S for side – not mono and stereo, as one might be tempted to think, though in practice the M mike records the mono component and the S mike adds the stereo element.

This middle and side arrangement has various advantages. It's easy for the recordist to know where to point the mike. It lets the recordist and sound editor suit the width of the sound to the situation – there's no point having a wide stereo panorama if all it does is drown the interviewee's voice. The editor can also treat the sound as mono when he or she is cutting; the level of the S component (the side recording that produces the stereo effect) can be set in the dub. Being able to edit in mono is important, because that's how most viewers will hear the programme. There's no point having stunning stereo effects if the mono signal suffers.

Most people think of stereo as a way of delivering thrilling effects – letting viewers hear as well as see the car roaring past from left to right. Or letting viewers hear that the violins in the orchestra are on the left and the double basses on the right. In practice, however, this sort of occasion, when the viewer wants to 'place' the sound, is not all that common.

The benefits of stereo are usually more general. It lets the viewer hear sound coming from all over the place (as in real life) and it helps to differentiate the main sound from the background sound. The general quality of sound in programmes also improves because programme-makers think more carefully about sound than they might do when there is only mono to worry about.

So what difference does stereo make in production?
In everyday bread-and-butter programme-making, not
much. But in any situation where the sound is coming at
you from all directions – when there is a crowd or a concert
or a choir or a collection of animals – stereo comes into its
own. Think of it as high fidelity sound.

SUMMARY
SOUND

*Ears can choose what to listen to; microphones can't.
There are four basic types of mike: omnidirectional,
figure-of-eight, cardioid and hypercardioid. The shape
and size of their nets vary.*

Gun mikes (hypercardioid) have to be pointed accurately.

*Personal mikes (omnidirectional) are noisy if the wearer
moves too much.*

*Hand mikes (omnidirectional) need to be held close
to the source of sound.*

Radio mikes give freedom of shot and movement.

*Think about the best way of using sound perspective.
If in doubt, record close sound.*

Make sure mikes are out of shot when they should be.

*Don't rely on the camera mike. Use it to record non-specific
sound for general shots.*

Record wild track on each location.

Exploit stereo when you can.

Lenses

Zooms

The zoom lens is the lens most commonly found on television cameras, both film and video. It is, in effect, a whole set of lenses because of its ability to change its focal length to order.

focal length   The focal length is the distance between the centre of the lens and the position inside the camera where the image is in focus. The more important thing to remember, however, is the link between the focal length and the angle of view. The shorter the focal length, the wider the angle of view; the longer the focal length, the narrower the angle of view. Focal length and angle of view are two ways of describing the same thing, namely, the width or narrowness of the window offered by the lens. Zoom lenses are often described by the ratio between their widest and

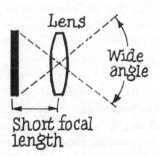

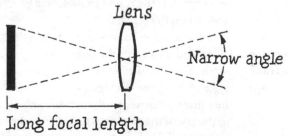

Focal lengths

narrowest angles. Thus a lens with a wide angle of 50 degrees and a narrow angle of 5 degrees is a 10:1 zoom (you say 'ten to one').

With a film camera it is more usual to talk about the focal length rather than the angle of view, but the principle is the same. So a zoom lens with a short focal length of 12mm and a long focal length of 120mm is also known as a 10:1 zoom (though logically one should perhaps say 1:10). You can get zoom lenses in a variety of short and long (or wide and narrow) combinations – anything from 6:1 to 20:1.

So what use can you make of this information about zoom lenses? The first point to note is that zoom lenses distort the picture at both ends of the zoom. The picture is most natural in the middle part of the range.

wide angle   At the wide-angle end the zoom makes the foreground and background look further apart that they really are, and the speed of something moving towards or away from the camera is exaggerated. So a small room will look bigger and action will look more dramatic if you take the camera in close and use the wide-angle end of the lens.

narrow angle   At the narrow-angle end the effect is like looking through a telescope. You see only a small part of the scene and the picture lacks depth and looks flat. Foreground and background look like they have been pushed together and are on top of each other. The background is also out of focus. So a distant runner coming towards you will appear to be running on the spot and people crossing the road will seem to be much closer to an approaching car than they really are (useful for staging near-miss accidents). When using the narrow end of the zoom, make sure the camera is on a tripod, as the tiniest tremble will produce exaggerated wobbles on the screen.

the difference between a track and a zoom   The runner who appears to stay on the same spot is the key to understanding the difference between a track and a zoom. The zoom gives you a closer shot by narrowing the angle of view; the track gives you a closer shot by moving the camera in closer, without changing the angle of view. So the zoom makes things flatter, puts the background out of focus and slows down movement towards and away from

ZOOM

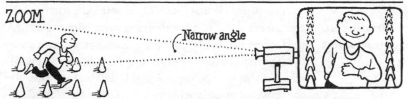

Narrow angle

END-OF-ZOOM SHOT: Runner appears to be running on spot. Background out of focus. Flat picture. Note position of cones.

TRACK

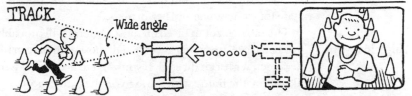

Wide angle

SHOT AFTER TRACKING IN CAMERA: Runner comes through shot and past camera more quickly. Picture has more depth. Foreground and background are in focus. Compare position of cones with end-of-zoom shot.

The difference between a track and a zoom

the camera (as described above). The track makes things seem further apart because of an important principle that is true, even if you aren't tracking: the closer you get to two objects, the further apart they seem. So if you want a room to look small, don't shoot in a small room; the camera will have to be so close to its subjects that it will make the room look roomy. If you confine your set to a small area in a large room, you will be able to move the camera far back enough to make everything look close together. You will also be able to use the narrow end of the lens, thus increasing the sense of being in a confined space. You will also have enough room for the crew to do their work without getting on top of each other – an advantage that they (and the performers) will appreciate.

The closer you get to two objects, the further apart they seem

The principle that the closer you are, the further apart things seem, also helps with movement. Moving from A to B takes exactly the same time whatever lens you are on, but if you move the camera in close and shoot on a wide lens, the distance between A and B will seem greater and the movement will therefore seem faster. So a fall, a leap or a punch will always look more dramatic on a wide lens that is close to the action – but make sure your close-up action is safe for cameraman and performers.

The normal zoom fitted on most cameras will probably give you close-ups as big as you need: most of them can fill the screen with a credit card. If you want to go even closer (like filling the frame with the logo on the card), most zooms have a 'times two' extender that will get you the shot. As you are working at the narrow end of the zoom, the card and the camera have to be rock steady to get a wobble-free shot. They also have to be about a metre apart. If the distance is less than a metre, you probably won't be able to get the card in focus.

Unless the zoom has a macro setting. The macro gives you a close-up at the wide-angle end of the lens and the minimum focus distance is negligible, so you can get very large close-ups in very confined spaces. Because you are at the wide-angle end, the camera wobble problem is much reduced and it's possible to hand-hold the camera for close-ups. But the depth of field becomes very shallow, possibly creating focus problems, and if the camera and subject are very close, it may be difficult to light the object.

Other lenses

The versatility of the zoom will give you all the shots you need for most programmes but it's worth checking what other lenses are available. Wide-angle lenses (with a short focal length) can give you an effective shot in confined spaces (a small kitchen, for example) and can also give impressive results in landscapes or looking up at tall buildings. The wider the lens, the more it tends to distort the edge of the picture – this is particularly noticeable when you introduce a camera movement into the shot, but the effect can be interesting (try tilting up and down the building). Another advantage of the wide-angle lens is that it is usually more efficient than a narrow-angle lens at transmitting light into the camera; it is what is known as a 'fast' lens. So in situations where there is not enough light for the zoom (where the zoom is too 'slow') the wide-angle lens can sometimes give you an acceptable picture.

telephoto At the other end of the scale from wide-angle lenses there are telephoto lenses of various sizes, some of them so long that they need a stand to hold them up in front of the camera. These long lenses, with a focal length of anything from 200mm to 600mm and more, are often difficult to use. They are less efficient at transmitting light into the camera (they are 'slow' lenses) and you therefore need a bright day to use them. But if it is hot, heat haze can obscure the picture badly; the effect can be attractive for a couple of shots but it soon becomes tiresome. The tiniest breeze can also make the lens tremble, which gives the picture an exaggerated wobble. All in all, telephotos are not for locations where you're in a hurry.

F-numbers and the depth of field
All lenses have a focal length. They also have an aperture

the lens speed (the opening that lets the light in). The amount of light entering the camera is governed mainly by the size of the aperture and the length of the lens (the longer the tunnel, the less light arrives at the other end). So these two properties are used to define the speed of a lens – how much light the fully-open aperture lets into the camera. The speed is expressed as the ratio of the aperture to the focal length: the f-number. So a lens with an aperture of 5mm when fully open and a focal length of 8.5mm has a ratio of 5:8.5 or 1:1.7 (divide both sides by 5).

F-number ratios are normally referred to simply as f-numbers: you might say we have been talking about an 'f1.7 lens'. This is an average speed for a standard lens. Telephotos are often much slower (and therefore have a bigger f-number) and wide-angles are usually faster (and therefore have a smaller f-number).

T-numbers

You might also come across the T-number (the Total Light Transmission Number) which takes into account the amount of light actually transmitted by a lens. There is often a slight variation, even with lenses of identical design.

F-stop and auto exposure

The cameraman can change the f-number on a lens to control the amount of light entering the camera – this is usually known as 'changing the stop'. The brightness in different parts of a scene may vary enough to need different f-numbers so the cameraman has to find a compromise for the conflicting demands or use the correct exposure for the part you are interested in and ignore the rest of the picture. Finding the best exposure in tricky situations is part of the cameraman's art.

The automatic exposure system built into most cameras works fine if the light is evenly distributed but is less reliable if it isn't. If there are bright and dark patches, the auto-exposure may produce a compromise that obscures the part of the picture you are interested in. If the camera pans through different light levels, the auto-exposure may make the picture flicker as you pan. Light reflected into the lens from a windscreen or wristwatch may trigger a momentary closing of the aperture that looks very strange on screen.

F-number settings

F-number settings are usually arranged so that each setting reduces the amount of light entering the lens to about half that of the previous setting.

f-number	1.4	2	2.8	4	5.6	8	11	16
amount of light entering lens	1	1/2	1/4	1/8	1/16	1/32	1/64	1/128

So the light entering the lens at a setting of f2 is ½ that at a setting of f1.4.

depth of field and throwing focus

One other point about exposure: the lower the light, the shallower the depth of field (the area of picture where everything is in sharp focus). Conversely, the brighter the light, the deeper the depth of field. But the depth of field is more likely to be a problem because you are using the narrow-angle end of the zoom than because of low light. The problem, however, can often be turned to your advantage by 'throwing' or 'pulling focus'. Supposing you have a close-up of a schoolboy lighting a cigarette. Behind him the picture is a blur. The cameraman throws focus from boy to blur, which sharpens into a disapproving teacher.

Focus on Boy.....throw focus to.......Teacher

In bright sunlight, when the camera might well be stopped down to f16, the depth of field will be deep and so it may be impossible to throw focus for the above shot. You may be able to get the effect you want by moving the camera a long way back so that you can use the shallow depth of field at the narrow end of the zoom. Or the cameraman could cut down the light entering the camera by using a neutral density filter (a ND filter) which reduces the light without affecting the colours. Less light makes it necessary to increase the aperture, thus reducing the depth of field, thus making it possible to throw focus ... perhaps.

Why perhaps? Dodges like this are not as straightforward as they sound – getting them to work is a mixture of art and science. It's this mixture that a good cameraman brings to the production.

Too much light is only occasionally a problem. You **shooting in** are far more likely to spend your time looking for ways **low light** to get acceptable pictures in locations where there is too little light, in a sombre cathedral or a dingy warehouse, for example. A proper lighting rig would require a recce, time, planning and money – resources that are in short supply for most everyday programmes.

So what can you do?

gain

If you are shooting video, you can use the 'gain'. This is an electronic process that boosts the available light and is built into the camera. Most video cameras have two levels of gain, usually 9dB and 18dB (decibels). They can brighten up a scene remarkably, but the drawback is noise or grain (the texture of the picture looks unsettled and busy, as if it is about to break up). At 9dB the noise is acceptable for most purposes; at 18dB, it usually isn't.

distagon lenses

With film you have two options for maximizing the available light. One is to use a faster film: some stocks make it possible to get acceptable pictures in half the light you need to shoot with ordinary stock. The drawback – once again – is more grain. The second option is to use one of the Distagon lenses. These come in various focal lengths with a maximum aperture of f1.4 (so they need only half the light of a f2 zoom). They are designed to be used with fast film stocks to get high-resolution pictures in very low light – 'if you can see it, you can shoot it'. The trade-off for being able to shoot in very low light is a very shallow depth of field and the focus problems that go with it.

SUMMARY
LENSES

Zooms

The zoom lens can change its focal length to order.

The shorter the focal length, the wider the angle of view.

The longer the focal length, the narrower the angle of view.

Zooms give their most natural picture in the middle part of their range.

At the wide-angle end
- *the distance between foreground and background is exaggerated*
- *the speed of anything moving towards or away from the camera is exaggerated.*

At the narrow-angle end
- *you see only a small part of the scene (like looking through a telescope)*
- *the picture appears flat and the background is out of focus*
- *movement towards or away from the camera appears to be slow.*

Difference between a track and a zoom

The zoom gives a closer shot by narrowing its angle of view. The track gives a closer shot by moving the camera in closer.

The closer you get to two objects, the further apart they seem. When the camera is closer, movement and action appear faster.

Big close-ups

Use the 'times-two' extender and macros to get close-ups of really small objects.

∨

Other lenses

Wide-angle lenses distort round the edges. Camera movement draws attention to this distortion, but the distortion can be interesting. Wide-angles transmit light well and can sometimes give you an acceptable picture when light is too low for the zoom.

Telephoto lenses need good light, no wind and not too much heat haze.

F-numbers and the depth of field

The f-number is the ratio of the aperture to the focal length. The f-number when the aperture is fully open gives the speed of the lens. The smaller the f-number, the faster the lens.

The auto-exposure may produce unsatisfactory results when conditions are tricky.

The lower the light, the shallower the depth of field (the area of picture where everything is in sharp focus). The depth of field is also shallower at the narrow end of the lens. Use this effect to 'throw' or 'pull' focus.

Use gain to shoot in low light. Or with film, use faster stock and/or Distagon lenses.

Clapperboard conventions

It's a pity that the clapperboard is so rarely used for video. It's a reliable, cheap and effective way of labelling shots and has much to offer if used in tandem with time code. Some benefits:

1. It tells everyone on the set (even if it isn't clapped) that you are now shooting and off-camera noise and movements are unwelcome.

2. Shot and take numbers on the clapper (10 take 1) are easier to remember and talk about than time code numbers (00:14:23:16).

3. It provides a visual marker in the picture that help you to see shot changes when spooling through at high speed.

Of course, you don't have to put a clapper on every shot. Use it at the start of a cassette and to mark a shot taken to record wild track sound. It's also useful when you come to choose the best of – say – six very similar takes of a short action; the clapper makes it easier to keep track of where you are. It's not unknown in such situations for the wrong take to go into the programme because the time codes are almost identical!

Here are the different ways of using the clapper.

For each sync shot
Hold the clapper in front of the camera, read out the shot and take number and drop the clapper arm. If using the clapper to label shots on video you don't

need to drop the clapper arm. Don't clap the board close to people's faces – it isn't polite and doesn't help their nerves.

End board

If you don't put the clapper
at the beginning of the shot,
put it on at the end – but
upside down. This tells the
editor that the board is an
end board. Announce the

shot and take number as before and don't forget to say 'End
Board'. Use end boards when shooting people (or animals)
who might be disconcerted by a clapper at the beginning of
the shot.

    If you are using film, note that the end boards take the
editor longer to sync up (he or she has to run through the
film three times instead of once). So don't use them too
often.

Sync to second clap

If for some reason camera
or sound miss the first clap
they may ask to do it again.
Read out the shot and take
number and then say 'Sync
to second clap'.

No clap

This is the normal way to use
the board for video and, if
you are using film, for shots
without sound. Hold the
board in front of the camera
with the arm raised. One
board will do for a group
of consecutive mute shots.

Mute end board

Use the 'no clap' procedure,
but hold the board upside
down.

Mike tap

On some formal occasions (during a speech or religious service for example) it may not be possible to use the clapperboard without interrupting the proceedings. But film-users will still want sync sound and the editor will need a sync point.

For these occasions you can book equipment that will record matching time code on picture and sound. Or you can use a mike tap. Pan the camera to the sound recordist (or get him or her to walk into the shot) and signal him to tap the mike. This will make a noise on the sound track which the editor can use to sync with the film.

SUMMARY

CLAPPERBOARD CONVENTIONS

The clapper has advantages even for video.

For normal shots read out shot and take number, then clap (the clap is not needed for video).

For end boards, hold the board upside down.

For mute shots, don't clap the board.

Use mike taps for sync shots on film when you can't use the clapperboard.

Vox pops and phone-ins

What do people think?

It's a question that should crop up regularly in television production offices, if only to remind programme-makers that viewers are people and public opinion is important.

What about including some public opinion in the programme? Actually letting the public have a say. It would certainly make a change after all those experts and officials.

But how do you reflect public opinion in a programme? Invite a studio audience? Organize a phone-in? Interview a spokesperson?

Vox pops

The vox pop is often the easiest and most entertaining way to reflect public opinion. It's also the most controllable way, because it's shot and edited in advance. This allows you to change its length (usually to make it shorter) or even drop it at the last moment if a live programme is threatening to overrun.

Vox pop stands for *vox populi*, which is Latin for the voice of the people. The recipe is this. Decide on the question you want to ask. (Do we have too many public holidays? How should we pay for health care?) Then go out on the street with a camera crew and put your question to about ten people – choose women as well as men, young as well as old. Then edit all the answers together.

You don't need to use the question more than once in the finished programme and you don't need to run all the answers at full length. Instead, look at the answers carefully and pick the heart of them only – perhaps two or three sentences, sometimes as little as two or three words. The

editing is important: the better the pruning, the more
powerful the vox pop. It's not very difficult, as you don't
have to worry about continuity or cutaways. Notice you
don't have to shoot any cutaways; you can just cut straight
from one person to the next.

You don't have to show all the interviews you shot or
show them in the order in which you shot them. Assemble
them instead so that each one makes its neighbour more
effective and don't forget to keep a good one for the end.
Some producers like to make sure that each contributor
looks to the other side of camera from the previous one
(so that the answers go cam. left, cam. right, cam. left, cam.
right and so on). But I think it's better to let the content of
the answers dictate the assembly order.

When you are interviewing for a vox pop you can of
course rephrase the question as you wish. If the first answer
is not very good, put the question in another way; it's your
job to get a quotable answer and sometimes you may have to
go on with one interviewee for quite a time before you get
it. This is especially true when you are talking to children.

If you are talking to a group of people and a lot of them
answer at once, pick one person to talk to first, tell camera
and sound who it is and then wait till they have found him
or her and are focused before you start. When you have
finished with that person, tell the crew who is next and
wait till they are ready before putting your question again.

And that really is all there is to the vox pop. It's a nice,
simple technique which if done well can give you lively 1½
to 2 minutes of programme. Don't make it longer, as one of
the great assets of the vox pop is that it can provide a change
of pace from the other sequences.

You can, of course, use the vox pop to tackle serious
subjects but its main value is as entertainment. Don't
mistake it for an opinion poll: you would have to interview
a lot more people and work out rules for choosing which
answers to drop and which to screen before you could say
your vox pop was even a rough survey of public opinion.
The most you can claim for a vox pop is that it illustrates
what people in the street are saying.

Phone-ins

Phone-ins are another way of including public opinion in a programme but, once again, you have to be clear (and make clear to your viewers) that this isn't a valid survey of public opinion. Your callers are a self-selected sample of the people who have chosen to watch your programme. But their views are often based on direct experience of the topic under discussion and are therefore relevant, even if they aren't representative.

GOOD MORNING, HOW ARE YOU? WHAT'S THE WEATHER LIKE? IT'S DRIZZLING HERE. HOW IS THE PRODUCER? I HOPE YOU ARE ALL HAVING A NICE TIME...

Telephone operators can remind callers to get straight to the point >

The usual procedure is to get people to phone in first with the points they want to make and then call back those who are chosen to take part. The contributors are then held on the line until it is time to say their piece on air. This preselection makes it possible to include a wider range of opinion than a first-come-first-heard policy, it also gives late callers a chance to be included. Furthermore your telephone operators can remind callers to get straight to the point and not hold things up by lengthy greetings and enquiries after the health of everyone in the studio.

Organizing phone-ins is a specialist business and you need specialist help and advice on questions such as:

— how and where should the phone-in be publicized before the programme?
— what is the likely response and how many lines are needed to cope?
— how do you select the callers to go on air?
— how do you deal with callers to live phone-ins who swear, use racist language or libel others?

Phone-ins can also be used to record viewers' votes (use different phone numbers for yes and no); to conduct a quiz; to accept money for a charity appeal or to take orders to buy something (home shopping). Phone-ins are usually a debit on the programme budget but can sometimes be turned into a credit if you negotiate a deal with the telephone company to split the revenue on calls made at premium rates (viewers must be warned if phone charges are going to be above normal).

Finally, on a more philanthropic note, phone-ins after the programme can be used to provide a talking factsheet or a helpline. Programmes often stimulate people to look for ways of changing their lives; helplines can provide backup.

SUMMARY

VOX POPS AND PHONE-INS

Vox pops

Let a range of people have their say by asking about 10 people the same question and cutting together the core of each answer.

Put the question at the beginning of the vox pop. You don't need to repeat it before each answer.

When interviewing, rephrase the question if necessary to get a good answer.

If talking to a group of people, give camera and sound time to focus on each contributor.

Vox pops can be used for serious as well as light-hearted programmes. They can be used to illustrate what people are saying, but they aren't opinion polls.

Phone-ins

Preselecting contributors and phoning them back helps you keep editorial control of the programme.

Get specialist help if you haven't produced a phone-in before.

Phone-ins after the programme can be a public service.

Shooting and presenting pieces to camera

The piece to camera (or standupper) says to the viewer 'I was there', and endows the reporter with instant, on-the-spot authority. It's also a useful way of conveying non-visual information, telling a story, or expressing a personal opinion that might sound odd in a voice-over commentary.

writing the piece

The key to success lies as much in the writing as in the delivery. Beginners try to pack in too much information and make their piece too long, with too much literary language. They should remember that viewers will hear the piece, not read it. The viewers have to understand it at the first hearing.

On the whole, pieces to camera should be left to professional reporters or presenters. But if for some reason you are delivering one yourself, make sure that you use spoken rather than written language. You can check this by reading it out loud several times. Does it sound like something you would say? Adjust the words to suit your personal style. If a sentence is too long, shorten it. If the rhythm is wrong for you, change it. If a phrase is too much of a mouthful, simplify it.

project your voice

When you record your piece, imagine you are talking to a friend who is standing just behind the camera (the cameraman, perhaps?). Or imagine yourself talking to two or three people on a windy day or in a noisy, echoing railway station. This gives you a rough guide to how much you need to project your voice – the right level depends on where you are and what you are saying.

recording the piece

Learn your piece by heart, and practice saying it until you can deliver it with meaning and confidence. If you are nervous in front of the camera, there are various ways of helping you through the ordeal. Prompt boards held up behind the camera with the text of your piece (or key words in the text) written in big letters can be most useful – if you've remembered to bring some card on location. Some reporters hang their script below the camera with a piece of sticky tape, which works well, provided you aren't short-sighted.

When recording, don't worry too much if you make a mistake (even veteran reporters make them); stop for a moment, compose your thoughts, look up and start again from the beginning. Don't waste time and energy apologizing to everyone in the team; they want to get a successful recording as much as you do and would far rather that you concentrated on getting it right. If you don't get it right after several takes, try shortening the piece or recording it in two sections with a different size of shot for each section.

prompting systems

Two mechanical memory aids are worth thinking about. The first is a location version of one of the studio prompting systems – invaluable if your piece to camera is complicated, indispensable if you have more than one to deliver. Experiment with the fonts, their size and the brightness settings until you find the best for the conditions and your eyesight.

The other aid is a small cassette recorder – a dictaphone or walkman with a recording facility will do. Record your piece at normal delivery speed and then play it back through one of those tiny earphones that can be tucked snugly into the ear without showing. With a bit of practice in front of a mirror you will find that you can follow the words in your ear and revoice them confidently and convincingly for the camera.

The way not to record your piece is to have some notes in your hand and refer to them as you go along; this gives the impression that you are not sure of what you are saying. Unless there are precise statistics or dates to be quoted. Then the glance down to check the figures from the notes in your hand shows commendable concern for accuracy.

If you are using one of the prompting systems, you might cunningly think of working in a glance to hand-held notes to disguise your use of the device.

what shots? What shots should you use for a piece to camera? If you are doing an 'I was there' piece, it makes sense to have a wider shot to show the location, or pan off the scene on to the reporter as he or she starts talking. If the piece is more than a few sentences long, shoot the whole text in a closer shot as well (without the pan if you used one); this gives you a choice of assemblies in the cutting room. You should make sure you have a close shot for any piece more than a few sentences long. When you are editing, wide shots frequently turn out to be too wide to hold for the whole length of a piece.

Don't make the presenter walk in shot unless there is a reason for it and the move from one interesting background to the next ties in with what is being said. On the whole, the value of a piece to camera is verbal rather than visual. If the happenings behind the presenter are more engrossing than the words, why is the presenter cluttering up the shot?

One tip to help knit your piece to camera into the whole programme. Don't refer to the subject of the piece directly in the first sentence. The shots before your piece will have introduced the subject – for example, windmills. Viewers will already know what's being talked about when your piece to camera comes up. So don't start your piece 'Windmills have become the most controversial part of the green revolution'. Instead say 'They have become the most controversial ...' etc. It feels odd when you are shooting it but looks and sounds right in the finished programme.

Finally, microphones. It's rarely necessary for the reporter to be holding a mike (in most situations an out-of-vision mike will do the job as well) but some reporters seem to gain confidence from clutching a mike as if it was their badge of office, like a mayoral chain. If that is so, make sure the mike looks good. An ugly, chipped lollipop, topped with foam, may not confer the image or authority reporters look for.

SUMMARY
SHOOTING AND PRESENTING PIECES TO CAMERA

In the hands of a professional reporter the piece to camera is a good way of establishing on-the-spot authority, conveying non-visual information or adding a personal touch.

The writing is as important as the delivery.

If remembering the text is a problem
- *use prompt boards, or*
- *stick the script on the camera, or*
- *use a teleprompt system, or*
- *a concealed cassette recorder with earpiece.*

Don't use notes in the hand (except for precise dates and statistics).

Shoot all pieces more than a few sentences long in a close shot as well.

To help the piece to camera knit into the programme, start the piece with a pronoun instead of the name of the subject.

If the reporter must hold a mike, make sure the mike looks good.

Walking and car interviews

Interviews with people who are on the move make a pleasant change from the more usual static setup. They are not particularly difficult to do if conditions are right.

The first requirement is a smooth path or road to walk or drive along. These are needed more for the cameraman than the interviewee. For a walking interview the cameraman has to shoot while going backwards or sideways – not the easiest way to avoid tripping up on bumps and holes (someone should guide him or her over such hazards). A bumpy road can destroy a car interview because it's so difficult to keep the camera steady without a specialist mount.

The second requirement is a consistent level of light over the area where the interview will be shot. Patches of bright sunlight or dark shade can be a problem as it's not easy for the cameraman to adjust the exposure manually while on the move. The situation is not much better if the camera is switched to automatic exposure. Most meters react too slowly or too visibly to produce an acceptable picture if the camera is moving through different levels of light.

walking interviews Most of a walking interview can be shot in two-shot – a mid-shot or close-up of the interviewee may be difficult to hold steady for long. But don't make the shot too wide, or the sound may be difficult to record. Usually camera and sound walk backwards directly in front of the performers (if the path is even, the cameraman can be pulled backwards in a wheelchair or on a trolley). Or camera and sound can walk a little to one side of the performers; this produces more of a profile shot. Make sure that the interviewee is furthest from the camera so that he or she is seen full-face as he turns to talk to the interviewer.

Now and then let the performers walk out of shot; remember that they should walk into the next shot from the opposite side of the picture. If the walk seems to be going on too long, you can arrange for the performers to stop at a convenient wall or bench and finish the interview there. All these shots and exits and entries should be worked out before you start to shoot. You can then adjust them – if necessary – as the interview develops.

You will need a lot of cutaways to edit a walking interview, especially ones that disguise the fact that your interviewee and interviewer have suddenly jumped down the street as the result of your cuts. Shots of walking feet and listening shots are useful for this. Otherwise shots from behind, shots from the side and long shots are helpful in the cutting room.

car interviews For interviews with people driving there are usually three possible camera positions. The cameraman can either sit in the front passenger seat, or crouch down on the floor where the front passenger's feet would be. Or the cameraman can sit in the back and lean forward to shoot across the front passenger seat (if the passenger seat has a headrest, make sure it can be removed or shooting from the back may be impossible). The driver can usually help the shot by sitting a little sideways to favour the camera. Don't forget that the driver should be wearing a seat belt.

You will have to do separate shots – from the back seat – of the interviewer sitting in the front passenger seat asking questions and listening. Other useful cutaways are shots of the driver's hands (steering, changing gear and so on); shots of the driver's eyes in the rear-view mirror (you will have to angle it specially); shots through the side and front windows of the area you are driving through, and shots from the roadside of the car driving past. If the road is smooth, the light is even and the car's engine isn't too noisy, you shouldn't have any problems.

One advantage with walking and driving interviews is that profile shots are acceptable. I'm not sure why – perhaps it's because the moving background means that the viewer doesn't have just half a face to look at. It's also the way one *Car interview shots* prefers to see drivers – in profile, with their eye on the road.

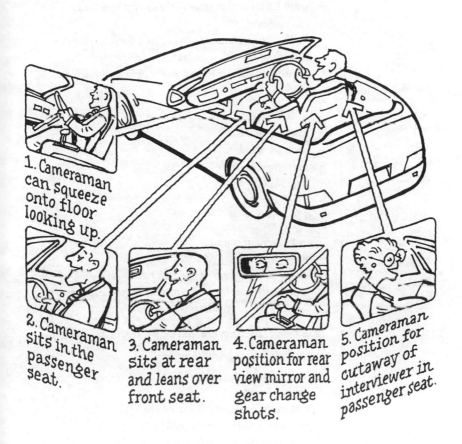

1. Cameraman can squeeze onto floor looking up.

2. Cameraman sits in the passenger seat.

3. Cameraman sits at rear and leans over front seat.

4. Cameraman position for rear view mirror and gear change shots.

5. Cameraman position for cutaway of interviewer in passenger seat.

SUMMARY

WALKING AND CAR INTERVIEWS

Walking interviews

Shoot walking interviews in two-shot to steady the shot.

The cameraman can
- *walk backwards in front of the interviewee and interviewer*
- *walk a little to one side (make sure the interviewee is furthest from the camera)*
- *be pulled backwards on a trolley or in a wheelchair.*

For cutaways shoot
- *walking feet*
- *listening shots*
- *shots from behind*
- *shots from the side*
- *long shots.*

Car interviews

The cameraman can sit
- *in the front passenger seat*
- *on the floor in front of the front passenger seat*
- *in the back seat leaning across the front passenger seat (make sure the headrest is removable).*

Don't forget the driver should wear a seat belt.

For cutaways shoot
- *interviewer listening*
- *driver's hands*
- *reflections in the rear-view mirror*
- *the view through the car windows*
- *shots from the roadside of the car passing.*

Profile shots are acceptable for interviews on the move.

Miming

The other name for miming is 'shooting to playback', which gives a more complete description of what the technique involves. It's a technique much used for pop videos, where the sound track is vitally important and the location and conditions that are ideal for shooting the pictures can be less than ideal for recording the sound. If you want to shoot a group doing their number on the edge of a cliff in a howling gale there is no alternative to shooting to playback.

the procedure   The theory is simple. Choose the song or piece of music you want the performer(s) to mime to. If there isn't a suitable recording already available, arrange to make one. This performance is known as the master recording. You then decide on the location(s) and the shots for each bit of the music. The sound recordist plays back the relevant part of the music to the performer(s) through a loudspeaker or through an earpiece and they sing in time with this playback. This performance is shot and recorded in sync and the editor uses this sound as a guide track when he or she edits the pictures to fit the master recording.

That's how it works but, of course, it's not as easy as it seems (it never is). You have to shoot generous overlaps so that the editor can make the cuts as smooth as possible. You have to be very careful when shooting close-ups of the singer if he or she is miming to a loudspeaker as sound travels so slowly that the singer has to keep a tiny bit ahead of the playback if the timing is to be precisely right. That's a difficult thing to do.

You can help by placing the loudspeaker as close to the
singer as possible, but it must stay out of shot. This can be
a problem with long shots; try and find somewhere to
hide the speaker near the singer and hope that the sound
recordist has enough cable to reach it from the playback
machine. Or consider whether a concealed earpiece might
be a better bet.

The most difficult thing is trying to find something
for the singer to do while he or she is miming. Wandering
round the local park, beach or beauty spot sniffing flowers
has been done before and really isn't original enough.

So go back to the music and think hard what it is about.
Can you think of an unusual location that might give it a
new slant? Somewhere that would add meaning to the
words or complement the mood of the music? Do the
words suggest a prop that might motivate some of the shots?
Would it help if you shoot the song in several locations?
In the middle of a crowd of shoppers? In a factory? On a
boat? Next to the airport? In the zoo? In a fantasy location
concocted out of smoke and lights? Does the singer actually
have to mime at all? Could you not shoot him or her just
doing something while the song is being played?

Finding settings for slow love songs is particularly
difficult and there should come a point while you are trying
to think of suitable locations when you ask yourself: why
do I want to shoot this song to playback anyway?

If a band and studio are available and you can't come up
with an original idea, why not record the song in the studio
and rely on songs that bring original locations to mind more
readily to provide the breath of fresh air you want for your
programme?

SUMMARY
MIMING

The procedure for shooting to playback (miming) is

1. Record a good quality master (if not using an existing tape or record).
2. Select the location(s).
3. Shoot the singer singing to playback and use the sound from this performance as a guide track.
4. Editor uses the guide track to assemble the shots in sync with the master recording.

Remember to shoot overlaps and place the playback speaker as close to the singer as possible (but out of shot).

Try and find original locations — not the park, beach or local beauty spot every time.

Picture composition

It isn't fair. Some people have a natural feel for composing a picture. There are cameramen who can walk and sway and pan and zoom and everything always sits beautifully in the picture, satisfyingly and perfectly framed. Their pictures seem to glow; you can't take your eyes off them.

Then there's the rest of us. We have to develop what sense of composition we have by thinking about what makes a good picture and learning to look.

things to avoid Probably the best way to start is to think about the things not to have in the picture. Chins resting on the bottom of the screen, heads bumping against the top, ears cut off at the side (remember the cut-off strip round the edge of the screen) – these are the obvious things to avoid. Flat-looking pictures with a background object (perhaps a bunch of flowers or a telegraph pole) sprouting from the top of someone's head, strong horizontal lines coming out of either ear – these are ridiculous and should also be avoided. Nor is the back of an interviewer's head and shoulders blocking half the screen in an over-the-shoulder two-shot particularly attractive. Keep the interviewer more to the side.

These are all obvious points. But they are things that everyone has seen on programmes because, strangely enough, there are people in television who never really look at the pictures they produce. Instead they just listen to the words and remember what they wanted to see in the picture and then let their brain direct their eyes to concentrate on that part only (in the two-shot example I have just mentioned, they don't see the head and

shoulders blocking the screen because they look only at
the interviewee). They don't see the shot as it really is.

The camera records everything impartially: its brains
must come from the cameraman, the director and the other
technicians, who all work together to compose shots that
lead the viewers' eyes to the important things on the screen.
This is done, of course, by using shot sizes, lighting, sound,
camera angles and movement, the position of people and
things in the screen, and so on.

In order to orchestrate these elements successfully you
learn should first of all devote some time to leaning to see things
to look as they really are, as impartially as the camera. Look around
you now. Look at the obvious things: I see a sofa, a reading
lamp (switched off), bookshelves and two pictures on
the wall. The camera would give more emphasis to the
lampshade (it's lighter in colour than the rest of the scene),
the red plastic toy on the ground (I like to see things
tidier than they really are), a blob of blackness where the
bookshelves are (they're not lit), and two gold-coloured
picture frames (the pictures themselves are too dark and
detailed for the camera to record). If I want to take a shot
of my sofa, lamp, bookshelves and pictures, I will have to
remove the toy (unless I want the viewers to notice it),
relight the scene and choose the angle from which I take
my shot very carefully.

Once you have had a little practice at seeing pictures
the way the camera sees them, it takes less and less conscious
effort and eventually becomes second nature. It's rather
like the warning marks at the end of each reel of film in the
cinema; some people have to have them pointed out to
begin with, but after that they spot the marks without any
conscious effort.

What else can you do to improve the look of your
pictures? Common sense and experience are the best
guides, but there are some general principles that can help.

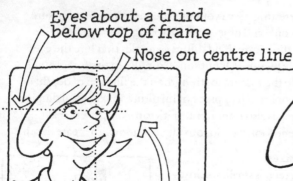

Eyes about a third below top of frame

Nose on centre line

Looking room

No looking room

1. Looking and walking room

A person's face (most shots are of faces) sits comfortably in the picture when the bridge of the nose (where spectacles rest) is about a third from the top of the picture. If the person is looking to one side, he or she should be slightly in the other side of the picture – he or she should be given what is called 'looking room'.

If he or she isn't given looking room, the picture looks unbalanced with the person crammed into one half of the picture looking out and a lot of dead ground behind his or her head.

Walking room >

In the same way a walking person needs 'walking room'. But you don't have to worry about giving a car 'driving room' because the central point of interest is really the driver of the car and not its bonnet.

2. Give pictures depth

Real life has three dimensions; the screen has only two. So you have to work hard to counter the screen's tendency to make things (especially landscapes) look flat and

uninteresting. Give your pictures depth by making sure
that people and objects aren't arranged in a straight line
across the centre. Find things or angles that lure the eyes
into the picture. Or put some 'dingle' in the foreground
close to the camera to strengthen the illusion of depth;
a bush or branch or piece of furniture makes ideal dingle.
Lighting is also important. If it's too even, it will make
the scene look flat. So introduce shadows to create depth.

Shot sizes

The screen is small; so close-
ups have more impact than
long shots. An unrelieved
diet of close-ups, however,
soon becomes indigestible.
On the other hand, don't
leave shots looser than they
need be – a 'dead' area left
unnecessarily round the
point of interest weakens
the impact of a shot.

Shot angles

Shots taken from normal
eye-height tend to be the
least interesting because that
is what the viewer sees every
day. This doesn't mean you

have to shoot everything from eye-catching angles, but
if you can add something to what the shot is saying by
choosing an original angle you should do so.

    The important things – if you want a well-composed
shot – are to decide what the main point of interest is and
then to frame the shot to lead viewers' eyes towards it.
The main point can be in the centre or at the side, in the
foreground or background. The camera angle, the lighting,
the way the camera moves, the relationship of the main
point of interest to other things in the picture, the way it and
they move – all these can then be used to make the viewers
see what you want them to see.

Make sure also that there are no competing points of interest. This will save you from shooting the sort of general shot that leaves viewers wondering what they are supposed to be looking at and asking themselves 'What is this shot trying to say?' But it's a question you should be asking yourself – frequently.

You can cultivate your sense of composition by looking at paintings and photographs. Where has the artist placed the main point of interest in the frame and why? Often a striking picture places its subject where you least expect it – try and work out how the artist has then balanced the picture to make it a satisfying whole. You can also learn a lot about composition by doing some painting and photography yourself.

In television, however, the pictures move and are accompanied by sound. To study the way this affects composition you have to watch programmes or go to the cinema. Don't limit yourself to films of your own culture; try Asian, African, Australian, Middle Eastern, South American and any other variety of film you can find. Picture composition varies between cultures and each culture should remain open to foreign influences while developing its own style. Just make sure that by the standards of your own culture you develop something that is good, and good-looking.

SUMMARY
PICTURE COMPOSITION

Avoid
- *chins resting on the bottom of the screen*
- *heads bumping against the top*
- *objects sprouting out of people's heads*
- *horizontal lines coming out of their ears*
- *the interviewer's back blocking half the screen in two-shots.*

Do
- *position the bridge of the nose about a third from the top of the screen*
- *give 'looking room' and 'walking room'*
- *give pictures depth by putting 'dingle' in the foreground and making sure the lighting isn't too even*
- *make sure shots aren't looser than they need be*
- *be on the look-out for original angles for shots.*

Ask yourself what is the shot trying to say?

Learn to look by studying paintings, photographs, television and films from all cultures.

Graphic design

Graphic design can contribute a huge range of material to your programme – the title and credits, supers for the names of people who appear in it, maps, diagrams, graphs, drawings, paintings, animations and slides.

talk to graphics early

The main rule about graphic design is simple: involve the designer early. Illustrations, paintings, diagrams and in particular animations take time to prepare.

If your programme is likely to have a lot of graphics, consult the designer at treatment stage. Computers have revolutionized techniques and styles and the designer will be able to advise you on what is appropriate, available and – even more important – affordable. Talking to the designer as early as the treatment stage gives you and the designer a chance to develop your ideas.

Don't worry too much about how to get the graphics on screen (that's the designer's job); be clear instead about what they are intended to say and do. The designer is trained to help you get your message over as long as you can explain what the message is.

Follow up your first consultation with the designer with phone calls and perhaps a visit to see how the work is progressing. Designers – being human – often put on one side anything that isn't urgent and you may need to do a little gentle prodding to make sure you get the benefit of your 'consult early' policy.

collect graphics early

The other general point to remember is to collect all your graphics at least 24 hours before you need them and to check them all personally. For news and topical programmes the time scale is often hours rather than days, but the principle of checking graphics before they go on air is still a good one. It must never happen that the first time you see the completed work is just before it goes on camera. Mistakes are always cropping up in unexpected places (particularly spelling mistakes) and you must allow time for finding and correcting them. You may also want to make changes – keep these to a minimum. For more complicated areas of graphic design such as animated sequences you will obviously need to view and discuss progress more regularly with the designer.

Text

titles, credits and name captions

If your programme is one of a series it will already have a style; so all you have to do is to give the designer the exact wording or the information you want in your graphics. If it's the first programme in the series or a one-off, go and see the designer personally and discuss with him or her:

– the style, size and colour of lettering. Upper or lower case?
– its position on screen. 'Top third', 'bottom third' or centre?
– how it relates to the background colour, picture or pattern
– how the captions will enter and exit. As a cut? Fade? Slide on from the side, top, bottom or diagonally?

name supers

Keep all your captions short and simple. With names of ordinary people you don't have to include titles like Mr, Mrs, Miss, Ms or Madam. But generals, admirals, bishops and other elevated people usually like their titles to appear.

Try and keep the number of credits to the minimum.

credits

Your station probably has a policy written somewhere which recommends who should and should not have a credit. Find out what that policy is and stick to it. It's tedious for viewers to have to sit through a never-ending list naming anyone who ever came near the programme while it was being made.

dates

With dates you don't need to mention the year if it's the present year. You don't need to write 'st', 'nd', 'rd' and 'th' after the days of the month. Remember also that people usually have to think for a moment before they can tell you what day of the month it is (if they know at all) and so it's helpful to give the day of the week as well: WEDNESDAY 19 NOVEMBER. Or if you prefer: WED. 19 NOV. Or a mixture of the two: WED. 19 NOVEMBER.

It's also best to give the name of the month rather than the number. Few people can tell instantly that 23/7 is in July – almost everyone has to do some mental counting first.

times When giving times of the day, don't be caught out saying things like TOMORROW EVENING AT 9PM. Nine pm is always in the evening. Either pm or evening is enough; you don't need to mention both.

Make sure you keep names and captions on the screen long enough for slower readers to take them in. A good way to judge how long is to read the caption slowly to yourself three times before taking it off.

making letters easy to read Words can be difficult to read on screen, particularly if there are a lot of them (when you are subtitling a foreign language film, for example). So *the first thing to do is to* make sure *that* every word adds *to the* meaning – drop those that don't. All the italicized words in the previous sentence can be dropped.

Then work on the presentation of the words and letters. Black or coloured edging added to the letters electronically in the studio can make them easier to read. If this isn't enough, you may have to ask the vision mixer to black out the portion of the screen behind the words to make them stand out more clearly. It's best always to err on the side of clarity, as many of your viewers will be watching badly tuned sets with inadequate aerials.

Maps and graphs

maps Maps should be simple, clear and stripped of all unnecessary information. You should mark on your map the names of all towns, rivers, mountains and so on which you mention in the programme. If you don't mention them, don't mark them.

graphs Graphs should also be simple, clear and stripped of all unnecessary information. They must have a title (JAPANESE

CAR EXPORTS) and their axes should be labelled clearly (CARS IN THOUSANDS on the vertical axis, YEAR on the horizontal axis). The message of the graph must be simple and immediately obvious or many viewers will miss the point – remember they can't dictate how long they can look at it, as they can with graphs in newspapers.

Don't forget that you can superimpose simple maps and graphs over pictures; this can improve their presentation greatly. But clarity must come before presentation. If the pictures get in the way of the message, use the maps and graphs on a plain background.

If you can animate graphs, so much the better. Work **animating** out the points you want to get across and give them to the **graphs** designer marked on the script or a step-by-step outline of the script. If you have second thoughts when you are finalizing the script and decide you want changes that affect the animations, talk them over with the designer. The changes may be difficult to make. If it's a straight choice between a graphic change or a script change, the words are usually easier to manipulate than the drawings.

Once again, the motive for animating graphs should be clarification – to steer the viewer through a line of reasoning or round a map or diagram that might otherwise be difficult to understand. Beware being seduced by computer gee-whizzery. There's no point animating graphs (or anything else) if it doesn't make the message clearer.

If you are using slides, check that they are clean. **slides** Enormous, greasy finger and thumb prints are all too easy to miss in the hectic atmosphere of the studio. But they are all too easy to see for the viewer at home.

Press cuttings

These are always a problem to present attractively. They are rarely the right shape for the television screen and almost always contain more words than you can expect the viewer to read. A graphics designer will be able to help you find the most effective – and cost-effective way – of presenting your quotes but here is a story showing four different approaches that might give you some ideas.

1. PRESENTER:
'Now a cautionary tale for anyone who's thinking of buying a new suit. It could cost more than you expect.'

Method 1:
pick extracts that
fit the screen as
well as the story

Ill fitting suits wreck wedding and put groom in court

THE long and short of bridegroom James Moore's ill-fitting wedding suit cost him his bride and a £50 fine yesterday.

2. VOICE:
'Ill-fitting suits wreck wedding and put groom in court. The long and short of bridegroom James Moore's ill-fitting wedding suit cost him his bride – and a fifty-pound fine yesterday.'

3. PRESENTER:
'And that doesn't include the cost of the suits. The first one Mr Moore bought was too small. So he dashed out and bought another – only to find it was too big. Teasingly, he told his bride-to-be:'

Method 2:
mask unwanted
words with
coloured plastic

4. VOICE:
'I'm not wearing this down the aisle. It's all off.'

5. PRESENTER:
'His bride, Miss Caroline Mortimer, believed him. So next day Moore and his relations waited over an hour for her to show up at the church.'

Method 3:
place cutting on
background
which makes it
look good

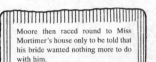

6. VOICE:
'Moore then raced round to Miss Mortimer's house only to be told that his bride wanted nothing more to do with him. In a fit of anger Moore kicked out all the lights on Miss Mortimer's car and ripped off both wing mirrors, causing over two hundred pounds' damage.'

7. PRESENTER:
'That lot landed him in court and cost him the fifty-pound fine. A last word from the would-be groom:'

Method 4:
ask graphics to
put your quotes
in captions

8. VOICE:
'I have lost two stones with the worry and embarrassment since it all began. I think I will remain a bachelor for ever.'

9. PRESENTER:
'Suit yourself, Mr Moore. Or perhaps not. After your problems you'd better stick to something more casual.'

Of course it would be wrong to use all four methods of presentation in the same story. Decide which style works best for the story or fits the programme style and stick to that.

The extra voice – or voices – to read the quotes are important, as the impact of the story is lessened if the presenter reads both links and quotes. Presenter and voice(s) will need to rehearse together to get a polished performance. Make sure also that the quotes are typed out correctly in the script and the voice reads them accurately. Missing out a phrase or reading words that aren't on the screen looks and sounds careless.

Finally, keep the quotes short and don't be frightened to split them into two or more screens. The impact of a well-written quote is lost if viewers can read ahead to the punch line. Shots 2, 6 and 8 in the example would all work better as two screens.

Photographs and drawings

It helps if these fit the proportions of the television screen (four units across by three units down), but obviously if they don't, you will have to frame them on camera as best you can. Photographs should be matt finish (not glossy) to avoid reflections from the lights. They should be mounted on stiff card by the graphic designer so that they lie flat – creased and wrinkled illustrations look awful and should never be allowed on to the screen.

stills You can successfully produce whole sequences using
sequences only photographs or drawings. In fact some situations are actually easier to cover using stills only. Suppose you want to show a child being taken out to see the Christmas decorations at night in a big city. A sequence like this can be expensive and difficult to shoot on video or film: lighting problems, overtime for the camera crew and the limit on the number of hours you can reasonably keep a seven-year-old out of bed could make this a tricky assignment. If you use stills, however, you have at your disposal very high-speed films and flash: a good stills photographer can take dozens of photographs in different locations in a fraction of the time a video or film cameraman would need.

You can record the child's
reactions and the sounds
of the Christmas crowds
at night on a tape recorder.
When the stills have been
developed, you pick the best
ones and put them on tape,
perhaps introducing a few
camera movements. You
then edit the shots and sound
track in the normal way
(without any sync problems
to worry about) and with
luck and the addition of
carefully chosen music and
effects you should end up
with a nice sequence.

Rostrum camera >

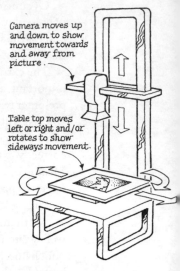

Camera moves up
and down to show
movement towards
and away from
picture.

Table top moves
left or right and/or
rotates to show
sideways movement.

rostrum camera

It is possible to put your stills on videotape or film using
a normal studio or location camera. But for really smooth
and accurate camera movements, and anything that's more
complicated than a zoom, it's best to have the stills shot on
a special rig known as a rostrum camera, which is designed
to give maximum control of camera movements over small
areas.

It's not usually necessary to be present when your stills
are being shot by the rostrum cameraman. But you do
have to give him or her exact instructions about what you
want. The best way to do this is to fix a sheet of see-through
paper over each still with paperclips, number the still and
trace the outline of some easily recognizable feature in
the still so that the rostrum cameraman can realign the
paper correctly if it moves. Then take another piece of
greaseproof paper and make a large right-angled triangle
(as shown in the illustration) to check that the shots you
mark up are the right proportions for the screen. Label
the opening and closing frames of each shot and specify the
speed of the movements by 'seeing' the movement on your

Screen ratio
triangle

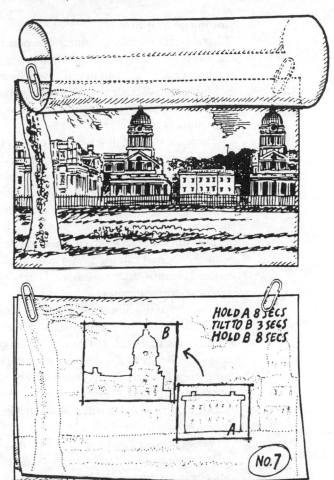

HOLD A 8 SECS
TILT TO B 3 SECS
HOLD B 8 SECS

NO.7

*Preparing
a photograph for
rostrum camera*

mental TV and counting how many seconds it takes. If you
still aren't sure how fast or slow the movement should be,
ask for two different speeds – the picture quality may suffer
if you adjust the speed during the edit. Don't forget to ask
the cameraman to hold each shot steady for about eight
seconds before and after each movement – here's another
chance to get three shots for the price of one.

Computer graphics

What about computer graphics? Whenever the phrase comes up, people tend to think of the latest wonder-machine or software, but in truth even the most humdrum graphics chore uses, or is controlled by, some form of computer technology. Computers are now as much a part of graphics as colour.

There are three basic categories of machines: those that create or modify pictures (Paintbox and its rivals); those that store and output pictures (still stores); and those that manipulate pictures (Digital Video Effects or DVE). Each new version of the different machines offers more and more functions beyond its basic category. Increasingly, the machines are also linked together in networks, so that graphic designers can use any bit of technology from their personal terminal and you can see the result played back on your desk-top computer.

To see what the designers working on your programme have available, ask for a demonstration. This will give you an idea of the input needed from you, how much work the designer will have to do, the time-scale and the charges for doing the work. Don't get carried away by the unlimited range of possibilities. Remember that your viewers' ability to absorb information has not grown in step with the computer's ability to produce it.

Finally, don't try and save money on graphics. Layout and lettering that look fine on posters and leaflets often look cheap on the screen. As with economy packaging in the supermarket, the whiff of cheapness may rub off on the contents of your programme. Quite unfairly, of course. But the danger is there.

SUMMARY
GRAPHIC DESIGN

Two general points

Talk to graphics early (what rather than how).

Collect graphics early to allow time for alterations and corrections. Check all graphics personally.

Text

Write out the exact wording you want and discuss with the designer lettering, position on screen, colour, background, mode of entry and exit.

Keep all captions short and simple.

Mention VIP titles only.

Keep the number of credits to a minimum.

People rarely know the day of the month or recognize the number of the month instantly. So name the day of the week and the month. Use short versions if you want.

Cut out redundant information
— TOMORROW EVENING AT 9PM.

Keep captions on the screen long enough for slower readers (read each one to yourself three times).

For legibility use black or coloured edging. Or wipe in a plain background from the studio mixer.

Maps and graphs

Don't include unnecessary information.

Give graphs a title and label the axes clearly. Animation or camera movements or cuts can help get your message across.

V

Superimposing simple maps or graphs over a picture can make them look good, but don't sacrifice clarity.

Animate graphs to make them easier to understand. Give the designer details and don't change them without consultation.

Make sure slides are clean.

Press cuttings

Difficult to show attractively. Try
– *using extracts that fit the screen (as well as the story)*
– *masking unwanted words*
– *placing the cutting on a good-looking background*
– *rewriting quotes on captions.*

Use an extra voice to read out the words exactly as shown on screen. Keep quotes short. Split into two or more screens to sharpen impact.

Photographs and drawings

Mount on stiff card. Photos should be matt.

Still sequences are cheap, relatively easy to do, and can be very effective if used with sound effects and music.

For rostrum camera shots
– *cover each still with see-through paper*
– *number each still*
– *mark up shots using triangle guide*
– *specify timings*
– *ask for holds before and after camera movements (three shots for the price of one).*

Ask for a demonstration of computer graphics.

Don't save money on graphics.

Whose programme is it?

It takes a lot of people to make a television programme: technicians, contributors, bosses and of course, you, the producer/director. Some of these people may get very involved with the programme, almost as involved as you. The cameraman, the editor, the presenter, the major contributor and your boss may even start to refer to the programme as 'my' programme. Don't worry about this; it's usually a good sign. Everybody likes to be involved with a winner. They shun a loser.

But what happens when you have an argument about the programme, or something in it? Whose programme is it then? Who has the final say?

It all depends with whom you are arguing. The first point to be clear about is that the programme is yours. You, the producer, are the only person who is involved with it from the day it begins to the day it is transmitted, and beyond. You are the person who will get all the blame if things go wrong. If things go right, there will be no shortage of volunteers to take the praise for 'my' programme.

So the programme is first and foremost yours. But this doesn't mean that you should be a petty dictator when dealing with the people who help you make it. Television is teamwork; you can't do it all yourself.

So in technical matters you would be foolish to disregard the advice of the cameraman, sound recordist or editor; they almost certainly have more experience to draw on than you. If you are having a dispute with a contributor, you probably know more about what's right for television than he or she does; listen to the points being made, but never allow the editorial control to slip from your hands. All the members of the team are experts only so far as their part of the programme is concerned. So the final decision in any disagreement with them is yours, because only you know how each part of the programme fits in with the whole.

Disputes with your boss are more tricky to resolve. In the first place you should prevent most of them arising by telling him or her at each stage of the production what you are up to, so that when it comes to viewing the edited programme or watching it being recorded in the studio, there are no surprises. If the boss wants to make changes you don't agree with, you are of course entitled to put the case for doing it your way. But in the end you will probably have to give way, because the boss is the boss.

Giving way is not necessarily a bad thing – don't underestimate the contribution a good boss can make. He or she knows the background to the programme but can also approach it with a fresh eye at a time when you may be so hopelessly caught up in the details that you find it impossible to stand back and assess the impact of the programme as a whole.

SUMMARY
WHOSE PROGRAMME IS IT?

Other people may call the programme 'my' programme but it is your programme. You are the only one who stays with the programme right through the production process.

If you disagree about something with
- *a cameraman, sound recordist, editor or other technician: listen to their advice, but the final decision is yours*
- *a contributor: again listen, but the final decision is yours*
- *your boss: you will probably have to give way. Minimize the chances of disagreement by keeping him or her informed at all stages of the production. Bear in mind his or her criticism may be valid as he comes fresh to the programme.*

Style in commentary writing

Words are first-class for communicating with people if used well. If used badly, or there are too many of them, they just get in the way.

So you have to make every word in a commentary count. Think of this while you are writing. When you have finished writing, go through the commentary crossing out all the words and phrases that won't be missed. When you have crossed these out, you will be left with a commentary that gets your message across simply, clearly and briefly.

drop the meaningless

How do your recognize the words and phrases to drop? The key is always the meaning. Many phrases don't mean anything, phrases like 'let's face it', 'if you ask me', 'you have to admit', 'when all is said and done'. They are expressions that people use to keep talking while they are thinking of what to say next; they should have no place in your commentary Sometimes these phrases can make a whole sentence: 'It is also of importance to bear in mind the following consideration ...' But they still don't mean anything, except perhaps listen, which you don't need to say any way.

Many words are also meaningless and therefore redundant: 'Well' at the beginning of a sentence; 'interpersonal' in the phrase 'interpersonal relationships' (how else do people have relationships?); 'cruelly' in 'he was cruelly tortured' (is torture ever less than cruel?); 'essentially' in the sentence, 'He was essentially a simple man'. Surely 'He was a simple man' is more powerful?

Give your commentaries clarity and impact by also dropping words that weaken their neighbours, words like 'quite', 'almost', 'perhaps' and 'about'. If you are sure of your facts, pick the appropriate word and let it stand without qualification.

don't describe the picture

You can go through your script and weed out most adjectives without losing meaning. If the object or person you are describing is in the picture, adjectives are unlikely to add much. For example: 'Ali Smith, a good-looking young bus conductor, found the bomb'. Far better to say 'Ali Smith, a bus conductor, found the bomb'. This leaves you room to add something about how, when or where Ali Smith found the bomb – or even tell viewers how old he is. Viewers can see for themselves if Ali Smith is good-looking. Don't describe the picture; add to it.

don't state the obvious

Check that you aren't stating the obvious in your commentary. Some examples: 'This tropical island set in the sunny blue sea will make an ideal holiday spot' (where but in the sea do you find islands?); 'At the end of the week he picked up his wages for the work he had done' (what else are wages paid for?); 'There are many sick people in hospital' (it would be surprising if there were not).

avoid jargon

Another thing to avoid is jargon. After researching a programme on airlines you will be familiar with airways jargon, like ATC, passenger sea miles, short-haul destinations, and so on. But don't expect your viewers to be. Jargon is a shorthand language for specialists. If you want to give your commentary an authentic flavour, use one or two jargon expressions but make sure their meaning is clear from the context and that they are explained in everyday language.

initials

Don't introduce sets of initials without explaining them at least once (ATC stands for Air Traffic Control). But viewers probably won't remember their meaning for long, especially if you have introduced other sets of unfamiliar initials like CAT (Clear Air Turbulence) and VMC (Visual Meteorological Conditions). If you have used ATC, CAT and VMC in the same piece, you are using too much jargon.

Sometimes initials stand for something so complicated that no one is much the wiser if you do spell them out –

paraphrasing is then more helpful than spelling out. Some examples: DNA, PVC, D-MAC, TNT, HMI.

use simple words

The word for a set of initials is acronym. It may be one of those words you aren't sure about, exactly the sort of word not to use in a commentary. Use simple language for television; keep the long words for your novel. Even minority programmes reach a vast number of people compared to other media and it's a safe bet that words like acronym, arcane, anodyne, ascetic and anomaly are not in most viewers' everyday vocabulary. They may understand the meaning from the context, but there are still good reasons for not using difficult words. Viewers don't enjoy puzzling out their meaning. While they're puzzling, they miss the next bit of the programme. Difficult words also send out a subtle message: if you don't use words like this, this programme is not for you.

clichés

Clichés are another thing to be wary of. In some ways clichés are comfortable and reassuring because they are familiar. Expressions like 'in this day and age', 'the dawn of time', 'kick-starting the economy', 'putting the finishing touches to', ill luck that always 'dogs' people, determination that is always 'ruthless' and 'a dream ticket' in politics communicate instant meaning. But is it the precise meaning you want to communicate? If it is, fine. Too often, however, the comfortable cliché that presents itself so quickly is only roughly right for what you want to say. A few moments' thought would produce a better arrangement of words that would express your meaning more freshly and precisely.

brevity is better

When you are writing commentary, keep your sentences short. If they average more than three or four lines, viewers may lose the argument. Try one or two sentences with fewer than five words; you will be surprised how direct and effective they are. It pays to simplify.

The same goes for words: short words are better than long words because viewers understand them more easily. So 'start' is better than 'initiate', 'show' is better than 'manifest', 'weather' is better than 'meteorological', 'stop' is better than 'terminate'.

Remember that viewers hear your commentary; they can't read it. Moreover they hear it once only, at a pace not of their choosing and coupled with pictures and sound effects that may compete for their attention. So the meaning of your commentary must be instantly clear. The way it is voiced is also important: a good performance will add clarity and nuance. But don't try to introduce sarcasm or irony. Unless you are a public figure well-known for saying the opposite of what you mean ('Five defeats in a row – a spectacular achievement!'), viewers won't know you are kidding.

write as you speak

Commentary is spoken language – the writing is only incidental, a means to an end, not the end itself. So literary language such as 'whilst' or 'amongst' or 'prior to' is usually inappropriate. The sentence, 'The People's Stadium, which was the stage for his greatest triumphs, was renamed in his honour', is literary rather than spoken. Try replacing the 'which' and the commas with dashes: 'The People's Stadium – the stage for his greatest triumphs – was renamed in his honour'. This is less literary. It's also easier to say and sounds more lively.

Because commentary is spoken, check what you have written by reading it out loud. Your ears will detect the awkward patches and padding. If you stumble when reading, the fault almost always lies with your pen rather than your tongue. If you find it difficult to put your thoughts down on paper clearly and simply, use the 'out loud' technique by telling someone out loud what you want to say. Most people talk more clearly than they write; so make your writing more like your talking and your viewers will understand you better.

Good writing is not just an extra refinement to round off your other abilities. It's more important than that, because in many ways your words are your thoughts. If your thoughts aren't clear, it will show up in your words.

SUMMARY
STYLE IN COMMENTARY WRITING

Make every word in a commentary count.

Drop
— *meaningless words, phrases, sentences*
— *words that weaken their neighbours*
— *most adjectives*
— *phrases and sentences that state the obvious*
— *jargon and clichés.*

Don't use too many initials in your programme.
Explain what initials stand for — if it helps.

Use simple words and some short sentences.

Commentary is spoken — not written — language.
Voice it carefully.

Don't use sarcasm or irony.

Check commentary by reading it aloud.

Make your writing as clear as your talking.

Legal problems

This briefing is not a guide for producers on how to stay out of trouble with the law; that would be impossible for any one book to provide because legal and broadcasting practices differ widely around the world. The only practical advice I can offer is that you should find out who is the lawyer for your station and refer to him or her whenever you think you are going to have problems. Don't wait till you are in difficulties; ask for advice before the problem arrives. Often a tiny change of procedure (sometimes just a tiny change of wording) will save you endless trouble later.

Which are the areas most likely to bring you into contact with the law?

shooting permission The most common pitfall is getting permission to shoot on location. Obviously you have to have permission to shoot on private property. In most countries you don't need permission to shoot the outside of private property as long as your camera is on a public right of way. But do you need permission to shoot on the public highway? In some countries you do. And what are the rules about re-creating crimes, using fake guns and dressing actors in police uniforms?

paying artists Does your station normally pay contributors to programmes? If so, how much? You obviously have to pay presenters, artists, actors, singers and so on, but does the fee cover rehearsals and repeats? And what about cassette, satellite and cable sales – do the artists' contracts cover these? Who fixes the fees and sends out the contracts? What about interviewees in current affairs and documentary programmes – are they paid? These questions are not only significant for your budget; they also have a bearing on the amount of interference you might have to accept from a contributor. As a general rule, editorial control should stay with you as the representative of the TV station, but what happens if someone agrees to give you an interview only on condition that he or she can see the edited interview before it is transmitted? Do you the producer have the authority to agree to such a demand? You need to know beforehand what to do.

safety   Programme-making can be dangerous, so always play safe. Never take risks on roads or with animals – domestic or wild. Heights, stunts, water and investigations are all potentially dangerous; get specialist advice and make sure an expert is present at the shoot, not only for the safety of your contributors and crew, but also for your own safety. An accident could be a very serious matter for you, even if you aren't personally hurt, as you may be responsible in law and therefore liable for a fine or even imprisonment. You should know what your responsibilities are.

copyright   Copyright is another area you should find out about. Generally speaking, if you use someone else's drama, short story, film, photograph, or music, you have to pay. But your station may have a special deal with the organizations which protect copyright and the policy may be to use only those items covered by the deal and never touch the rest. Obviously it's worth knowing what the arrangements are.

libel   Libel is probably the most serious legal mess you can get yourself into. The dangers, definitions and defences for libel are complicated, but don't be put off finding out what the practice in your country is; you'll find it a fascinating subject. You may be surprised to discover that in your country, as in Britain, truth is only a complete defence to a libel action if you can prove it. So your research for investigative programmes has to go beyond the needs of the programme – it has to satisfy the law as well. It's no use just knowing that you are right …

SUMMARY
LEGAL PROBLEMS

Practical advice

Find out who your station's lawyer is and refer potential difficulties to him or her before they get serious.

Areas in which you need to know your local law
— *location shooting permission*
— *artists' contracts*
— *editorial control*
— *safety*
— *copyright*
— *libel.*

Who are the viewers?

Is anyone out there?

It's not a question that producers ask themselves every day. The answer leads to other questions, which in time lead into an area of broadcasting policy over which producers have little control. Anyway, you may say, you are much too busy finishing your programme to think about such problems. You may even believe that whether the programme attracts one viewer or a million doesn't make much difference to the process of making it ...

But it ought to. It's important every now and then to step back and ask yourself (as your bosses should constantly be doing): who is this programme for? The young? The old? Graduates or non-graduates? Government officials, academics or managers? Or workers and their families?

Your answer to these questions affects a lot of things in the programme. It affects the subjects you choose: the young don't have the same things on their minds as the old, vips don't have the same concerns as workers. It affects the language you use on air: the educated don't always speak the same language as the uneducated and the two don't necessarily understand each other. It affects the sort of people who appear in your programme: should they be mainly officials or ordinary people? It affects the type of music you broadcast: should it be traditional or imported, classical or pop? It affects the sort of sport, dancing and drama you show, the sort of programmes you import. When you start thinking about it, it affects virtually everything.

Of course when you start asking yourself 'Who is this programme for?' the answer is not difficult to find. For general programmes the viewers will come from across the spectrum, with more young or old people, men or women, depending on the subject. They will be not so well educated rather than well educated, simply because most people are not so well educated.

So it seems silly to waste the most successful medium for mass communication ever devised by doing programmes on subjects that wouldn't fill a lecture hall – subjects like the velocity of money or motivations for work, which even academics and executives find difficult to turn their minds to. By all means tackle these subjects occasionally on television, but do so only occasionally, and then in ways which a sizeable chunk of your audience finds interesting. The rest of the time you should produce programmes that interest ordinary people. These are mainly programmes about people (their life, their loves, their work, their successes, their failures, their adventures, their hates, their pleasures, their children, their pets), and programmes with people (singing, dancing, telling jokes, playing sport, cooking, taking part in competitions). People are interested in people.

'Ah, yes, but our station is run by the government and they like us to spend most of our time talking about problems of national importance,' you say. That may be so, but it's up to you (and the broadcasting authorities) to see that the programmes of national importance don't crowd out the programmes with popular appeal. If they do, the viewers will turn to satellite, cable, cassettes or the broadcaster across the border and your station will stand as a symbol of a government that has lost touch with its people. When the government realizes that hardly anyone is watching the programmes of national importance, they will criticize the broadcasters for not doing a good job – and they will be right. Though, to be fair, they should accept part of the blame themselves.

How does all this affect you as a humble producer? There are two lessons that you can take away:

1. Choose subjects for programmes that interest you, not subjects you are paid to be interested in.

2. Remember who your viewers are and make your programmes appeal to as wide a section of them as possible. TV is a mass communication medium.

SUMMARY

WHO ARE THE VIEWERS?

Young or old? Graduates or non-graduates? VIPs or workers?

Your answer affects
- *the subjects you choose*
- *the language you use*
- *the sort of people who appear on TV*
- *the music you choose*
- *the mix of programmes you broadcast.*

People like programmes about people.

Governments like popular, successful TV stations. So choose subjects that interest you. Make your programmes appeal to as wide a section of the public as possible.

TV is a mass communication medium.

Working with actors

Actors present a particular challenge to programme-makers. You can choose contributors to other programmes but you can't tell them what to say. Actors, on the other hand, are under your control. Words, gestures, movements, costume, make-up – everything about actors comes under your direction. Yet they bring their own creativity to the programme; they are not automata. The challenge is to find the balance between their creativity and your control.

studying the script   You have to be extremely well prepared to do this successfully. The first place you should turn to for inspiration is the script, which we will assume has been written by someone else and has to be followed faithfully. Your job is first to try and make the script work as it stands; if later during rehearsals you find it doesn't work, that is the time to suggest or make changes. When you first look through the script you should read it solely for pleasure. Only then when you have enjoyed the script yourself, should you start working to let the viewer share your enjoyment.

Start by going through the script two or three times in great detail, thinking about the most effective way for each character to look and move, and considering the most effective way for each line to be spoken and covered on camera. It is not necessary at this stage to make final decisions about each point. A careful review of the possibilities is all that is needed. You must leave room for the actors to make their creative contributions.

casting   This preliminary study of the script will give you ideas for casting. If the budget for your production is large enough, it's worth employing a casting director to help you. He or she will know better than you which actors are available and what they can do. This specialist knowledge can save you a lot of time and heartache. Good casting is a prerequisite for success. If you get it right, half your problems are over. If you get it badly wrong, you will have to work flat out just to avoid a disaster.

auditioning

You should hold an audition open to anyone who wants to come – there's always the chance of finding new talent. Give each candidate a scene or speech to perform and see what they make of it. Don't trust your memory, but make notes about each actor as you go along: how well they perform and how well they suit the part physically. Looks are important, but in the long run being able to put the part over is more important than looking right.

rehearsals

Once you have chosen your actors and arranged for contracts to be issued, give everyone the script to study for a few days. The first rehearsals can be in any convenient and quiet place and may be nothing more than a read-through with each actor doing his or her part and you listening. An actor's idea of the character on the page may differ from your own but listen carefully: his or her interpretation may bring out aspects you have missed. This is the fascination of working with actors. By listening, discussion and experimentation, together you should arrive at a performance that is better than any of you would have achieved alone.

Putting on drama is team work, but don't forget that you are the captain of the team. It's difficult to lay down precise guidelines how to get the best out of your team – every leader has his or her own methods. The main thing is to let everyone contribute and then mould these contributions to fit in with your overall interpretation of the work.

working out the shots

As rehearsals proceed you should start thinking in more detail about the shots. If you are making your programme away from the studio you should already have chosen the locations. If you are recording in the studio you should have a floor plan showing the layout of the set. Now use your

mental TV to imagine the actors in each setting, where
they will stand, sit, walk, kneel or lie down. Then think
about where you will place your camera or cameras to
cover each action – and each reaction. The reaction is often
as important as the action, so you need both. Make a sketch
showing each shot and/or camera position. It doesn't
matter if you can't draw. Pin people, diagrams and arrows
are enough.

storyboard
You should end up with a storyboard and/or sketches
of the camera positions for the whole script. It will be a lot
of work, but the work will result in a better programme.
It will make you think how each character should act and
react at each stage in the story. It will give you advance
notice of problems and time to think of a solution. And
even if on the day you don't shoot each shot as you planned
it, your thorough preparation will give you the overview
that enables you to spot the best solution.

rehearsing
movements
Once you have worked out positions and movements,
start introducing them into your rehearsals. You don't need
the full set to do this. Chairs, tables, books, masking tape or
chalk marks on the floor – any of these will do to mark the
positions of props and scenery on the actual set. The size
and layout of your makeshift set should be as close to the
real thing as possible.

In rehearsals from now on the actors should practise
all their moves as well as their words. This will let them
get the 'feel' of the area where they will be performing and
also gives you the chance of viewing the action from the
positions you have planned for your camera. You may well
discover better positions and movements for both actors
and camera.

long, static
scenes
Try and avoid long stretches of dialogue during which
the actors don't move; very static scenes are difficult to
make interesting on the screen. But if you have a long
stretch of dialogue, don't give up and just cover everything
in one general shot. Even if people are only sitting and
talking, their relationship changes at each stage of the
conversation. When chatting off-camera this change is

revealed in the way they interact: leaning forwards or backwards, looking at or away from each other, coughing or just settling into a more comfortable position. You should encourage your actors to reproduce this sort of subtle detail in front of the camera. You can then use these small but revealing signs of a changing relationship to make decisions about which actor to show on the screen at each point. If you get your cuts right, your viewers will unconsciously absorb this interaction or 'body language' and see the characters in the play as real people going through a real experience. And even your long, static scenes will be worth viewing.

Understanding body language also helps you to motivate the actors' moves. This motivation is important: without it gestures and movements round the set tend to confuse rather than illuminate what the play is trying to say. So give your actor a reason to walk across the room (perhaps he's playing a meticulous character and wants to uncoil the phone cord). Give your actress a reason for leaning back in her chair (she is getting bored with the conversation). Often the motivation for the actors' behaviour lies in something that took place before the drama began (the actress finds the actor's role reminds her of her father, whom she didn't get on with, and she therefore finds him a switch-off). The viewers may never know about this subtext, but that doesn't matter. The point about the subtext is that it gives the characters context, which the actors can use to decide how to perform a given action.

motivate movements

One other point about acting. Don't let your actors

don't allow
overacting
overact. The television audience is made up of many units of one or two people watching at home and so your actors should perform as if they were playing to one or two viewers sitting no more than a couple of metres away, not an audience of tens of thousands. TV drama is the art of the raised eyebrow, not the grand gesture. Your actors don't have to project their emotions as stage actors have to; they should just behave in character as naturally as possible and let the camera take the message to the audience.

shot sizes
Most of your drama (perhaps as much as two-thirds) can be shot in mid-shots or close-ups. These make the viewers feel they are part of the action far more effectively than loose, general shots that discourage involvement and keep viewers at a distance. But you will also need two-shots or the occasional long shot to show where people are in relation to each other.

positions in
the screen
The position in the screen for each actor in these wide shots is important, as some parts of the screen are stronger than others. For example, a person giving an order should be in a dominating position (in the centre of the screen or in the foreground) and a person receiving an order in a weaker position (at the side or in the background).

There are no hard-and-fast rules about the strong and weak parts of the screen, as the values of the different parts change as the position of the camera changes or the distance between the people in the picture changes. It's enough for you to be aware that these relationships exist and to know that you can use them to give your drama impact.

clever-
clever shots
Try and avoid very tricky shots (for example, an action covered only by showing its reflection in a glass bottle) unless they really help the story along. Too often clever-clever shots draw attention only to themselves and don't do much for the play as a whole. As a general principle you should aim for a succession of smoothly flowing, well-lit shots that tell the story effectively rather than proclaim their own brilliance. On the other hand, don't shoot everything square-on at normal eye-height. Look for high shots and low shots that give interesting new perspectives. Think also

how you can involve the viewer in the action by 'seeing' it with the camera from each character's point of view.

studio productions

The procedure for doing a drama in the studio is the same as for any other studio programme. When you have finally decided on all your shots, put them into the script and have the script typed out in the usual layout. You still need to do your shot-by-shot run-through in the studio even though you have been rehearsing with the actors for some days. Things always look different when you're actually in the studio and the technicians also need to rehearse their roles.

For studio productions it's sensible to record the play in large chunks with as few stops as possible and follow the order in which it was written. This gives the actors the chance to get into their parts and forget the television technology all round them. If anything goes wrong, carry on to the end of each section and then go back and repeat the bit which went wrong so that you can edit in the correct version later.

drama on location

For single-camera shooting you will have to break the whole play down into individual shots and light and shoot each one separately. You can save time by shooting all the scenes in one area one after another, just altering the lighting a little. But don't do this if it confuses the actors because you are jumping about the story too much. They are the people your viewers will see and so their needs must be given priority.

SUMMARY
WORKING WITH ACTORS

Start with the script. Read it first for pleasure. Then work through in detail, thinking how each character should look, move and say the lines. Start thinking about shots.

Finding the right cast is half the battle. Hire a casting director to help you. Hold auditions.

At rehearsals work with the actors to mould their ideas to fit your interpretation of the work. Storyboard shots and/or sketch camera positions. Begin to rehearse movements on a make-shift set.

Observe the actors' body language and use it to fine-tune your shooting plans. Give actors subtext to help them motivate their moves and actions. Don't let actors overact; 'small' performances work better on camera.

Avoid clever-clever shots. Aim for smoothly flowing, well-lit shots that tell the story effectively.

Give your actors' needs priority. They are the people the viewers see.

You want to work in television?

Getting a job in television is difficult. There are always large numbers of people wanting to work in the industry and so you must make yourself stand out from the crowd.

your degree The first requirement therefore is a university degree. The subject of the degree doesn't matter but obviously if it's a subject you are genuinely interested in, your grade will be better – which won't harm your prospects. Television needs people who know about life and the arts (sociology, anthropology, health, welfare, drama, literature) and understand the world (government, politics, science, economics, business). But recruiters won't pay an enormous amount of attention to the subject of your degree; they are more interested in who you are, what you have done, your experience of work and what makes you tick.

media studies Unlike medicine and the law you don't need a vocational degree to go into television. Mass communication and media courses are fine but treat these subjects as worth studying in their own right, not as the back door to a job. The practical training you get on these courses is helpful, but in the long run the value of your degree to your employer (and you) is that it lets you study something deeply and teaches you to think. Craft skills are useful but they aren't an education.

There are, of course, other ways of demonstrating that you know how to use your mind, so don't despair if you didn't go to college. If you didn't, find out what jobs you would be considered for and apply for those. It may be possible to transfer to production later.

useful experience

If you have a degree, you still have to make yourself stand out from the crowd of eager graduates. The best way to do this is to show that you done something worthwhile in a field that is relevant or vaguely relevant to television. Obviously to be able to say that you have made (or helped to make) a short video or film makes you stand out head and shoulders above everyone else; it doesn't matter what it was about or what equipment you used, the important thing is to have done it. Writing, producing or directing a play (amateur or professional), putting on an exhibition (perhaps of your photographs?), organizing a fair or festival, or any other evidence of organizing or creative ability will give you a head start. A background in student or professional journalism is impressive. Radio experience is a definite plus.

the best targets

To whom should you apply? The obvious person is the appointments or personnel officer: phone the station to find out the correct title and the name of the person you should write to. It's probably more productive, however, to apply to the executive producers or editors in charge of individual programmes, or the independent producers who supply the programmes. They are the ones who need the workers and decide whom to hire. Don't apply only to prestige programmes shown at peak viewing times – they can take their pick of experienced people, so the competition is bound to be fiercer. Make a point instead of viewing the day-time, night-time, schools and study programmes you have probably never even heard of and write to the ones you are interested in. They need staff to make them just as much as prestige shows. You don't have to wait for a job to be advertised before you write. Production companies and producers often need extra people in a hurry and you should position yourself to benefit from this unscheduled recruitment. Read the trade press regularly to see which producers or companies have been contracted for new series. It stands to reason that they are likely to have some openings.

CV and summary

Work hard at your CV (curriculum vitae). It should contain all the usual things: education, prizes, jobs, achievements and so on. Check there are no spelling mistakes and make sure it does justice to any experience that is even vaguely relevant for the job. Then put a summary page on the front. This should have on it your name, address, phone number and a few sentences outlining your achievements and ambitions. The summary makes life easier for anyone who has to wade through job applications (no harm in being helpful) and should be designed to get people interested in you. With luck they will take that interest further by going through the details on the other pages of your CV and inviting you for an interview.

Does your summary work? Try it out on one or two people and ask if they would invite you to come for an interview. You may want to make some changes after these tests.

If you haven't heard anything for a week or so after you send in your application, follow up with a phone call to check that it landed on the right desk and enquire if all is well. If the moment seems right, you might even ask if you could come in, though this might be considered a bit pushy. Maybe the programme is looking for someone pushy – in the nicest possible way, of course.

Having lots of programme ideas will not give you as great an advantage as you might expect. Whatever viewers may think, TV stations on the whole are not short of ideas – they are short of money, air time and perhaps the energy to introduce new ideas. So presenting your own list of ideas is unlikely to excite anyone who might hire you; he or she is more interested in evidence of your potential ability to turn ideas into programmes. By all means work out a list of good ideas but keep it for the interview, not for your letter of application.

Whatever method you use to show your potential, it has to be backed up by knowing something about television. To do this you have to watch it intensively, putting yourself into the programme-makers' shoes and working out where they

have been successful and where they have failed and what
you might have changed. Get to know the names of a few
producers and their programmes; if you know who is going
to interview you (phone and ask) try and find out what
they have made. Also read the television critics regularly
and consider the strength and weaknesses of their
comments. The object of all this is to be so well briefed
that when you go for an interview you are as well informed
as anyone already in television. Not a know-all, but
pleasantly knowledgeable.

the interview   It's impressive (and flattering) for anyone in television to
meet someone who has paid the medium the compliment
of studying it intelligently and sympathetically. If you
have done this, you'll find you have lots to talk about at
the interview, which will be a refreshing change for your
interviewers, who usually spend their time having to ask
questions like 'Why do you want to get into television?'
Incidentally, one way to answer that question is to say:
'I saw that programme two nights about …' (pick a well-
made programme about something you are interested in)
'well, that's the sort of programme I would like to make.
Though, perhaps, I wonder why the programme didn't
go into another aspect of the question, namely …' How
can they resist you?

If you are offered a job, don't worry if it's for only a few
days or weeks. Accept it anyway. It will give you valuable
experience and look good on your cv. It might well lead
to something longer term – many a career has started with
a five-day contract. But don't be surprised if your career
turns out like many careers in acting and is made up mostly
of contracts a few months long, with contracts of a year or
more the exception rather than the rule.

If you are turned down at first, keep trying. If you are
leaving college, haven't yet managed to land a production
job in television and have to earn a living while you are
trying, journalism and radio are the best havens – if you
can get a job there. Be very careful about accepting a non-
production job in television if you have the formal entry

requirements (like a degree) and are really determined to get into production. There is nothing wrong with non-production jobs. But if being a producer is what you are determined to become, starting as a secretary or floor manager can put you back a long time, as everyone gets into the habit of thinking of you as a secretary or floor manager. And how many existing secretaries and floor managers are already in the queue to transfer to production?

SUMMARY
YOU WANT TO WORK IN TELEVISION?

Get a degree – the subject doesn't matter.

*If you can't go to college, apply for any job you can get.
It may be possible to transfer later.*

Make yourself stand out from the crowd of applicants by
- *making (or helping to make) a short film or video*
- *writing, producing or directing a play*
- *putting on an exhibition*
- *organizing a fair or festival*
- *showing evidence of creative or organizing ability*
- *working in student or professional journalism or radio.*

*Phone to find out the correct title and name of the person
to apply to. Apply also to executive producers or editors of
individual programmes, or the independent producers who
supply the programmes. Apply to off-peak programmes as
well as prestige shows.*

*You don't have to wait for jobs to be advertised. Read the
trade press to see who is getting contracts for new series.*

*Test your CV and summary before sending it out. Do they
work?*

Follow up your application with a phone call.

*Prepare for job interviews by viewing and reading about
programmes and producers. Research your interviewer(s)
and their work.*

*Accept any job you are offered, even short-term jobs.
Many careers consist mostly of short-term jobs.*

*Keep trying. Think twice about accepting non-production
jobs.*

Glossary

AM (amplitude modulation) a method of transmitting information by varying the amplitude (strength) of a regular carrier wave (but leaving its frequency unchanged) in response to variations in the strength of the input signal. See *FM*

action 1. any performance or event taking place on camera. 2. the command to start the same

ad lib unscripted, improvised

amplitude the strength of an electrical current or signal

analogue recording recording video or audio as a continuous electrical signal – as opposed to digital, where they are recorded as a stream of binary numbers

animate 1. to create the illusion of movement on screen by separating it into a series of steps and shooting one frame at a time. 2. to add computer-generated movement to artwork

answer print first fully graded colour print made from cut neg

aperture the opening in the lens through which light enters the camera

assemble edit to copy shots onto a tape that does not have a pre-recorded control track

audio another word for sound

audition to ask actors to perform in a scene or role in order to assess their suitability for a part in a production

available light light already on location – as opposed to lights brought by the camera crew

B & B see *black and burst*
BCU see *big close-up*
back light light (usually hard) placed behind interviewee to separate him or her from the background and add sparkle to the hair

barn door adjustable flaps on lamps used to control where the light falls

basher (hand basher) portable battery light

big close-up (BCU) 1. very close shot of a face, cutting off the top of the forehead and the lower part of the chin. 2. very close shot of an object

bit a single digit – either 1 or 0 – in binary notation, the counting system used by computers. The word bit comes from *binary digit*. See *byte*

black and burst (B & B) encoded TV signal with chrominance and luminance set at zero (the picture is black) containing pulses and other information needed for synchronizing video equipment or tapes. See *control track*

black edging outlining letters on screen to make them easier to read

blonde 2-kilowatt light frequently used on location

buffer shot shot inserted between two shots to disguise a discontinuity of direction (crossing the line)

byte a group of eight binary digits (see *bit*). Eight bits (either 1 or 0) give 256 combinations, which are assigned to letters or numbers, thus making it possible for computers to handle writing and conventional arithmetic

CCD charge coupled device – the name for the light-sensitive chip inside the camera

CSO see *colour separation overlay*

CU see *close-up*

camera card a list given to a studio camera operator showing details of the shots assigned to his or her camera

camera left and right left and right as seen from the camera's point of view

camera script a detailed script for a studio programme noting each shot, which camera it is on, the camera position, sound, lighting, details of recorded inserts, etc.

caption straightforward graphics, usually with lettering

cardioid microphone microphone with heart-shaped area of sensitivity

carrier high frequency regular electrical wave that can be modulated in amplitude or frequency to carry a signal

cassette 1. case containing magnetic tape for audio or video. 2. the tape itself

casting assigning actors to roles

chromakey electronic technique for replacing part of a picture with material from another source

chrominance signal the colour information part of the TV signal. See *luminance*

clapperboard board used at beginning or end of a shot to label it with shot and take numbers and (for film) to mark the points for synchronizing picture and sound

clock electronic counter recorded on a tape before programme material to serve as a label and count-down timer

close-up (CU) 1. shot showing head from collar upwards. 2. close shot of an object

colour balance procedure to ensure that a camera or monitor is combining the three primary colours in correct proportions

colour difference signal technique for reducing the amount of information needed to encode colour information in the TV signal

colour separation overlay (CSO) another name for chromakey

colour temperature the colour of light, measured in degrees Kelvin

commentary out-of-vision narration, usually ad lib for outside broadcasts

component recording technical standard in which the luminance and chrominance information is recorded separately, giving better quality and making it easier to apply special effects. See *composite recording*

composite recording technical standard in which the luminance and chrominance information is encoded as one signal before recording. See *component recording*

compression computer techniques used to reduce the amount of information that needs to be processed in order to record, playback or transmit pictures. See *JPEG, MPEG*

conforming the video equivalent of neg cutting – in other words, using the off-line edit decision list (EDL) to produce the transmission copy from the master material

continuity 1. consistency of dress, hair, props etc. between shots or scenes. 2. channel logos, announcements, trailers etc. between programmes. Often referred to as presentation

contrast range between the brightest and darkest part of a scene or picture

control track electronic pulses recorded on a tape to ensure recording and playback machines run at the correct speed, thus enabling trouble-free video and audio transfer

crab to move the camera sideways over the ground

credits list of people's names acknowledging their contribution to the making of a programme

crossing the line reversing continuity of direction in successive shots, thus confusing viewers' sense of direction

cue 1. a signal to performers or crew to start the action. 2. a section of continuous commentary read without pausing for sync sound, music or effects

cue dot 1. unobtrusive dot in top right corner of screen used by presentation as countdown to the next programme. 2. also used on film to signal an impending reel change

cutaway shot used as buffer between two other shots to avoid a jump cut. See *jump cut*

cut-off the area about 2cm wide round the edge of camera viewfinders and studio monitors that most viewers won't see on their sets

cycle one complete oscillation of alternating current (AC). The number of cycles per second is measured in hertz. UK mains electricity operates on 50 cycles a second (50Hz), US on 60 (60Hz)

cyclorama (cyc) floor-to-ceiling curtain in the studio used to provide a background

D1 ¾inch digital video format – component. See *component recording*

D2 ¾inch digital video format – composite. See *composite recording*

D3 ½inch digital video format – composite. See *composite recording*

D5 ½inch digital video format – component. See *component recording*

DAT digital audio tape

decibel (dB) logarithmic measure of gain or loss in video or audio. Sound levels are usually expressed in dBA, a log scale of intensity. Loudness roughly doubles every 10dB. See *gain*

depth of field the area of a shot in sharp focus

digital recording recording video or audio as a stream of binary numbers – as opposed to analogue, where they are recorded as a continuous signal. All copies of a digital recording are effectively first generation because digital passes on the specifications for the signal, not the signal itself. See *generation*

digital video effects (DVE) manipulation of pictures to resize or produce effects such as page-turns, mosaics, etc.

director creative and artistic leader of a production, responsible for directing and coordinating the actors, technicians and designers. See *producer*

dissolve gradual transition from one shot to another. See *mix*

Distagon a range of lenses designed to be used with fast film to get high-resolution pictures in low light

Dolby technical system for reducing electronic surface noise and hiss named after Ray Dolby (1933-) its US inventor

dolly 1. camera platform on wheels or track used for moving shots. 2. also used as verb denoting the move itself. See *track*

drop-out an imperfection on videotape causing fleeting loss of signal

dub 1. to transfer or copy video or audio from one tape to another. 2. the production (usually in a specialized dubbing theatre) of the final sound track for a programme. 3. to create a foreign language version of a programme

dubbing chart diagram prepared for the dubbing mixer showing details, timings and transitions of all the elements needed to produce the final sound track

dubbing mixer the technician responsible for balancing and combining the various elements (recorded sound, commentary, additional music and effects) that go into the final sound track

EDL (edit decision list) a list of time codes and other technical information from the off-line edit. The EDL can then be used to conform the on-line copy

edge numbers See *key numbers*

editor 1. technician editing video or film. 2. senior producer responsible for a regular programme

effects (FX) 1. sounds other than music or speech either recorded during the shoot or added during the dub. 2. short for digital video effects (DVE). See *digital video effects*

emulsion 1. light-sensitive coating, the less shiny side of film stock which sticks to a moistened finger. 2. magnetic coating on sepmag

encoding technical conversion of luminance and chrominance signals into form suitable for broadcasting. See *NTSC, PAL, SECAM*

end board sync point or shot label marked by clapperboard held upside-down at the end of a shot

establisher general view (GV) shot showing the layout of a location

executive producer senior producer, often in charge of a series of programmes being made at the same time

exposure 1. the quantity of light entering the camera through the lens. 2. amount of media publicity given to someone in the public eye

exterior any shot taken out of doors. See *interior*

extro studio link or comment referring to an item in a magazine programme immediately after it has ended. Also known as outro. See *intro*

eyeline the line of sight of a person on camera

FM (frequency modulation) a method of transmitting information by varying the frequency of a regular carrier wave (but leaving its amplitude unchanged) in response to variations in the strength of the input signal. See *AM*

field electronic scan lasting 1/50th of second (1/60th in the US) on alternate lines of the screen. Two interlaced fields make a frame. See *interlaced scanning*

figure-of-eight microphone microphone sensitive to sound coming from in front and behind but not from the sides

filler light soft light used to make shadows less dark

fine cut final stage in editing

flicker irritating flash between video or film frames, eliminated from electronic pictures by scanning each frame as two interlaced fields; and eliminated from film by showing each frame twice

floor plan scale diagram of studio layout and facilities, used both to show the position of the set and to work out the deployment of cameras, artists, etc.

f-number the ratio of the aperture of a lens to the focal length. The f-number when the aperture is fully open is used to indicate the speed (the light-gathering power) of the lens. The smaller the f-number, the faster the lens (the greater the light-gathering power)

focal length the distance between the optical centre of the lens and the plane inside the camera where an image at infinity is in focus

frame 1. a single, complete television picture, made up of two fields, scanned onto the TV screen every 1/25th of a second (1/30th in the US). 2. each exposure in a length of film

freeze frame a single frame from a sequence of moving pictures that is repeated on screen to make it look like a still photograph

frequency number of cycles a second, measured in hertz (Hz).

One Hz = one cycle per second. See *cycle*

f-stop aperture setting on lens, described by an f-number. Also known as stop

GV general view shot of a location

gain picture control on electronic cameras that boosts the picture signal (typically by either 9 or 18dB), for use in low light to make dark scenes appear brighter

gallery control rooms used by director, vision-mixer, PA, lighting and sound supervisors and assistants to direct and operate the staff and equipment in the studio

generation each successive copy of video or audio tape. The master is first generation, a copy of the master is second generation, a copy of a second generation is third generation ... and so on. See *digital recording*

glitch momentary defects of picture or sound

grading film lab adjustment of the exposure and colour balance of the neg to get the best possible print

graphics any drawings, diagrams, captions, photos, animation, etc. supplied by a graphics designer

grip person who operates the dolly or other equipment used for moving shots

gun mike highly directional hypercardioid, the mike most frequently used on location

h/a see *high-angle shot*

HDTV (high definition television) high quality pictures on 1000+ lines on a wide screen in 13 x 9 instead of the usual 4 x 3 proportions

HMI light (hydrargyrum medium iodide) light with colour temperature similar to daylight

hard light light casting shadows with hard, distinct edge. See *soft light*

head electro-magnetic device for recording picture and/or sound signals on magnetic tape (writing) and also playing back the recorded tracks (reading)

helical scan spiral-shaped path of videotape round the drum holding the heads, which enables the tracks to be recorded diagonally on the tape

hertz (Hz) measure of cycles per second named after Heinrich Rudolf Hertz (1857-1894), the German physicist who first produced electromagnetic waves artificially. See *frequency*

Hi8 non-professional 8mm tape format sometimes used for broadcast

high-angle shot (h/a) shot taken from above looking down

hypercardioid microphone highly directional microphone with narrow area of sensitivity. See *gun mike*

insert edit 1. to edit shots or sequences onto a tape with pre-recorded control track. 2. to replace a shot with one of identical duration

interior any shot taken indoors. See *exterior*

interlaced scanning scanning system in which each frame is scanned as two (or more) fields, one field consisting of even-numbered lines, the other of odd-numbered lines. See *field*

international sound track music and effects track without commentary or dialogue used to produce a foreign language version of a programme. See *M&E*

intro studio link or introduction to the next item in a magazine programme. See *extro, outro*

iso recording recording the output of each camera in a multi-camera setup on separate recorders for editing later

JPEG Joint Photographic Experts Group – digital compression standard for still pictures, used in most post-production machines. See *MPEG*

joiner device for precise cutting and joining of film and sepmag sound

jump cut a cut that juxtaposes two shots which noticeably violate continuity of place or action. See *cutaway*

key light the main light on the subject, usually a hard light in order to provide depth and modelling

key numbers manufacturer's numbers built into the edge of film stock, used by neg cutters to match neg to cutting copy. Also known as edge numbers

kilo- 1. 1000 of something. One kilohertz (1kHz), for example, is 1000 hertz or cycles per second. 2. when used as a measure of computer memory (as in kilobyte) kilo equals 1024

l/a see *low-angle shot*

LS see *long shot*

leader length of stock at the beginning of film and sepmag rolls, used for lacing up and synchronizing the rolls on machines, often with countdown numbers for accurate cueing

line-up engineering check of equipment before transmission or recording

linear editing video editing system in which selected pictures and sound are dubbed from a playback onto a record tape. The scope for changing

edit decisions is for all practical
purposes limited to the shot
that has just been edited, since
changing the duration of earlier
shots makes it necessary to
re-create all subsequent edits.
See *NLE*

link presenter's introduction
(or back reference) to an item in
a magazine programme. See *intro*

location anywhere outside the
studio used for shooting a
programme

locked-off shot shots taken with
the camera in exactly the same
position which can be edited
to make people and/or objects
appear and disappear against an
unchanging background

log a list of time codes and/or shot
and take numbers of shots

long shot (LS) 1. shot including
head and feet of a standing
person. 2. shot taken from a
distance

longitudinal time code time
code recorded on a separate
track. See *VITC*

looking room area of the screen
on the side to which a person is
looking, used to balance the
composition of the shot in the
frame. See *walking room*

low-angle shot (l/a) shot
taken from below looking up

luminance the part of the TV
signal conveying brightness
information.

M & E (music and effects) sound
track containing sync dialogue
(usually), music and effects but
not commentary.
See *international sound track*

MCU see *medium close-up*

MPEG Moving Pictures Experts
Group – digital compression
standard for recording, playback
and transmitting colour video.
See *JPEG*

MS see *mid-shot*

macro setting on zoom lens for
very close shots

magazine programme a
programme with a number of
different items linked by one or
more presenters

medium close-up (MCU) shot
showing head and shoulders
above the armpits

mega- 1. a million of something,
as in megahertz (MHz), one
million cycles per second.
2. when used as a measure of
computer memory, mega-
equals 1,048,576

mid-shot (MS) shot showing head
and upper body, cutting just
below the elbows

mix gradual transition from one
shot or sound to another

mixed light mixture of daylight
and artificial light

monitor TV set used for viewing
recorded programmes and
output of cameras but unable
to receive off-air broadcasts

multi-camera shooting with
more than one camera, as in
the studio or for an outside
broadcast. See *PSC*

mute shot shot taken without
recording sound

NLE (non-linear editing) digital
editing system that stores edits
in a decision list and replays the
cut sequences by assembling
them instantly from shots stored
in its memory. This gives the
user complete freedom to
change edit decisions whenever
and wherever, since all changes
are changes to a list, not to a
physical entity. See *linear editing*

NTSC 525-line encoding system
for colour TV signals devised
in 1953 in US by National
Television System Committee
and used in US and Japan and
some other countries

NVQ National Vocational Qualification – national standards of competence in production and craft skills in the workplace set by the broadcast film and video industry. See *SNVQ, Skillset*

narrow-angle lens lens with long focal length used for close shots of distant objects

negative film (neg) the original stock exposed in the camera. After processing in the lab, light parts of the scene appear dark on neg and vice versa. Colours appear as their complementaries

neutral density filter (ND) filter that reduces the light entering the camera without affecting colours

Nicam stereo digital compression system developed by the BBC for transmitting stereo sound. Nicam stands for near instantaneous companded audio multiplex (since you asked!)

noise unwanted sound or vision signal

OB (outside broadcast) see *outside broadcast*

OOV out-of-vision commentary. Pronounced as in (h)oove(s)

off-line edit pre-edit, usually on a cheaper non-broadcast format machine. See *on-line edit*

omnidirectional microphone microphone sensitive to sound from any direction

on-line edit edit on a broadcast format, often using an EDL from the off-line edit to conform the on-line material

outro studio link or comment referring to an item in a magazine programme immediately after it has ended. Also known as extro. See *intro*

outside broadcast (OB) multi-camera recording or transmission made away from the studio

overlap (action) to shoot as much of the action as can sensibly be covered from each camera position, thus giving the editor a choice of shots of the same action and a choice of cutting points

PA (production assistant) highly trained person who runs the producer/ director's office and helps with all aspects of production and post-production both at base and on location

PAL (phase alternate line) encoding system for colour TV signal. The UK version uses 625 lines at 50Hz

POV abbreviation for point of view

PSC (portable single camera) as routinely used on location. See *multi-camera*

pan horizontal swing of camera to right or left, short for panoramic (shot). See *tilt*

paper edit preliminary edit decision list worked out on paper after viewing and logging rushes

planning meeting meeting called by producer/director and production team with the technical team and designers to go through details of the planning for a studio recording/transmission or for a complicated location shot

presentation channel logos, trailers, announcements, etc. between programmes. Often referred to as continuity

primary colours red, green and blue (often referred to as RGB), which are added together in different proportions to produce the range of TV colours

prime lens lens with fixed focal length. See *zoom lens*

producer person in overall charge of a programme, especially its organisation and finance. See *director*

profile side view of face when only one eye is visible

prop any movable object or furnishing used for a programme

RGB see *primary colours*

radio microphone cableless mike fitted with tiny transmitter giving user maximum freedom of movement

redhead standard 1 kilowatt light used on location

reversal (film) fast turn-round film – replaced by video – where the stock exposed in the camera was the stock that was cut and used for transmission. See *negative film*

rostrum camera device for shooting graphics with precise camera moves. The camera moves up and down on columns and looks down on the graphics, which are on a moveable table top

rough cut first assembly of shots during editing, preferably made off-line

rubber numbers numbers printed on the edge of film stock and sepmag after they have been synchronized to help identify them if they become separated during editing

run-through pre-interview discussion between interviewer and interviewee about the lines the interview might take

rushes pictures and sound before editing; the raw material for the edit

SECAM colour encoding system for TV signal used in France, Russia and some other countries. The name comes from the French for Sequential Colour with Memory

SNVQ Scottish National Vocational Qualification – NVQs in Scotland. See *NVQ*

S-VHS ½ inch super VHS format. See *Hi8*

sepmag separate magnetic audio track used in conjunction with film

sequence one or more shots edited together to portray an event

set scenery and props for a programme, usually in a studio

shooting ratio ratio of material shot to material transmitted

shot a continuous recording or length of film taken by one or more cameras

shot list 1. list of shots planned for the shoot. 2. log of shots that were actually taken, with their time codes. (1 and 2 may differ!). See *log*

Skillset the training organization for the broadcast film and video industry and head body for organizing and implementing NVQs. See *NVQ*

soft light light casting shadow with soft, indistinct edges. See *hard light*

spacing blank film stock added to picture or sound roll to fill gaps and thus ensure the rolls stay in sync

spreader three-armed rubber mat designed to be placed under tripod legs to prevent them slipping or damaging carpets or the floor

star filter camera filter designed to make lights appear to radiate like stars

steadicam harness and camera mounting designed to take the wobbles out of handheld shots

stereo two-channel sound system arranged to convey position of sound sources. See *Nicam stereo*

stop aperture setting on lens, described by f-number. Short for f-stop

storyboard strip cartoon drawn to prepare for a tricky sequence or complete shoot

striping recording black and burst on a tape. See *black and burst*

sync (synchronize) to adjust the relationship of picture and sound so that they are exactly in time with each other

TX short for transmission

take each successive recording of a shot

talkback sound link between the studio gallery and the crew on the studio floor

telephoto lens lens with long focal length used for close shots of distant objects

teletext information display system transmitted in 'spare' lines of the TV signal between fields

tilt vertical swing of camera upwards or downwards. See *pan*

time code frame numbering system (hours, minutes, seconds, frames) giving each frame a unique number which can be read and displayed by post-production machines. Time code can be set to record elapsed time or time-of-day. See *Longitudinal time code, VITC*

T-number f-number adjusted to take into account the actual amount of light transmitted by a lens

track camera movement over the ground, usually with the camera mounted on a platform running on a track. See *dolly*

treatment a sequence by sequence breakdown on paper of the programme as envisaged after research and before the shoot

two-shot shot with two people in it

user bits labelling system that is part of time code, consisting of 8 characters that can be set to numbers (0-9) or letters (A-E)

VCR video cassette recorder

VHS Video Home System – ½ inch non-broadcast format

VITC (vertical interval time code) time code recorded as part of the picture signal. See *longitudinal time code*

V/O see *voice-over*

virtual studio computer-generated background and objects – for use with live action in a real studio – that can be re-computed in real time to show changes in perspective when the cameras move

voice-over commentary where speaker is unseen, often used in advertisements. See *OOV*

vox pop technique of shooting and editing together a succession of people answering the same question. Derived from Latin *vox populi*, the voice of the people

walking room area of the screen in front of a moving person used to balance the composition of the shot in the frame. See *looking room*

wide-angle lens lens with short focal length giving wide angle of acceptance

wild sound sound recorded without a matching picture and therefore not in sync

zoom lens lens with variable focal length. See *prime lens*

Index